Letters to My Israeli Sons

BY THE SAME AUTHOR

The L-Shaped Room
An End to Running
The Backward Shadow
Children at the Gate
Two is Lonely
One More River
Sarah and After
My Darling Villain
Dark Quartet, the Story of the Brontës
Path to the Silent Country,
Charlotte Brontë's Years of Fame

FOR CHILDREN:
The Adventures of King Midas
The Farthest-Away Mountain
I, Houdini

ANTHOLOGIES:
The Real Thing
Is Anyone There?

Letters to my Israeli Sons

THE STORY OF JEWISH SURVIVAL

Lynne Reid Banks

A GROLIER COMPANY

Franklin Watts
New York/London/Toronto/Sydney
1980

804
B22l
1179
2/12/85

The author would like to thank Dr. Martin Gilbert for his personal help with the maps, particularly those that appear on pages 14, 40, 162, and 186, and for his permission to borrow from his own atlases.

The author would like to acknowledge Eleanor and Herbert Farjeon and J. M. Dent Ltd for permission to quote "Richard the Lion-Heart" from *Kings and Queens.*

Copyright © Lynne Reid Banks, 1979

Maps, Copyright © W. H. Allen

This book or parts thereof may not be reproduced in any form whatsoever without permission in writing.

Library of Congress Cataloging in Publication Data

Banks, Lynne Reid.
Letters to my Israeli sons.
Bibliography: p.
Includes index.
1. Jews—History. 2. Zionism—History.
3. Palestine—History—1917-1948. I. Title.
DS118.B348 1980 909' .04924 80-12658
ISBN 0-531-09934-2

First printed and bound in Great Britain by W & J Mackay Limited, Chatham, for the Publishers, W. H. Allen & Co., Ltd.

First published in the United States in 1980 by Franklin Watts, Inc.

All rights reserved
6 5 4 3 2 1

Contents

MAPS

For Adiel, Gillon and Omri
Stephenson

Remember, as you read, and as you live:
Nothing is ever simple. Nothing.
The more it looks black-and-white,
the deeper you should dig
to find the gray.
Gray sounds dull.
But it is the color of the mind.

Foreword

Jerusalem,
July 1976

My dearest boys,

Your father has just taken you off to the municipal swimming pool and I am sitting at my desk with several free hours ahead of me to begin writing these letters to you which I hope will end up as a book. It's really the first chance I've had to begin work on them since we arrived in Jerusalem more than two weeks ago. At the age you are now —ten, nine, and nearly eight—perhaps it's too much to expect you to settle down in this strange new environment without demanding pretty constant attention from your parents. Certainly you've left us with very little time for the work which we came here to do!

I want to write a book about the Jews and Israel for teenagers. It was while I was watching the three of you, each in your own way getting the feel of your native country again after five years in England, that I suddenly thought that the teenagers I want to write for are—you. You three, not as you are now—still children, more interested in swim-

1

ming pools than history, in food than people, in games than atmosphere; but you as you will be in another five years.

By that time Israel should mean more to you than just a faraway place to spend the summer—a place full of strange animals, high temperatures and occasional adventures to go home and "shvitz" about to your friends. When each of you is *bar mitzvah* (and though I am not Jewish, which means that, strictly speaking, *you* are not, I mean to give you all some form of that ancient Jewish coming-of-age celebration)—when in turn you become thirteen, I would like to be able to hand each of you a book by your mother which will tell you, very personally, why I think Israel should be important to you. Even though that mother is an unrepentant Gentile.

And since your book may be read by others as well as you, perhaps I had better explain a little of my own background so that they will understand the peculiarities in our family. Perhaps these facts, which you take so much for granted, may become more real to you, too, when you read them.

When I was eleven, near the age Adiel is now, the Second World War started, and I was sent off to Canada with my mother and cousin as an evacuee. I wish in many ways that I hadn't been, because, as it turned out, Hitler never did invade Britain; little children like me were not turned into goose stepping, brain-washed Hitler Youth, denouncing their own parents and "*heil*ing" the Führer. Our house was not bombed, it only had a few windows broken when a big blockbuster fell into the reservoir behind our suburban road. The war, in fact, with all its horrors, would no doubt have been a great adventure to me if I had been allowed to experience it, as it was to most kids of my age. And I missed it. Of course I had the experience of life on the Canadian prairies instead. But looking back, I feel that after all I would have learned more, grown more, in my own country during her time of trial than I did in that comfortable, kind, safe country which gave me sanctuary.

But it's quite possible that if I hadn't been cushioned by living that soft easy life, while Europe was in agony and turmoil, then the shock of what I found out on my return would not have affected me as it did, and my whole life might have taken quite another road.

I won't go into all the shocks. The two that affected me straight away were: the sight of London in ruins from the bombing, and the sudden realization of the hardships my aunts and my father had been suffering while we'd been living in comparative luxury.

I remember the silly incident that first woke me up to this. The day after we got back we all had tea at our old home (looking pathetically shabby, with the lawn dug up to grow vegetables) and afterwards my mother washed up in our kitchen for the first time in five years. She took down a packet of soap powder while she talked to her sisters. One of them was speaking, and suddenly she stopped, gasped, and rushed to the sink to catch my mother's arm. "You mustn't use so much soap!" she exclaimed in a shocked tone. "That's almost a week's ration!" My mother looked deeply ashamed. I couldn't quite understand it. After all, it was a natural mistake; no one was really angry with her. It was some time before I realized that she was ashamed because she had missed the war, even though they had all practically forced her to take us to Canada in 1940.

But I was in for a worse shock than that.

Like most young people I was able to adapt quite quickly to my new (or rather, old) surroundings, and I soon picked up the threads of life again. I wanted to be an actress—I had nothing much else in my head at the time, nor for long afterwards—but I also wanted to be happy and have fun, and I often went to the "movies" as I still called them (I had quite a Canadian accent).

One day I was sitting in a cinema. In those days, before television was bringing news-in-pictures to every home, there was always a newsreel before the main film. The news at that time was all about the aftermath of war in Europe, and suddenly before my eyes was film which had just been released, of the concentration camps of Belsen and Auschwitz. The film had been taken by American army cameramen when they broke into the camps.

Sometimes one still sees these films, or stills taken from them. You will see them some day, though not, I hope, until you are older—they are not for young eyes. They are not for any human eyes, in my opinion, but then the actions which created the subjects for those pictures were not human either—yet they were performed by creatures who called themselves human beings.

I suppose I had known about the camps before—heard or read about them. But it is one thing to hear and read, another to see. Tough American soldiers vomited and fainted when they saw the real thing. Sitting in the cinema, waiting for some Hollywood musical to come on, I did not vomit or faint. I sat there with the rest of the audience in silence, and the newsreel ended, and the musical came on, and after it I came out and went home I suppose, though I don't remember that. But something was changed in me forever.

"My childhood was over," people tend to say about such an incident. Well, my childhood, or my youth, was not over. At least not outwardly. I mean that I went on having fun, being happy, being silly, wasting time, thinking about trivialities, and so on. The way a pregnant woman goes on perfectly normally before she knows that a seed has taken root in her that will change her life for good. And that, I now realize, was something like what had happened to me.

The seed grew slowly. I became very interested in Jewish people. Jews had been butchered in the millions—by Germans, yes, and I wasn't a German, but also by non-Jews, and I *was* a non-Jew. Why had "we" done that to "them"? Even my own, darling father—the mildest, the gentlest, the kindest of men—had remarked in my hearing when I was a little girl: "How odd of God to choose the Jews." That was anti-Semitism, wasn't it? How could anti-Semitism come so close to me, close enough so that I felt—however irrationally—that I *had* some responsibility for the Nazi atrocities? If nothing worse, had I not been sitting in comfort in Canada, enjoying myself in the most selfish fashion, while all these unspeakable things had been going on? I hadn't even shared the dangers and difficulties that civilians, and children, endured in England. *I had not even had to save soap.*

The Nazis had boiled down Jewish fat to make soap for German housewives. . . . When I found out things like that, I just could not think about them. I rushed back to my tap-dancing, speech lessons, parties and general fun-and-games with a sense that I was escaping some inner confusion too huge to be faced. The two worlds—mine, and that of the Jews of Europe—were impossible for me to reconcile. People like the ones I knew could not, it seemed to me, belong to the same species as the Nazis. It did not make sense. So I went to drama school, and concentrated on make-believe.

But I watched out for Jews. I noticed them. They fascinated me. In 1949 I fell in love with one.

He's dead now, so you'll never meet him, but he had a great influence on my life. He was able to answer a lot of the questions that had been faintly troubling me. He told me about the Jewish religion. And it was he who first talked to me about Israel.

The War of Independence had just ended. Your father was in it, fighting for his life and the life of the new State, but of course I didn't dream of that. I listened to what this other boy told me about how the Jewish refugees of Europe had been kept out of the only place they had to go to—Palestine—by the British, who were supposed to be in charge there, and how they had got in illegally, and how at last the British had withdrawn and the State had been declared. He told me about the immediate attack by five Arab armies from the surrounding countries, and how no one had expected the Jews to last more than a few weeks—but in the end, after a year of fighting, they had won.

He was Jewish and he was very proud of the Jews of Israel —"a new sort of Jew," he called them. I was not clever enough at the time to understand what he meant—to put two and two together through his eyes: the Jews who had "allowed themselves" to be wiped out by the Nazis, and these others who had not allowed themselves to be wiped out by the Arabs. I was not *nearly* clever enough to realize, as I realize now so many years later, what a much-too-simple view of the "two sorts of Jews" my Jewish boyfriend took.

He fired me with this two-dimensional view of Israel—a brave new country, a country for the survivors of the concentration camps, a place where Jews could be themselves without fear or favor. Even after I stopped being in love with that young man, I fell deeper and deeper in love with the heroic idea he had given me of the new land of his people.

I longed to see it. But it was years before I did. Too many years. Silly to waste regrets on the fortnights I squandered on student trips to Austria, Switzerland, France; the frivolous summer holidays in gay little villas in Positano, or sticky hotels in Majorca. It was many years before I finally got here—only when I'd written my first novel and had a little lump of money in my hand that I wanted to do something important with.

During those years Israel had been, as it were, a kind of obsessive hobby. I read about it, dreamt about it, talked about it. I looked out for Israelis and asked them questions. I even tried to learn Hebrew! Everyone laughed at me. They thought I was crazy. Perhaps I was. It was as if some kind of destiny had a grip on me. And when I got here at last, instead of being disappointed, instead of being brought down to earth, I found a magic land, more exciting, more challenging, more mysteriously fascinating and beautiful even than I had expected.

Later—much later—I came to know that it was not perfect, that there were flaws. Terrible flaws. But by that time it was too late. My honeymoon with Israel was over; I was married to it. And that—that feeling of being committed to it forever—strangely enough came *before* I married, or even met, your Israeli father. Before I went to live in a kibbutz. Before any of you were born. So it must be something in the country itself, which, as Shakespeare says, "grappled me to its heart with hoops of steel," never to let me free again.

I have written a lot about Israel, in one form or another. Four of my novels have been concerned with it, at least partly. I've written articles and stories about it. But I've never written a book before which was concerned only with the Jews. I feel—especially here, in Jerusalem—so involved, so close to the country that it seems dangerous to write about it. Fiction is one thing; but now I must write its history for you, I feel afraid. I want so much to be honest and to be fair. I don't want to write propaganda! And yet I want you to understand. So this must be a very personal book, even though I shall try my best all through it not to let my love for my subject distort my view or my writing. Because, even more important to me than you three coming to love Israel as I do, is that you shall not love it blindly, but as wisely, as bravely and as perceptively as possible.

Perhaps I'm hoping for too much. You're young, and will still be very young when you read this. When I was young, I either loved totally or I didn't love at all. I could not qualify my commitments with a recognition of faults in the people or the places that I loved. But perhaps your generation will be more mature than mine. I shall write in that hope.

LETTER 1

In the Beginning

At the risk of putting you off right from square one, I'm afraid I must begin at the beginning. And the beginning is the Bible.

We have done our job as practicing atheist parents all too well. At this moment you are the biggest bunch of little bigots about religion that could be found anywhere—even among the zealots! Which was not what we intended, but perhaps you will have become less extreme in your godlessness by the time you are older. I hope so, because at the moment you're shutting yourselves off from many interesting places, people and things. And you will never understand the origins of your native country if you don't read the Old Testament.

Still—don't worry. I shall deal with that aspect of my history briefly, because, although it has a good deal of importance in the minds of some people, to my mind more recent events carry much more weight.

The idea the Jews have of themselves as a special people

began with the agreement (called "brit" in Hebrew, "covenant" in English) which God is reported to have made with Abraham around 4,000 years ago.

Abraham, whom the Jews call "our Father," is also looked on by the Arabs as their father. He had two sons, Ishmael and Isaac, both by different women (Hagar, an Egyptian, and Sarah, from his own tribe) from whom the two "nations" are supposed to have descended.

As I expect you know, human civilization began in the Middle East, probably around the Nile. Later came the first Jews, or Hebrews, and by the way, the names "Arab" and "Hebrew" probably come from the same root word, a very ancient one meaning "nomads" or "wanderers."

And wanderers your forefathers were on your father's side (on mine they were no doubt caterwauling Celts covered with blue dye who became civilized a long time later!). They had a rough time trudging about the desert with their scrawny flocks. To keep alive in that savage environment and climate they had to keep together, and to do that they had to invent customs, laws and beliefs.

Of course they were extremely primitive, in their ways and in their ideas. Primitive peoples have always invented explanations for the things they saw or experienced, to make those things less terrifying. I've often wondered why it gave them a greater sense of security to invent supernatural beings who were in charge of every object and happening around them, when these gods behaved in such a capricious and often cruel way. But even today we can see that for a lot of people, it's more comfortable to believe that *someone* is in charge, even if privately they don't always care for the way he runs things.

The Jews and the Egyptians both claim to be the ones who first invented the concept of a sort of super-God; but when the ancients of Egypt first did so, they didn't at the same time make him replace all the little sub-gods—they simply set him above them, making him their chief and the little gods his deputies who looked after their own departments—wells, trees, crops and so on.

But somewhere along the line, a tribal leader whom the Bible calls Abraham, seems to have come up with the revolutionary idea of doing away with all the godlings and having one single all-powerful God *instead*, concentrating all the power over their lives into the hands of a being they couldn't see and had simply to trust.

The compact I mentioned included the promise that God would show his people—Abraham's descendants—special favor, if they obeyed him; and in particular, that he would give them large tracts of land at the heart of the then-known world. This area has had a lot of different names: Canaan, Judea, Palestine, and now Israel. At that time it was Canaan. Abraham, and his son Isaac, and *his* son Jacob, were promised in turn that their "seed" should inherit this "land of milk and honey" some time in the future.

But not then. At that point there were very few of them. So the twelve sons of Jacob, great-grandsons of Abraham, drifted into exile in Egypt.

Gradually their descendants fell into something very like slavery, though it was not the sort of slavery that black Africans went through in America. They had to work desperately hard, it's true; they were beaten and driven and ill-used. But they had their own communities, and—apart from the legendary edict, when one Pharaoh panicked, ordering the killing of all the boy babies—no one tried to break up their families or destroy their way of life, or interfere with their religion. And that religion, though inevitably it got all mixed up with the idol worship and rituals of the Egyptians, kept as its basis the old idea of one God and his promise of a land of their own.

Nevertheless they had a very hard time of it, and it must have seemed strange to them that their all-powerful God kept them in bondage to these pagans century after century. Tradition promised them a savior who would lead them out of Egypt and back to their land, and they had to live on that. But as the years passed, and they sank deeper and deeper into poverty and degradation and servitude, they must have wondered if their God hadn't abandoned them.

What had they done to deserve such a punishment? If you read the part of Genesis which deals with the sons of Jacob, founders of the Twelve Tribes, you may think they did some pretty wild and wicked things. But a punishment of 400 years of slavery seems a bit stiff, and must have caused bewilderment, even resentment, in the Hebrews, much as the ghastly persecutions suffered by the Jews of our own times at the hands of their enemies bewilder believers today. Where was their God then?

According to the Bible, God has always punished his chosen people more harshly, and just about as often, as their enemies. But they have gone on believing in him and loving him. They always believed—and so do religious Jews to this day—that their own errors and sins were to blame for all their tribulations; that their God punished them most because he loved them best and wanted them to be perfect. And got angrier, it seems, than any human father when they proved to him repeatedly that they weren't.

Well, so the Hebrews suffered "under the Egyptian yoke," building the pyramids among other monstrous tasks, for 400 years. And at long last, along came Moses.

Was Moses a real person? We have no proof that he lived, only the story in the Bible. He could be just a legend. But then so could Jesus. When one of you asks me, "Do you believe in Jesus?" I always answer that I do believe he lived. I believe it because it's easier to believe *that*, even without proof, than to believe that a world religion sprang out of nothing.

Anyhow, this much I can definitely say. If Moses did live, and if he was anything like his biblical image, he was a most extraordinary and brilliant man, more so than Jesus, in my opinion. He had a staggering vision: of leading an entire people (several hundred thousand by that time, despite the later Pharaohs' laws about killing all the baby boys) out of slavery into freedom. He had the power to convince them that it was worthwhile—or at least to browbeat them into obeying him, and that was no easy task, when you consider that, after perhaps fifteen generations of servitude, they had no tradition of free thought or independent action, and no knowledge of what lay ahead of them. Only tales of an endless desert which must somehow be crossed.

Not only did Moses manage all this, with or without the help of miracles, but, having got them clean away, he then dragged and drove and inspired them through that awful —and I mean awe-ful—desert, staggering from water hole to water hole fighting off marauding tribes, keeping them fed, keeping them moving, keeping them from turning back. Because even the most horrible punishments for escaping may have come to seem more attractive to the poor, hungry, frightened rabble than the endless nightmare of their desert ordeal.

Little by little he brought the Israelites (as they were calling themselves by then because they were descended from Jacob who changed his name to Israel) up again into the Land of Canaan, which they believed their forefathers had been promised by God.

The generation which left Egypt was not the one which finally came "home."

It seems unfair that the last slave generation had to die out before their children reached their goal at last. But hundreds of years in Egypt had degraded them. Even God was disappointed, and Moses was furious. At one point during their desert wanderings, Moses went up into the Mountain of Sinai (no easy climb, as you know!) to collect from God some very high-minded commandments. And while he was up there, the Children of Israel, left leaderless below, got impatient and frightened. They remembered the comforting little god-figures they'd worshiped in Egypt —things you could see and touch. And so they collected up all their gold trinkets and melted them down and made

them into a golden calf. When Moses came down with the
new laws, written on stone tablets, he found them all flat
on their faces around this idol. He flew into a rage. Was it
for this he'd brought them out of Egypt? He smashed the
tablets in front of them and went up and got some more,
a good deal more concerned with ritual and discipline and
less with faith, which he (and God, presumably) considered
more fitting for these poor-spirited people.

They just could not rise to the level of Moses' tremendous new idea, his vision of a new approach to religion
which has influenced every Jew and Christian who came
after him. It was this: instead of having a special caste of
priests to act as go-betweens, ordinary people should know
all the mysteries and communicate directly with their God.
The God of the Hebrews was to be the God of all of them
equally, and he, Moses, had wanted to share his knowledge
of God with them "complete and unabridged," so to speak.

But the business with the golden calf proved (what a less
inspired and more practical man would have known) that
they just weren't up to it. They wanted—as many people
still do today—the security of feeling that their priests were
holy and set apart, more in touch with God than they were.
And they wanted statues to focus their prayers on.

Well, Moses wouldn't give them statues—that was utterly
forbidden in the commandment which banned the making
of graven images. But he gave them the tablets of the law,
and let them decorate them and lug them about in beautiful
crafted containers everywhere they went.

The word. Not an image of God, but his word they were
allowed to worship. I expect that a lot of them, like Rachel
when she left home with Jacob, still kept their little Egyptian idols hidden away in their tents; and who can blame
them? People need objects. Look how the Catholics go on
today with all their saintly statues and holy pictures and
relics and what-not. And the ancient Hebrews were having
a much rougher time than most Catholics are now.

True, they were tough; they had endurance. But they

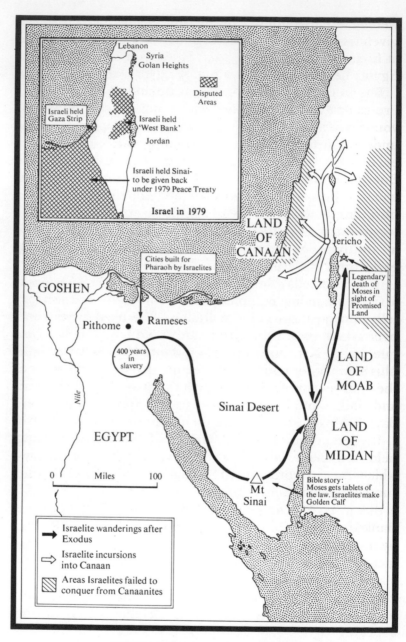

Israel in 1979

- Lebanon
- Syria
- Golan Heights
- Disputed Areas
- Israeli held Gaza Strip
- Israeli held 'West Bank'
- Jordan
- Israeli held Sinai—to be given back under 1979 Peace Treaty

LAND OF CANAAN

Jericho

Legendary death of Moses in sight of Promised Land

Cities built for Pharaoh by Israelites

GOSHEN

Pithome · · Rameses

400 years in slavery

LAND OF MOAB

Sinai Desert

LAND OF MIDIAN

Nile

EGYPT

0   Miles   100

Mt Sinai

Bible story: Moses gets tablets of the law. Israelites make Golden Calf

→ Israelite wanderings after Exodus

⇒ Israelite incursions into Canaan

Areas Israelites failed to conquer from Canaanites

Biblical Return from Exile

weren't used to going hungry—the Egyptians had always given them enough to eat. And they weren't good fighters at first—how could they be? They'd never had to fight in Egypt.

But they had learned to fight by the time they got to the Promised Land at last. They were a new kind of Hebrew— young people who'd been born in freedom, untainted and undemoralized by their parents' and grandparents' experience in Egypt. They regarded Canaan as their homeland. But there were people there already—the Canaanites, tribes settled on the land who were not about to be driven off it. Where have we heard that before? Isn't it the same tragic situation as today—two peoples (more, if you count all the tribes separately) fighting for the same territory, each firmly believing it to be theirs by right?

The Bible tells that the battle for the Promised Land was a single campaign master minded by Joshua. Archaeology tells a different story. The skirmishes were local and spread over a long time. In the end the Hebrews still hadn't conquered all of it. But they held a large area in the middle, plus some other patches. The Canaanites still held most of the fertile coastal plain (where Tel Aviv, Jaffa, Ashkelon and Haifa—and the kibbutz where you were born—are today).

It's rather important to compare on two maps the area held by Israel today with the so-called Promised Land which the Israelites—with or without God's assistance— succeeded in making their own, 3,500 years ago. The point is that if the Jews of today—religious Jews—claim the West Bank as part of the biblical Land of Israel, the Arabs can, by the same token, point to the part of the coastal strip that includes Tel Aviv and say, "But on that basis you can't claim *that*—that never belonged to your ancestors." It's very much safer not to base territorial claims on the Bible, because not only are they unprovable, but they can backfire.

For many years the running battles went on. The Hebrews tried to expand out of the rather poor, dry, mountainous areas they'd conquered inland, and the Canaanites struggled to hold them back or push them out.

If your forefathers hadn't developed a method of building watertight cisterns, they wouldn't have survived in those barren areas at all. But even in those times they were an ingenious lot. Determined to settle, they found ways of producing crops on land which had never been fertile before. Again, you can easily see a parallel with the Israelis of today.

At the same time they were constantly harassed by other tribes, and their own were by no means always available to help each other in times of famine or war. Their survival as a people even then is incredible. You can say God held them together, if you like. But I put it down to sheer human endeavor—ingenuity, endurance, courage.

By the time several hundred years had passed since the Exodus, the Children of Israel must have been a very different people from the dependent, demoralized, weak-willed rabble which had straggled through the marshes after Moses to an only half-wished-for freedom.

Of course it's possible that Moses is a myth, but in a way that isn't important. It isn't even important whether the Exodus and other events told in scripture really happened "just like that." Something like them happened; and the visionary ideas attributed to Moses came into being round about that time.

What really matters is the effect that these stories have had on the Jews down through the ages.

In order to understand Israel today, we must understand this: it has been the absolute belief in these people and these events which has caused a whole chain of undeniably true historical happenings right up to the present day.

After all, who really knows if Christ and *his* miracles existed? These, too, have no historical proof, outside the pages of the New Testament. What matters is how people's *belief* in them shaped history.

The belief in God's promise to Abraham, in Moses and the Exodus, in the trials and triumphs of the Hebrews of old, lies at the root of the deep desire of the Jews of our time for their homeland; the desire which took them back to Israel in our own century, just as it took the ancient Israelites back over 3,000 years ago. Belief in God's covenant with Abraham was by no means the only factor which brought modern Israel into existence. But it was a fundamental one, as you'll see.

LETTER 2

Conquests and Exiles

The "Conquest" of Canaan by the Children of Israel wasn't a conquest at all, in the sense of a successful war followed by a period of peace. It seemed that the Promised Land was never to be given freely by God to his chosen people—they had to keep struggling for it; and they haven't stopped till now.

In those early days the enemies were the surrounding tribes, such as the Philistines and the Moabites (who feature in some of the most famous Bible stories—Goliath, and Ruth, for example). And the Hebrew tribes, from Dan in the north to Simeon in the south, were constantly fighting them. These tribes, which took their names from Jacob's sons and grandsons, were quite scattered, and couldn't always come to each other's help. And their God didn't always help, either. Sometimes he did, but at other times there could be a very savage crackdown when he was displeased.

One thing that might fairly have irritated him was that

sometimes the Israelite tribes even fought each other: being basically one people has never prevented quarrels and divisions among Jews! But after a time it began to be obvious that only by sinking their differences and banding together, at least in bad times, could they hang on to what they had. So leaders of a kind began to emerge.

First there were the Judges, such as Deborah, Gideon and Samson. They were chosen to lead in times of war, as a sort of focus for people's loyalty, and afterwards they were expected to step down. Their children didn't inherit. But later came kings, much like the kings we know about in Europe, who had courts and armies and who passed on their power to their sons.

The first of these was Saul, and the greatest was David. But there were plenty of lesser-known ones, which, if you went to school in Israel, you would study as you now study the Williams, Henries and Georges of England. The Old Testament would be your history book.

The thing that makes them interesting is that they emerge as real men, with all sorts of faults. Even David, the great and the beloved, after whom so many Jewish children are named, did some fairly frightful things, like falling in love with the wife of one of his captains and then sending the captain out to certain death on the battlefield. And that was not the only dubious thing he did! But none of them were saints, which may be why we believe in them and keep their stories alive.

My own favorite king, of course, is Omri (why else would I name a son after him?). Omri is not a king favored by religious Jews because he tolerated pagans and wouldn't allow them to be killed or driven out by the Israelites. He stabilized the kingdom and brought prosperity to his people by making treaties with the surrounding "nations." Israel in his day was actually called The Land of Omri. But all that Omri had built up was thrown away by his son who married the treacherous, scheming Jezabel. And so it goes on, and fascinating reading it makes.

But it's just as well, if you are interested in history as well as legend, to check the Bible stories against the findings of archaeologists. These confirm some of the stories and debunk others.

Quite soon after Solomon (David's son) had built the first Temple in Jerusalem, the squabbling tribes split into two kingdoms. One was called Judah, which is where the name "Jew" comes from. The other, further north, was called Israel. But, just as today, powerful neighbors had their greedy eyes on this area and were determined to get their hands on it as well. Among them were Egypt, Assyria and Babylon.

And what do we discover but your ancestors, so convinced that God was on their side and so busy quarreling with one another (not to mention lapsing from time to time into soft living!) that they didn't take proper heed of the dangers threatening them.

About 760 B.C., when Israel was at its most prosperous, Amos the Prophet suddenly started predicting catastrophe: the destruction of the Temple—the defeat of Israel—the death and dispersion of its people. And Isaiah, in Judah, foresaw peace beyond that, and God in all his glory. (It's worth reading the prophets because a lot of what they predicted came about. There are sects today beavering away, trying to decipher their secrets and find out what's still in store for us.)

When Amos, and other very brave and outspoken prophets, predicted calamity, it may not only have been because they were urging the kings and people of their nations to mend their morals and avoid displeasing God. They may have been worldly-wise enough to realize that they were badly placed geographically.

One major source of trouble was (and still is) that the land of the Jews happened to lay right on a main road, so to speak, between the mighty empires to the north, east and south of it. Apart from anything else, if Egyptians, or Assyrians, or Babylonians wanted to march on each other—

which they frequently did—Israel was terribly in the way. It was a perfect nuisance to have to subdue the wretched Israelite tribes before the big armies could get to grips with each other. It was obviously more convenient to possess these intervening territories, subduing their populations and breaking up their cult centers so that any who were left alive couldn't regroup.

And so it happened that in the seventh century B.C. the Assyrians came swooping down and conquered Israel (the northern kingdom), and about 150 years later the Babylonians did the same to Judah. The crushing of Israel was the worst, because none of the inhabitants survived. The Babylonians were not quite so thorough. They also massacred thousands and destroyed the first Temple; but a remnant of the people of Judah were carried off in chains to Babylon.

It is from this remnant that most of the Jews of today descend. I say "most" because there were quite a lot of conversions down through the years, in particular a group called the Khazars, a fierce Tartar warrior tribe in what's now southern Russia. They converted to Judaism about 1,200 years ago, and although a lot of them converted again to Christianity when the Russian state came into being, some people claim that a majority of Jews of Russian ancestry (which includes you three) descend from these Khazars. But no one can prove who descended from whom, so if you prefer to consider yourselves as "sons of Abraham" there's nothing to stop you.

Back to the poor exiled remnant of Judah, sighing by the waters of Babylon. I've always thought that it was this second taste of exile that put the iron into the Jewish soul and into Jewish literature. The biblical version of this period produced a psalm which was turned into a prayer. It is so important, it wouldn't hurt you to learn it. It's sustained many, many generations of your forefathers while they were cut off from the land of their origins (or, if they were Khazars, from the land of their longing). Certainly it is not only the beautiful, mournful part of Psalm 137 which helps explain the *kind* and *depth* of attachment the Jews have felt down through the ages to their Land. One has to read the psalm to the end to understand that there was more than sadness and yearning, more even than determination to remember and one day go back. There is also fierce hatred for their enemies.

> Sitting by the rivers of Babylon
> We wept at the memory of Zion.
> We hung our harps on the willows,
> For we had been asked by our captors for a song.
> They who had decimated us demanded entertainment!
> "Sing," they said.
> "Sing us the songs of your country."
>
> How could we sing the Lord's song in an alien land?
> If I forget thee, Jerusalem,
> Let my right hand forget its cunning!
> May my tongue cleave to the roof of my mouth
> If I ever forget thee,
> If I do not remember Jerusalem
> Above my chief joy.

Now here comes the fierce part:

> Lord, do not forget what our enemies did
> On the day they took Jerusalem!
> How they said, "Destroy her!
> Down with her to her foundations!"
>
> Woman of Babylon,
> Happy will that man be
> Who treats you as you have treated us!
> Happy he who takes and dashes
> Your infants against a stone!

Well, that's pretty horrific. But you have to take the rough with the smooth in the Old Testament—they were savage times. *Whenever* you come to consider hatred and acts of revenge, ancient or modern, you always have to measure them against the acts that came first (in this case the destruction of the Jews' holy of holies, the massacre of their people, their forced journey into a strange land). And also remember human nature, which is often not far from its primitive beginnings, even nowadays when we are supposed to be civilized.

Jesus's instruction to his followers to "love your enemies and do good to them that hate you," turn the other cheek if someone strikes you, and so on, has always aroused incredulity in all but the most saintly Christians. It isn't "natural." Is it even desirable? I've never been able to decide. You'll have plenty of opportunity later in these letters to consider Jews who *did* resist their enemies, and Jews who didn't, and decide for yourselves which you admire most.

That second exile was shorter than the one in Egypt. The "happy man" the Jews yearned for in the psalm, who would avenge them, was Cyrus, King of the Medes and Persians, who in 539 B.C. conquered Babylon. He told the Jews they could go home, and home they went—some of them. Oddly enough, just as today, there were those who were too comfortable in their exile by that time and when they *could* leave, didn't choose to. The ones who went rebuilt the Temple on its old site, where it was to stand for the next 600 years.

After the Persians came the Greeks, and it was from this period—which is called the Hellenistic age—that the story of the Maccabees comes. Do you remember acting it as a play one Hanukkah? The Jews were prepared to put up with Greek rule, but the Greeks wouldn't be satisfied until every people they conquered was "Hellenized," in other words, turned into imitation Greeks. That meant that, apart from eating and dressing and living like Greeks, the Jews were expected to worship Greek gods as well. They drew the line at that. Well, some of them succumbed, of course. Some only pretended to, and secretly went on keeping up their

own religion. Others ran away into the desert. And others
flatly refused to bow down before the idols, and were killed.

And some plotted rebellion.

The Maccabees were the leaders. They were the guerrilla
fighters of those days.* They were few and poorly armed,
and the Greeks were mighty and had every battle aid you
could think of, including elephants they'd brought from the
East. It infuriated the powerful, invincible Greeks that they
couldn't break the will of this tiny group of Jews. They
would send huge armies into the hills where the Jews were
hiding; but the Maccabees (the word means "hammer")
would pounce on them when they least expected it, deal
them a sharp hard blow and vanish again into the rocks.

In the end, against all the odds, the Jews defeated the
Greeks and recaptured Jerusalem. The Greeks hadn't actually destroyed the Temple, but they had defiled it, in Jewish
eyes, by replacing all the Jewish religious objects, the Ark
of the Law and the sacred lamps, with pagan statues. But
the Maccabees threw the idols out and sanctified it again for
Jewish worship. Hanukkah, the Feast of Lights, originated
in this legend: a little jug of oil, which was all the pure oil
they had, kept the Temple candelabrum burning for eight
whole days (until more olives could be pressed) although
it was only enough for one day.

Nevertheless, the Jews learned a lot from the Greeks,
some of it good and some bad. The best thing would have
been if the Jews could have steeped themselves in Greek
philosophy and art without getting tainted by her hedonism
(which means living for pleasure). Actually, they picked up
a good bit of both, and the Greeks learned something from
them too, even though each people appeared to hate and
despise the other. Eventually the Greek era ended, and the
Romans took over.

---

*Guerrillas may be loosely distinguished from terrorists thus: guerril-
las fight the enemy's army, terrorists make war against civilians.

During the time of Roman rule, Jesus lived and died—at the hands of the Romans of course, not of the Jews themselves, as the Catholic Church (among others) has put about ever since. Mind you, the "establishment" Jews of that time, the rabbis who were struggling to hold on to their rights to run their own affairs under Roman rule, did to some extent encourage the Romans to do away with this troublesome member of their own race. He was preaching ideas too far removed from orthodoxy for comfort, *and* attracting far too many followers. But to blame the entire Jewish race for the death of Christ on the cross would look absurd to us now, if it were not for the amount of suffering that's been caused by this "excuse" for persecuting the Jews down through the ages.

Thirty-three years after Christ's death, when his ideas had already spread throughout the Roman and Greek empires, the Jews found they couldn't stand the Romans any longer.

In my view there was very little about the Roman Empire to admire. I remember dragging your father into the Coliseum when we were visiting Rome together. He stopped dead at the entrance like a horse that smells blood, and wouldn't go in. He looked round the great ruined tiers of the amphitheater, echoing and eerie and somehow cold, despite the Italian sun. "This place stinks of cruelty," he said.

It's true. One of their own historians said about them, "They make a desolation and call it peace." They built fine roads and amazing buildings, they fought and organized efficiently and put on splendid pageants. But they had no real culture or morality. They were brutal, superstitious, corrupt and hideously cruel. Nowhere in their history was this more obvious than in their dealings with the Jewish uprising.

Rome was like Goliath, and Judah, or Judea as it was called by then, was David. But their struggle was not so quickly over; and in the end, Goliath won. But not before the great Roman legions had been thoroughly humiliated many times by the tiny Jewish force. Incredibly, it took *four years* and a loss of thousands of soldiers before the Romans finally threw everything they had at Jerusalem in the year A.D. 71. They surrounded Jerusalem and tried to starve the Jews into submission. It took a year, and still they held out, so finally Titus, son of the Emperor, stormed the city, massacred its starving inhabitants by the hundreds of thousands, and carried the survivors off to Rome to sell into slavery.

They also destroyed the Temple for the second time. King Herod had restored and beautified the Temple and built a new wall around it. It is the last remaining side of this wall that can be seen there today; and it is this destruction that is mourned by the Jews on the holy day called Tisha B'av. If you visit the Western Wall, all that is left of the second Temple, on that date, you can see the Hassidim rocking and praying and mourning that fatal day. But in a way it was a triumphant day too. None of the other peoples enslaved by Rome could have held the legions at bay for four years and so shamed mighty Rome that when the victory came, they built a giant arch for Titus as if he had conquered half the world afresh. If you ever go to Rome, don't visit the Coliseum, where many of those brave survivors of the siege were fed to wild beasts for the amusement of Roman degenerates. Visit the Arch of Titus, and think of it as a Roman tribute to the Jewish people who so nearly got the better of them.

No Jews were allowed to enter Jerusalem after that, and the Romans renamed Judea Syria-Palestina. But still the Jews were not completely crushed. Small groups of guerrillas fought on, while their brave resistance caused other subject peoples to gather themselves together to oppose a Rome they no longer thought of as invincible.

We won't get to Massada this trip. I'm not sorry. I want you to see it when you're old enough to understand its meaning, not before. Now, it might look like no more than a huge, bare slab of rock in the desert, and perhaps I couldn't find the words to impress you with its history.

In A.D. 73, two years after the fall of Jerusalem, about 1,000 Jewish men and women were still holding out against the Romans, in the fortress built on the mountaintop by Herod. They were completely cut off in this remote spot, no help could reach them; yet they held out until the Romans, maddened by their stubborn resistance, painstakingly built a ramp of earth right up the side of the mountain up which they could march and bring their siege-machines. It took months, while the Jews above watched the ramp growing higher day by day until it reached the top. But when the first Roman troops marched up it, they found nothing to carry off in triumph to Rome except dead bodies. Every Jew was dead. They had all committed suicide rather than submit. Now, when an Israeli soldier completes his training, he is taken to the top of Massada to take his oath which includes the words:

"Massada shall not fall again."

LETTER 3

The Beginning of the Dispersion

Even Massada was not quite the end of the Jewish resistance. The famous Bar Kochba revolt, in A.D. 132, was still to come. Bar Kochba actually managed to recapture Jerusalem, and held it for the Jews for three years. But the end was coming—the end, and a strange beginning.

Hadrian recaptured Jerusalem, which was not in complete ruins after its long ordeal, tortured Bar Kochba to death, and banned the Jews from the capital he now called his own and renamed Aelia Capitolina.

It's hard to understand what the loss of Jerusalem, and especially the Temple, meant to those Jews of old. It was so much more than just blocks of stone to them. It had been the absolute focal-point of their lives—not only spiritually but in a practical way. To begin with, they believed with all their hearts that the "divine presence"—God, whose name was so holy it was never spoken—inhabited the Temple, and that when it was destroyed and defiled by the Romans, this presence left it—and where was it then to be found?

No loss of any human life could possibly be compared with a loss like that. It deprived them of the root of their spiritual being, the source of their Jewish identity—almost of their reason for living. It also robbed thousands of them of their livelihood, because so many had been connected with serving the Temple, one way or another. It had been the absolute kernel of their lives, and what they were left with was bare existence. They were bereft—a derelict and despairing people.

This was obviously one of the "dangerous corners" for Jewish survival. It was the point at which most nation groups would have just given up, assimilated, or gone under in some other way. But they didn't.

Banned from their holy of holies, they lingered in Palestine, keeping as close to it as they could, until the next fatal step was taken—the conversion of the Emperor Constantine to Christianity.

In no time the same Romans who had once thrown Christians to the lions in the Coliseum were rushing pell-mell to get baptized. The Roman Empire changed gradually into the Byzantine, which evolved after Constantine moved his capital to the city of Byzantium (now Istanbul in Turkey). And it was now that the Jews were really banished from all of Palestine, because these new Christians felt Judaism was a rival faith. After all, Christ was a Jew! If the Jews refused to recognize him, that threw doubt on his having been the real Messiah.

It is this—the Jews' refusal, all through the centuries, to accept Christ—which has so maddened the Christian church that it has never been able to let the Jews alone. Up till today, there are still missionaries who are trying to make them "see the light." . . . Do you remember those posters I pointed out the other day, just off King George Street, warning Jerusalemites about a certain family of Christian missionaries "trying to steal our children's souls"?

And so began the great Jewish experience of life in other

people's countries which is called the Diaspora,* which
means "dispersion." It was to teach them the lesson of
rootlessness, the nightmare of separation from the land
they considered their own. It was also to establish them as
a unique people—the only "nation," "race" or whatever
you care to call it, which kept their separate identity, religion and customs while scattered all over the world without
a territory of its own to hold it together. How they did this
is more of a miracle to me than any number of holy lamps
burning without oil.

Religious Jews believe that God accomplished this miracle through the Torah, their holy book of history and laws.
But how on earth did the Torah survive, with the Jews
scattered all over the Roman Empire and later driven further and further away from the lost center of their faith?

It was men who worked that miracle. Wise, far-seeing,
courageous and determined men—rabbis. It was one of
these—Yochanan Ben Zakai—who, even while grieving for
the loss of Jerusalem, was practical enough to move the
center of Jewish learning to Jabneh, a town outside Jerusalem. There he concentrated all the knowledge, wisdom and
history of his unhappy people, and kept it from getting lost.
He gathered together scribes who copied the holy scrolls
and somehow made sure that each group of the spreading
exiles carried one with them. Other rabbis came later who
realized that without more laws, written down and dis-
tributed among the scattered Jews, the great treasure of
Judaism would be forgotten. So they began to write the
Talmud.

The idea of the Talmud was to make a kind of fence of
rules around the main laws given in the Torah, rules that
stood away from the basic law so that nobody would even
come near to breaking it. The Torah, for example, forbids

---

*Much material for these letters was taken from Werner Keller's book,
The Diaspora, a wonderfully detailed and readable account.

cooking meat in milk. So the Talmud forbade eating them together at all, or even cooking them with the same utensils or using the same dishes.

In this way all the basic laws of Jewish prayer, holy deeds *(mitzvot),* diet and ritual were hedged in with hundreds of little customs and forms and observances which kept the minds of pious Jews concentrated and their hands busy in "righteous ways" from morning till night—at least that was the intention.

Petty and unnecessary as much of it may seem to us now, it was a brilliant inspiration at the time. Without it, Judaism would have been worn away, just by the friction of everyday living among alien nations. Many Jews today, incidentally, keep to the old traditions chiefly because they feel bound to these rules which held a nucleus of their people together through thick and thin for 2,000 years.

These scrolls of the law now took the place of their Temple and their land in the lives of the Jews. It was the same story as when Moses gave the Israelites the sacred tablets to carry through the desert, as a symbol of God and a substitute for a home. Wherever they now wandered—and they wandered far and wide, north into Europe, south into Arabia, west to Spain, east to the Orient—the Torah and the Talmud were carried as a sort of portable nationhood.

In addition to the variety of trades Jews had always followed, including farming, a large number of them now became merchants, and in this role they began to influence the whole development of civilization. Wherever they went they carried with them the seeds of the old, civilized Hellenism they had learned from the Greeks, together with their own idea of God and morality, and above all their obsession with learning.

In many places and for long periods they were the only people who could claim any kind of culture. Some of the peoples they lived among hated and feared them for it, as primitive or ignorant people tend to fear those more en-

lightened than they are; but others saw the worth of the
Jewish strangers, made them welcome, and put their special skills to use.

In the meantime, something of great importance had
happened. Mohammed had founded Islam.

Islam began about six centuries after Christ. In an incredibly short time it had swept across half the known
world: from Central Asia to the Atlantic coast of Africa, it
spread like a forest fire. The Moslems knew they owed
something to the Jews as the first believers in one god; they
called him Allah, which means "the God" and gave the Jews
credit for "discovering" him. They wanted the Jews to
recognize Mohammed as Allah's prophet. When they
refused, the Moslems—like the Christians—decided an-
grily that they were not fit to live in their holy land (the
Arabian Peninsula) and drove them out with barbarous
cruelty. The Jews fought bravely—and that was the last
time they ever organized a military defense, till modern
times.

Still, in all other parts of the new Moslem Empire, the
Islamic conquest had good results for the Jews. For the first
time since the Dispersion, they found themselves living in
a united empire which tolerated them, calling them "the
People of the Book." The restrictions the Romans had put
on them were taken off, even the one banning them from
Jerusalem. But they weren't allowed to rebuild the Temple,
the site of which was now a heap of rubble and filth.

The Moslem invaders, having driven out the Byzantines,
sought out this spot which had been the holy of holies to
the Jews. A great rock, defiled with dung, jutted up from
the mound, a rock steeped in Jewish legend and soon to be
steeped in Moslem myths as well. Here Adam had been
created, Cain had killed Abel, Noah's Ark had grounded.
. . . And before long, most sacred of all to the Moslems,
it would be believed that the Prophet Mohammed had risen
to heaven from the same spot. Factually, it had been the
Temple's altar-stone while the Temple still stood.

Now the conquering Caliph Omar ordered a shrine built over the Rock. This was soon replaced by a building which remains one of the most beautiful on earth—the Dome of the Rock, whose golden glint dominates every view of the Old City.

While that shrine stands there, the Jewish Temple can never be rebuilt—a bitter thing for religious Jews, who have to be content to say their prayers by the one remaining wall of Herod's Temple.

LETTER 4

Down into Darkness – Jews versus the Church

By the time Islam was well established, the dispersed Jews could be found in all the three main world centers: Byzantium (around Turkey, roughly), Islam (all over Arabia and North Africa) and feudal Europe. This last had been held by Rome, but had, by A.D. 500, been overrun by Vandals, Goths, Huns and suchlike barbaric tribes from the east, who made savage laws against the Jews. But Islam was still spreading. Before long the Moslem armies had burst out of their deserts, conquered the Byzantines, and took most of Spain from the Visigoths.

A better age now dawned for the Jews. True, the Moslems regarded them as second-class citizens. They had to pay special taxes, and here, for the first but not the last time, we find them forced to wear a badge of identification, sewn to their clothes. But they no longer had to wander; they had freedom to set up schools and develop their talents. They were recognized as a learned people—a people obsessed by learning—and some of them got important

34

posts in the governments of Egypt, Baghdad and Spain. There were Jewish men of science, philosophers and poets. And so, for two hundred years, Arab and Jew, Islam and Judaism, managed to co-exist, uneasily, but, on the whole, productively.

In Europe, too, the Jews had been making their mark. The Christian Church made laws to try to curb them, but the fact was, it couldn't manage without them. They found their way into government posts and, because of their learning, their gift for languages and above all their connections with several continents and cultures, they became an indispensable link between the Moslem and Christian worlds.

Jews suffered less than most others under feudalism. Though they were technically the chattels of the crown, at least they weren't in the category of the serfs. They were owned body and soul by the landlords, who were under the lords and barons, who were under the king, and the Church was in there too, struggling for power over them all. But the Jews didn't exactly fit into any category, so, providing they paid their taxes and kept the laws that could be applied to them, they managed to bypass a lot of the restrictions.

Then came the Crusades.

Don't let anybody feed you any nonsense about the noble Crusaders, Richard "the Lionhearted," the days of chivalry and all that rubbish. Richard was an appalling king, and the rabble he took off to the Holy Land with him were for the most part beneath contempt.

Of course you know the whole idea of the Crusades—to take Palestine and especially Jerusalem back from the "infidel" (meaning, people who didn't believe in Christ—needless to say the Moslems call anyone who doesn't believe in Allah an infidel, too). Any serfs who went crusading were given their freedom, any sinners were promised forgiveness. That meant that every villain (as well as every villein), all the rogues and vagabonds and adventurers, in general the scum of the earth, flocked to the standard.

What this brutal horde of so-called Christians did to the Jews on their way southeast doesn't bear writing about. They were off to kill the infidels, and who better to sharpen their swords on than the "Christ-killing" Jews? They murdered and tortured and robbed them wherever they found them, all through Europe and Turkey, leaving a trail of blood and horror never to be forgotten or forgiven.

They did worse when they got to the Holy Land—those who did get there; I'm happy to report many of them died on the way. You remember the verse about King Richard?

> To hew and hack
> The paynim black,
> To flay and fell
> The infidel
> To make short work
> Of the Murky Turk
> And draw the gore
> Of the dusky Moor—
> This was the first and favorite art
> Of reckless Richard the Lion-Heart.*

Not only that, but to burn, to destroy, and especially to steal. Many a British family fortune was founded on the gold brought back from Byzantium and Palestine. Altogether not one of Christianity's more creditable episodes.

This went on from the eleventh to the thirteenth centuries, A.D. And oddly enough, during that time of the worst persecutions the Jews had suffered since the Romans, those who had established themselves in Andalusia, southern Spain, were having a golden age. The Crusaders didn't go that way, and the Moslems allowed the Jews freedom to practice every trade, craft and science.

Everyone benefited from this tolerance, and it's well worth mentioning here that wherever and whenever Jews

---

*Eleanor and Herbert Farjeon, *Kings and Queens*

were given this degree of freedom, their adopted countries benefited. This was not God blessing those who accepted his chosen People! It was because the Jews, with their energy, industry and talent, their wide knowledge of different cultures and languages, and their genius for science and trade, got goods flowing, money circulating and—most important, you may think—minds opening up. On the other hand, where Jews were persecuted, held down, or driven away, economies suffered drastically and cultural levels invariably dropped.

Some great Jewish scholars, such as Moses Maimonides, made their contributions to civilization during this splendid era of cooperation and enlightenment in Spain, which lasted for several hundred years around the start of the second millenium. Between them, the Arabs and Jews, and to some extent the Christians of Spain, explored all fields of study, opening up research into everything from natural sciences to philosophy. Their discoveries and their shared scholarship paved the way for the Renaissance ("rebirth") which was to come at the end of the Middle Ages. This is the unfailing result of cooperation and tolerance, when different cultures, nationalities and religions work together instead of wasting their strength in persecuting each other. You'd think this would be obvious. The immense horrors of the Dark Ages of medievalism proved that this simple lesson had not been learned. It still hasn't.

The Crusades were just the beginning of the long nightmare which descended on the Jews of Europe at the end of the eleventh century. Christianity and in particular the Catholic Church were responsible for much of the butchery and mayhem; superstition (always just under the surface of any religion, particularly one rooted in myth and mystery as Christianity is) played a very active part. But there was a strong element of human greed in the persecutions of the Jews.

I said that wherever Jews settled prosperity followed, and the Jews prospered too, especially under feudalism. Their prosperity was useful to the rulers of their countries, who were always needing to borrow money, or better still, get it by taxation. But when orders from a pope or an archbishop, or a popular movement based on some superstitious rumor about Jewish anti-Christian practices, resulted in an upsurge of feeling against the Jews, the kings and emperors were only too delighted to encourage persecution. They were very willing to see the Jews first taxed till they could pay no more, and then killed or exiled so that their property and possessions could be added to the royal treasuries.

The fact that when the Jews had gone, they were invariably missed, and had to be speedily invited back again, was another lesson nobody ever seemed to learn. And the Jews themselves were oddly slow in discovering that the promises of greedy rulers were not to be trusted.

After horrendous massacres in Germany, France, Italy and Britain, in which literally hundreds of thousands of Jews were brutally tortured, burned, hanged, driven out or reduced to total poverty, they would be invited back sometimes within a few years—long before the memory of their dreadful sufferings could have faded. Some guarantees were usually offered, although the conditions for their return were often humiliating: having to wear special clothes; not being allowed to practice any trade but money-lending; not being permitted to own property or mix with Christians, and so on. Yet, incredibly, there were always some who went, just as there were Jews who actually went back to Germany after the holocaust of Hitler.

It is hard to understand, and perhaps it *can* only be understood in terms of a once-proud and justly self-confident people who had been brought so low by years of terror and decimation that their spirit and their pride were broken. The image of the cringing, fawning Jew—"Uriah Heep"— was a product of centuries of such appalling treatment at the hands of Christians that the wonder really is that they had enough spark left in them to continue calling themselves Jews at all.

There was nothing they were not accused of, nothing
they did not endure. It was said that they stole the holy
bread which Catholics believe is Christ's actual body, in
order to squeeze blood out of it. Communities of Jews who
had been living peacefully for generations all across
Europe would be set upon by mobs roused to bloodthirsty
fury by one priest claiming that his holy wafers had been
sacrilegiously stabbed by a Jewish knife. It was also said,
and much more often, that they murdered Christian children and used their blood in barbaric rituals.

Two cases out of hundreds may be enough to show how
Jews have suffered from this one superstition. In Vienna, in
1181, three boys disappeared while playing on the frozen
Danube River. Christians testified to having seen Jews lure
the boys into a house and butcher them. Three hundred
Jews were burned at the stake before the spring thaw came
to reveal the unmarked bodies of the drowned children.

Then there was the case of Simon of Trent. Simon was
a child of two, whose body was found by a Jew in the year
1475. He ran at once to the local bishop to tell him. This
bishop lost no time in having all the town's Jews arrested
and tortured. Having obtained "confessions" in this way,
he had them burned. Meanwhile Simon's body had been
embalmed and churchmen claimed it was working miracles.
He was declared a saint. He continued to be regarded as
such by the Catholic church until *1965,* when solemn investigations aroused doubts as to his powers.

At one stage the skies of Europe were literally black with
the smoke of fires in which Jewish homes and synagogues,
often forcibly crammed with the Jews themselves, or mountainous bonfires piled with Jewish men, women and children, were burned.

The Black Death, the worst plague the world has ever
seen, made matters worse for the Jews when it spread west

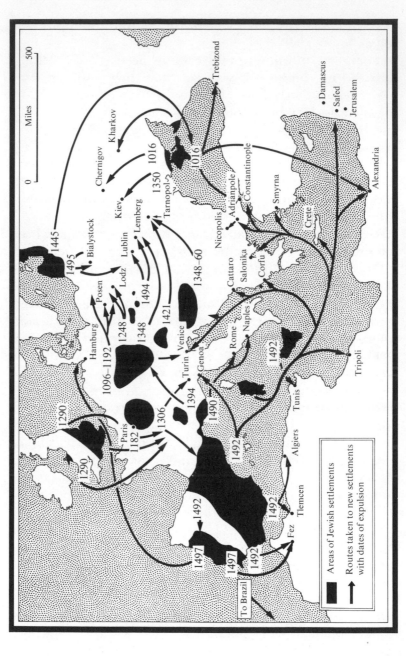

Miles

0   500

Damascus
Safed
Jerusalem
Alexandria
Trebizond
1016
1016
Constantinople
Adrianople
Smyrna
Crete
Nicopolis
Kharkov
Chernigov
1016
Kiev
1350
Tarnopol
Lemberg
1494
1348
1421
1348–60
Salonika
Corfu
Cattaro
Naples
Rome
Venice
Genoa
Turin
1394
1490
1492
1492
Tripoli
Bialystock
1495
1445
Lublin
Lodz
Posen
Hamburg
1248
1096–1192
1306
Paris
1182
1290
1290
1492
Tunis
Algiers
1492
Tlemcen
1492
Fez
1497
1497
1492
To Brazil

■ Areas of Jewish settlements

↑ Routes taken to new settlements
   with dates of expulsion

600 Years of anti-Jewish Persecution

from China in 1348. Jews who kept the old Talmudic laws were cleaner than their fellow citizens, who knew nothing whatever about hygiene. The dietary laws prevented them from eating the filthy meat and offal that Christians ate. They may therefore have been more resistant to disease than others. Though thousands of them died, the Jewish dead were still perceptibly fewer than their Christian neighbors.

In their terrible fear of death by plague, the Christians turned on the Jews with renewed fury. They accused the Jews of *causing* the plague by poisoning wells, or by magic. This gave them a new excuse to destroy them, and to the Jews who died of plague were added the ones who were murdered for "causing" it.

Only one sort of Jew was spared—the ones who agreed to be baptized. This is why there are those who say that the price of Jewish survival was too high, because, in those days, they were always offered that alternative. Inevitably, some took it, but in no country except Spain were there any mass conversions. The majority preferred death. Many threw their own wives and children into the flames to avoid the utter defeat of forced conversion—and many children were dragged from the arms of their doomed parents by Christians who considered it their sacred duty to baptize these little heathens and bring them up in the "true faith."

But if you think that it would have been better to accept conversion, to stop being Jewish, first consider the Marranos.

The Marranos were the descendants of those Spanish Jews who flourished in the Andalusian golden age. It is important for you, Israelis born in a time of hostility between Jews and Arabs, to remember that it was when Jews and Arabs respected each other and worked together that both nations reached their highest peak of civilization.

At that time, and for centuries afterwards, Christianity stood for intellectual repression. The Catholic Church

ruthlessly opposed any kind of advance in knowledge. It
was when the Church grew powerful in Spain, at the very
end of the fourteenth century, that the golden age ended,
for Jews and Moslems alike.

A fanatical priest called Martinez began to rouse the
people under the slogan "Christian Spain for the Christian
Spaniards." He accused the Jews of being the enemies of
God, and urged their destruction quite openly. Jewish
quarters in the main cities were attacked and a reign of
terror spread over the whole countryside. Jews were tortured and murdered, their property stolen, their synagogues razed, their children sold as slaves.

And here, where they had been so happy and so respected, where they had contributed so much, the violent
turnabout was too much for them. Thousands and thousands converted. The Spanish called them "conversos."
Only Jews called them "Marranos." That word means
"swine" or "the damned."

Still—better than death, you might think. Better than
being reduced to beggary, better than exile. But two generations later, the bills came in.

I didn't set out to attack the Catholic Church, but I find it
impossible to write the history of its relations with your
people without shuddering. In fairness I should say that
there were a few good and just Catholics, even during these
terrible centuries. There were even a few popes who sent
out orders insisting on fair trials for Jews, protested against
the wrongness of forced conversions and tried to stop the
slaughter. But these weak attempts to stem the tide of hatred the Church itself had let loose usually failed.

Here and there a light shines: a town whose council reso-
lutely protected its Jews; a bishop who sheltered them from
the mob in his own palace; an enlightened ruler who
refused, at the risk of being cast out of the Church, to join
in the general persecution. But they are like the little candle

in *The Merchant of Venice*—shining in a black night, like "a good deed in a naughty world." By "naughty," Shakespeare meant wicked. And one would think wickedness and inhumanity could go no further than it did in the twelfth, thirteenth and fourteenth centuries.

Yet in the middle of the fifteenth century, a new wave of terror broke out in Spain. This time it was directed against the "New Christians"—the Marranos, who had been promised that if they gave up being Jews they would have nothing to fear.

The fact was, though, that conversion hadn't lessened their skills. They had risen in all the professions now legally open to them. Whoever rises in the world arouses jealousy and resentment in those who don't. These ex-Jews had tried to hide in assimilation. But hatred sought them out.

And many had not truly become Christian. They kept up their Jewish practices in secret. The Church suspected this. The "accursed" people it had tried to wipe out by swallowing them up were now stuck like a bone in its very throat. It determined to vomit them up and destroy them forever.

So it used its most monstrous weapon of all: the Inquisition.

I won't go into details. They are too appalling. It is enough to give the basic facts. The Inquisition was an official organization set up by the Pope in various countries, to uncover what were called "heretics"—that is, anyone who deviated from the established beliefs of Christianity. Or anybody who seemed to deviate. Or anyone who was accused by anyone else of deviating. Or, in fact, any person whom any other person wanted to get rid of, either to repay some grudge or to seize his property.

It had to look legal, so there were "trials." If an accused man refused to confess, he was tortured until he did. If he held out against torture he could be killed for "obduracy" —stubbornness in refusing to confess. Men were tortured into denouncing others, who in their turn were con-

demned. Then they were burned alive, in public. The burnings were called "auto-da-fé"—acts of faith. They were
performed with full religious ceremonies, blessed by the
Church of Rome.

This evil work was carried on in the name of Jesus Christ,
the gentle savior, whose whole message was: love each
other, treat others as you want to be treated.

Before long the count of the dead was over 30,000. Most
of them were Christians whose beliefs differed, however
slightly, from the orthodox. But the sufferings of the converted Jews of Spain were terrible enough to prove, the first
of many proofs, that assimilation is not the simple solution
to the Jewish problem that one might think.

Ironically enough, such unconverted Jews as were still
living in Spain were left alone. They could not be called
heretics—they were unbelievers. But that didn't mean they
were safe forever.

In 1492 the Spanish king, Ferdinand, decided to expel all
his Jewish subjects for "reasons of state." Yes, in 1492.
Every schoolchild learns that date. It was the self-same year
that the self-same Spanish king was launching forth one of
Spain's greatest sons on his famous voyage of discovery:

> In fourteen hundred and ninety-two
> Columbus sailed the ocean blue . . .

And what was Columbus, according to common report?
Columbus's parentage is a mystery but a belief has always
persisted that he was the son of a Marrano woman—a Jew,
in fact. But his departure from Spain was very different
from that of 100,000 Jews who, banished from their native
land, sought refuge in neighboring Portugal.

That refuge was no refuge at all.

After a few years the Portuguese king wanted to marry a
Spanish princess in the hope of ruling both countries. Her
priest told her to make it a condition of the marriage that
the king get rid of all the Jews of Portugal. The king didn't

want to agree because some of the key men of his court were Jews. But in the end ambition won.

So the Sephardim—the Spanish Jews—were exiled *en masse,* a fate which had already happened to the Jews of France a century earlier, and the Jews of England in the time of Edward I.

Once again the landless, uprooted, unprotected people of Moses became what they have been called for 2,000 years—the Wandering Jews.

LETTER 5

Protestants and Ghettoes

The refugees spread out. Most of them went to North Africa and the Ottoman (Turkish) Empire, which had taken over from the Byzantines. Others stayed in Europe and swelled the communities still existing there in Poland, Holland, southern France and northern Italy. A few crossed the Atlantic and became the first Jews to help settle South America. Many died of hunger and despair, sailing about the Mediterranean seeking a refuge.

And some returned to Palestine. They set up religious and scholarly communities there. There was no thought yet of Israel as a homeland. True, they prayed, "Next year in Jerusalem!" But it was no more than a remote longing, as if for heaven. There were still more hard lessons to learn about the price of being a people without a land.

The coming centuries—the sixteenth, seventeenth and eighteenth—were not too bad for those Jews who had had the wisdom (or the luck) to seek refuge among their fellow-Semites the Arabs, or the Moslem Turks. Many of the

Sephardic descendants of the golden age in Spain did as you'd expect—they rose to important positions in their new countries. They became diplomats and counselors, and especially physicians, to the sultans. They thrived once again as merchants, bankers, traders and craftsmen. It's true that toward the end of the sixteenth century, when the Turkish Empire began to decay, the Jews there lost some of their prestige and began to be taxed and restricted. But at least they were not persecuted. Things did not go so well for the Ashkenazi* Jews of Europe.

In the middle of the sixteenth century came the Reformation. This is the word used in history for the beginnings of Protestantism. It was started in the early 1500s by Luther in Germany, Calvin in France, and John Knox in Scotland. Essentially they were all "protesting" against the domination of the Pope and the doctrines of Catholicism, which had been accepted unquestioningly (more or less) for hundreds of years.

From the Jewish point of view, there are two main points to make about it. The first is that when we look in horror at the Jewish persecutions in that era, we must keep a sense of proportion. Jews never suffered at the hands of Christians as much as Christians now suffered from each other. It's important to remember that it was an age of *general* religious fanaticism and violence.

When Protestantism began to take hold in Northern Europe in the mid-sixteenth century, all hell broke loose. The Catholics went quite mad at the idea of another Christian sect opposing their authority. There were hideous massacres of Christians by Christians, not to mention a proper war, lasting thirty years, in which Protestants and Catholics made away with each other on a scale and with a ferocity which makes the slaughter of Jews up to then look almost trivial by comparison.

*Ashkenazi is the term used to describe the fairer-skinned Yiddish speaking Jews of France, Germany and Russia.

The other interesting thing was that different branches of Protestantism (like all reform movements it immediately split up into sects!) had different attitudes toward the Jews. The Calvinists were fairly tolerant. The Lutherans, on the other hand, took their cue—or cues—from Luther himself; and Luther, for all his courage and cleverness, was a very sick man.

To begin with he used the sufferings of the Jews as a propaganda weapon against Catholicism, saying how badly they'd been treated and suggesting that if Protestants would treat them more fairly they would surely give up their wrong ideas and convert. When they didn't, Luther reacted much like Mohammed, who had also hoped to win the Jews over by tolerance. In his disappointed rage, Luther turned bitterly against the Jews, reviving all the old myths and lies and calling for repressions and cruelties against them worse than those thought up by his Catholic enemies!

In *The Merchant of Venice,* Shakespeare, writing in sixteenth-century England, introduced a character—Shylock, the Jewish moneylender—through whom we can see exactly how Jews were regarded in Europe, then and for years to come. On the one hand, the Church saw to it that they were degraded and despised. Punitive laws reduced them to miserable living conditions, forced them to wear special clothes so that Gentiles could easily identify them, and, in short, did all it could to destroy their self-respect and dignity.

They even made laws to keep down their numbers. It was illegal for more than one child in any Jewish family to marry. Huge taxes were imposed for the privilege of bearing children. It's no biological accident that Shakespeare's Shylock only had one daughter.

But, at the same time, the Jews were valuable to the economy. Merchants, princes, even the Church itself—in secret, of course—borrowed money from them, even while "spitting on their Jewish gabardine," as Antonio (one of the goodies) does in the play.

And all the time the Jews were being urged to convert. In the end of Shakespeare's "comedy," the Duke's judgment on Shylock the Jew for seeking the death of the Merchant is that he shall be reduced to beggary and, in return for his life being spared, shall "presently become a Christian." This was the ultimate aim of all the pressure and harassment—to wipe out this "foreign body" from the Christian map of Europe.

Until this could be done, one way to contain the Jews, to keep them handy for exploitation and yet prevent their coming too closely into contact with their Christian neighbors, was to confine them to special areas of towns. These Jewish quarters were called ghettoes.

I once gave a talk to a school at which most of the pupils were Jewish. At the end there were questions, and one girl asked: "What's the difference between a kibbutz and a ghetto?" I must say I was shocked—no Jewish child should be so ignorant. You can't understand anything about the Jews of today, let alone about Israel, without knowing not only what a vast gulf separates the two types of Jewish communities—kibbutz and ghetto—but what the true meaning of the ghetto was.

The origin of the word itself is lost. Some say it meant "foundry" because the first ghetto was near a foundry in Venice. Some say it meant "little quarter." But to every Jew of Europe it means something more like "prison." Its sound rouses echoes of poverty, overcrowding, isolation, degradation and misery.

Sometimes the ghetto had only one street, with its own tiny synagogue, kosher butcher and cemetery. It was walled in, and had a gate which was locked at night. Within this narrow, fetid area, where sunlight seldom came, the Jews lived crowded together, working desperately, paying out taxes for every move they made, constantly repressed, constantly harassed and afraid. Yet they clung to their religion and traditions like spiritual torches to keep back the encroaching darkness.

They might only leave the ghetto when the Gentiles allowed it. Even then they had to pay the hated "body-tax" —the same one the Gentiles paid for bringing their livestock into the cities.

Outside, no Jew could own property. Indeed, all ghetto property was owned by Christian landlords. They could do no business except what suited the Gentiles. And that meant usury—money-lending—and nothing much else, apart from tailoring, peddling and a few handicrafts, all "despised" occupations.

They were little better than kept serfs. Of course they deteriorated as the Israelite slaves had in Egypt. But at least now they had their Torah, their Talmud, and a history of glorious achievements to keep their pride flickering. They had little else except their belief in their God—and each other. The deep, abiding compulsion of Jew to help Jew, which had begun with old laws obliging Jews to ransom Jewish slaves, was strengthened under these grinding conditions. They were all "members of each other."

A close look at these ghettoes is necessary, because it was in them, and particularly those in Germany, that modern anti-Semitism had it roots, and modern Israel too, for nothing develops national feeling faster than oppression.

To see how German Gentiles regarded the Jews in the late eighteenth century, we can look through the eyes of Goethe, one of the great writers of his country. He was a boy of eleven when he first visited the ghetto in Frankfurt. At first he just peeped through the gate into the long, narrow street. What he saw made an impression on his mind which lasted all his life.

Tall, dark houses, shutting out light. A dirty narrow street, crowded with people, many of them working on their doorsteps to get a little air. But what people! Pale, thin, hunched, in black threadbare clothes, with nervous movements and shuffling gait and timid, sick-looking faces . . . They were alien. They were ugly. Through the boy's mind as he gazed "floated the sinister old fables about the

Jews' cruelty to Christian children," that he had read in the old chronicles.

When he plucked up courage to enter, the poor Jews on all sides jostled and pestered him to buy things from them. He sensed their indecent eagerness to sell, not realizing their hunger and desperation. Disgusted and afraid, he fled, and as he fled he had to pass—what any Jew venturing out of the ghetto also had to pass—a large picture which the municipality of Frankfurt had ordered to be painted on the archway of a bridge. It showed a dead Christian child, his body stabbed in a dozen places by Jewish shoemakers' awls. Under it was written: "In the year 1475, the infant Simon, two and a half years, was murdered by the Jews." There was also a picture of a pig, trampling on a Jew.

That cartoon was typical of carvings and pictures "decorating" towns all over Germany, showing Jews doing all sorts of disgusting and terrifying things. Such images, received in childhood or by simple ignorant people, could not help prejudicing them. Goethe himself, brilliant as he was, took years to get over it. "Only later," he wrote, "when I made the acquaintance of many intellectually gifted, sensitive men of this race, did respect come to join the admiration I cherish for the people who created the Bible."

But how many Germans had the opportunity to be "cured" of their deep-rooted prejudice by meeting gifted Jews?

The condition of Jews living closer to the center of Catholicism was even worse.

In Rome itself, the ghetto hung on the banks of the Tiber, squeezed between the river (which often flooded) and the city walls. Often the ghetto gates were locked, even by day. The community was so desperately poor that the women sat all day sewing buttonholes, one of the only occupations open to them. They were taxed for everything, even for eating unleavened bread at Passover.

Jews were attacked on their own streets by hooligans; stones were thrown at them wherever they walked outside, as a matter of course. They were forbidden to speak to Christians and were flogged if they spent a night outside the ghetto. They were constantly harassed and humiliated, even to having to wear special yellow hats so that the people could recognize and revile them more easily.

A Frenchman visiting Italy at that time wrote: "The question is always asked, when will the Jews at last convert to Christianity? But I ask: when will the Christians be converted to tolerance?"

In 1776 the brand new United States of America (only thirteen of them then) had declared their independence and announced equality for all. Jews across the Atlantic found themselves equal citizens for the first time since the days of pagan Rome, and took their rightful place among the builders, colonizers and organizers of the great new hopeful free nation of America. And at the same time, apart from the few "court Jews" exploited by arrogant, greedy, ambitious kings and princes for their intelligence, initiative and moneymaking abilities, Jews in Europe were at their lowest ebb.

These descendants of the heroic Maccabees—of the dignitaries of courts of Islam—of the poets, philosophers, astrologers, sought-after physicians and diplomats of Andalusia, men and women of a people which had proved its worth to human society over and over again whenever it was given the opportunity—this great nation had been reduced to huddles of hunched, pale, ragged, frightened creatures of the shadows. Outside the ghetto gates, the bullying mob waited, ready to jeer and spit and throw stones at them, to break into their pitiful domains and abuse them, insult their women, steal their few possessions. And the few, the very few Gentiles who pleaded for them before the all-powerful courts and church councils were mocked or ignored.

When their own desperation led the Jews themselves to petition a pope, listing the miseries and burdens of their lives and praying for relief, the answer was the same. The mockery of silence.

LETTER 6

The Coming of Enlightenment

Before dealing with the rest of Europe, we ought to take one more look at the mid-eighteenth century scene in Spain and the Spanish colonies in South America. And a horrifying scene it was.

Hard as it may be to believe, the Inquisition was still going on. (It was not finally halted by the Catholic authorities until the 1820s.) Year after year, century after century, this abominable evil went on—not steadily, but like the grim periodic convulsions caused by some brain disease of the Church. Its blighting tentacles reached across the Atlantic, and those Marranos and Sephardim who had tried to begin a new life in South America were seized in spasmodic outbreaks of religious fanaticism. The tortures, trials and burnings at the stake continued just as if the Dark Ages had never passed. For Spain they still hadn't. Spain's sorry condition in our century can be traced directly to the things she did in those times, not only to the Jews and Christian "heretics" but to the highly cultured and peace-loving Indians of South America, whom her Conquistadors (conquer-

53

ors) cheated, robbed and massacred without mercy—all in the name of Christ.

It is interesting to notice that even while Spanish adventurers were bringing back fabulous treasures stolen from the Incas, their mother-country was sinking into economic stagnation. No amount of gold compensates for loss of brains, skill and energy in trade. By killing and exiling the Jews, the Spaniards (and Portuguese) had rid themselves of one of their chief assets. In their perverted effort to save souls they crippled their own economy.

Now let's look again at Europe. A new order was on its way. There had been nearly 300 years of religious upheaval, in which, as I said before, more Protestants and Catholics had killed each other than either had ever killed Jews. All of northern Europe had been won over to Protestantism. The overriding power of the Catholics was broken. But in the countries in the south where they still held sway, not all the great rational thinkers, such as Rousseau and Mirabeau and Montesquieu, could prevail on Rome to relax its iron hold on the Jews. It took Napoleon to do that, not by high-minded ideas but by force.

However, there were two countries in Europe at that time—one destined to go over to Protestantism, one still rabidly Catholic—where Jews were not only tolerated but were very happily established for many years. One was Holland and the other, Poland.

The situation in Poland is especially interesting for you, because it's probable that you, along with most of today's Ashkenazi Jews, descend from that thriving, learned—and doomed—community.

The Polish rulers, like the Dutch, were more concerned at that time about the benefits the gifted and hard-working Jews could bring to their economies than with the grumblings of the Church, which still kept warning of the dangers to Christians of living near Jews with their "false religion" and "wicked customs." For centuries the Polish Jews lived in peace and prosperity. By 1650 there were 500,000 of them.

Every Jewish boy and many girls in Poland were highly educated. (I might mention here that literacy among the Jews was always high, at times when it was low among the surrounding peoples.) The Polish community was obsessed with learning. Great Talmudic study centers were set up, and students flocked to them. Little boys of thirteen could often recite the first five books of the Bible, plus the psalms, by heart, and discuss the difficult points like little professors.

The main language was Yiddish, a mixture of German, Hebrew and a few Slavic words. Hebrew was only used in prayer, and women were not considered fit to learn it. (I regret to say that the attitude of religious Jews toward women has always left a great deal to be desired.) The Spanish Jews, on the other hand, spoke Ladino, a kind of Hebrew-Spanish, and this was one way to tell them apart.

As usual where the Jews were allowed to live in peace and freedom, many rose to important positions, but in the case of Poland this proved to be their undoing. In the middle of the seventeenth century, an unparalleled disaster fell on this learned community.

The tragedy of the Cossack massacres had something different in it from any that went before. Here, for the first time I believe, the murderers who fell on the Jews had some real cause to hate them, other than superstition and greed. Not that it in any way justified what they did to them.

The fact was that over the years, the Polish landlords had spread their hold over other lands, now parts of Russia, but then separate countries. The poor peasants who lived in these lands were no better than serfs. Naturally they hated the bailiffs and brokers who collected their taxes and rents. And many of these tax-collectors and bailiffs were, I'm sorry to say, Jews.

So when the people finally rose up and rode to defeat their Polish oppressors, they regarded the Jews, with some justice, as their enemies too.

A terrible slaughter began and went on for eight dreadful years. It was worse than anything that had happened to the

Jews before. The Cossacks and Tartars from the Ukraine and the Crimea were barbarians, mad with anger. They committed atrocities more horrible than anything the Inquisition had dreamed of.

Thousands upon thousands were killed, tortured and enslaved. No Jew was safe. A whisper of the approach of a Cossack troop sent them fleeing in panic from town to town. Hundreds of small Jewish villages, called *shtetls,* were wiped out, as the tides of war washed back and forth across the Russian borders. Once again the peace and prosperity of a settled Jewish community was destroyed, and its inhabitants scattered.

The Jewish folklore of Eastern Europe is steeped in terror of the Cossacks and their leader Chmielnicki, who was to them the very devil himself. The great Russian-Polish Jewish writers who came later—Shalom Aleichem, Isaac Bashevis Singer and others—who wrote so lovingly and tenderly about the *shtetl* Jews, show on every page the shadow of the horrors of those unspeakable times, and the pogroms which followed 200 years later, in the time of the tsars. For the Cossack raids were not the end of the nightmare for your unhappy ancestors.

Gradually, over the years, the persecutions reduced these Jews, not only in numbers but in the quality of their intellectual life. No peoples' history shows more clearly the error of the Christian belief that suffering is God-sent to improve and ennoble human beings. All the advancement in learning was lost, and the Jews there fell into strange superstitions of their own.

Their need for a savior was so overwhelming that they began to see Messiahs everywhere. Of course that willingness to be led produced all sorts of fanatics and frauds, claiming to be the Messiah. One by one they all proved to be fakes, and in their disappointment the Jews fell further and further into despair. Then, for the first time, they began to dream of redemption in their Holy Land. But they had no energy or courage left to take an active step.

Mistakes of a different kind were being made by the much happier and more secure Jews of Holland. The Dutch had received some of the English Jews thrown out by Edward I in 1290, and they had been joined by Sephardim* from Spain and Portugal. These Jews did well, for and by their adopted country. No Cossacks came to persecute them. As Holland turned Protestant, the Jews there felt even safer than before, and were able to concentrate on their lives and professions.

When in 1656 Oliver Cromwell was trying to get English commerce back on its feet, after the bad times of those two useless Stuart Kings James I and Charles I, he turned to the Dutch Jews and permitted a number of prominent Sephardic families to settle in London. From them descended some of the famous families who were later to have such an influence on world affairs.

Of the Sephardim who stayed in Holland, quite a few were Marranos who, as soon as they escaped from Catholic repression, had gone back to Judaism. And they went back with a vengeance! They became more orthodox than the orthodox. As their rabbis interpreted the laws in an ever narrower and stricter way, to make up, perhaps, for the years when they'd had to pretend to be Christians, it became more and more difficult for a Jew to be a free-thinker. In other words, there grew up in the Jewish center of Amsterdam a type of Jewish religious fanaticism not unlike the Christian kind, in which anybody who dared to think differently was proclaimed a heretic.

Of course there was no Inquisition. But the Amsterdam rabbis—like every other powerful group utterly convinced of its own rightness—took it upon themselves to punish these Jewish heretics in their own way, by rejecting them and casting them out of the community and the synagogue.

---

*Sephardi means Spanish and is used to distinguish the supposedly "dark" Jews who migrated to Spain, Africa and the Far East from the Ashkenazi Jews of Europe.

I'm telling you this in case you should think that Jews are incapable of bigotry, blindness and fanatical intolerance. They are, as a matter of fact, more capable of it than most, as you can see when you look at modern Israel. The difference, though, between them and the Christian fanatics is quite obvious. The Jews hardly ever descended into the barbarism of deliberate physical cruelty. But they managed to cause their "rebels" a lot of suffering just the same.

One of them, a Marrano who tried to return to his people and failed because he could not narrow his thinking down to the limits of orthodoxy, was humiliated and outcast to the point where, in the end, his mind cracked and he shot himself. His name was Uriel da Costa.

But he is not so famous as another Jewish rebel, Baruch Spinoza, one of the great philosophers of the world. A brilliant young man, he was the shining hope of the Amsterdam Jewish community of 300 years ago. But to the rabbis' dismay he turned to rationalism. That is, he doubted everything that couldn't be proved, which meant, of course, doubting that the Torah was given to Moses by God, doubting religion altogether. He could no longer obey the laws of Judaism. Like da Costa, he was excommunicated—cast out of the faith. But unlike da Costa, he didn't mind. He moved away from Amsterdam to another city, where he lived out his life very quietly, polishing lenses for a living and meanwhile continuing to study, write and improve his mind. His few friends were all Gentile freethinkers. The Jews never forgave him, and it is only quite recently that some have admitted their mistake. Yet even now, more than 300 years after his death, one can find orthodox Jews defending the intolerance of their ancestors towards one of the most outstanding Jewish thinkers of all time.

Meanwhile, in France, Italy and Germany a new spirit was stirring—at long last! A spirit of humanism and progress. Christianity was under attack from rational men; all sorts of exciting new ideas were coming to the surface, like bubbles rising in a stagnant pool. A new tolerance was being urged, new talk of "freedom" and "rights."

A little Jew, humpbacked and frail from a childhood spent struggling to study in the eternal darkness of a German ghetto, broke out of it in the mid 1700s and breathed the fresh wind of enlightenment that was beginning to blow through all the suffocating religious bigotry and backwardness. His name was Moses Mendelssohn.

When he saw what was afoot, he became obsessed by the plight of his people, left rotting in the ghettoes. He saw that unless the Jews, who had once led the way in intellectual advancement, made contact with Gentile society, they would be left behind in a cultural backwater—as the *shtetl* Jews of Eastern Europe were.

Mendelssohn knew that language was the key to progress. As long as the Jews were walled-up in the "ghetto tongue," Yiddish, they would never absorb the new culture. So he did a remarkable thing. He translated the Torah (the first five books of the Bible) into German, but he wrote in Hebrew letters so that the Jews could learn German through reading what was already so familiar to them.

This translation was snatched up all over Europe, in spite of furious opposition from the conservative Polish rabbis. It marked a turning point. The ghetto Jews, just as Mendelssohn had hoped, went on to read other German books —books of science, and secular (non-religious) philosophy. The long isolation began to crack like ice. The Jews were coming out.

One thing worried Mendelssohn. Might the emerging Jews not be overwhelmed by the now-superior culture of the Gentile world? The eternal offer—"Convert and be accepted"—still confronted them, as it always had. And now, after so much inequality, it was more tempting than ever to the stifled hopes and intellectual ambition in many of them. What has been called "the march to the baptismal font" began.

Yet Mendelssohn's chief fear—the swamping of his people in the great tide of Gentile enlightenment—did not happen. The majority stayed Jewish. In any case the emergence from the ghettoes was only a trickle at first.

Moses Mendelssohn died in 1786. But he had opened a door, through which a number of humane and farsighted men followed him, pleading for tolerance for the Jews. A playwright called Lessing wrote plays in which, to everyone's amazement, Jews were shown as cultured, virtuous and wise. Another writer, Christian von Dohm, wrote a paper drawing public attention to the terribly unjust conditions and restrictions imposed on the Jews, saying that such laws were not only hangovers from the Dark Ages but very stupid policies from a practical point of view. The Jews had always benefited their adopted societies when they were given freedom—why not free them now and take advantage of their talents?

Often we look back on shocking abuses of past ages, things like the burning of "witches," slavery, child labor in mines and factories, and so on, and wonder how on earth people put up with them. Were these things not obviously evil? Why were they tolerated by ordinary, decent people?

The fact we have to recognize is that human societies have a kind of collective conscience, and that this conscience has to be awakened gradually to wrongs which a few enlightened individuals have been aware of for a long time. These individuals, who lead the way, are usually writers, politicians or preachers—men who can reach people through words.

Nowadays it's easy for new ideas to spread, through television and the other media of mass communication. But in the old days it could only be done slowly. Even travel was terribly slow. It took time for books to be carried from place to place. A gifted speaker could only address a few hundred people at a time, instead of millions, as today. What is remarkable is that a very few men, such as Mendelssohn, Lessing and Christian von Dohm could, in quite a short time, arouse public conscience as they did so that, even before the French Revolution (1789–1815) brought emancipation to the Jews of Western Europe, ordinary people had had their minds prepared to look at the Jews with new eyes.

But in the eastern countries of Europe, no new rational light was dawning. The Jews were all but defeated by their endless ordeals at the hands of the Cossacks. The survivors huddled together in their *shtetls,* robbed even of the resilience that had always enabled them to rise again out of their own ashes. It's hardly surprising that, when a certain rabbi brought a new message, they were ready to receive it.

The rabbi was called Baal Shem Tov, and his message, contradicting the whole of Jewish tradition, was this: *Learning is not what matters.* What God wants of his people is faith, simpleheartedness, and unquestioning obedience to all the laws he gave to Moses.

In other words, the exact opposite of Mendelssohn's message, which was a challenge to the Jews to come out and join in the forward march of history. Baal Shem Tov said, in effect, "Leave history alone. Never mind what the goyim* do. Don't try to improve your lot. Have faith. Stick to the old ways. Then the Messiah will come." This mystical movement, which spread all over the deprived communities of Poland and Russia, was called Hassidism.

One hot Sabbath, we walked through the ghettolike streets of Mea Shearim, the orthodox quarter of Jerusalem, and you saw today's followers of Baal Shem Tov in their distinctive clothes, beards and hats, going about their straight-and-narrow lives in the midst of a modern city. Another day we saw two little boys with sidelocks strap phylacteries to their skinny arms and pale foreheads to say their morning prayers in a bustling railway station. You wondered at it; perhaps you despised it. It does seem strangely out of place in today's world. But it is possible to

*Literally "the nations," but Jews use it to mean all non-Jews.

have sympathy when you know the unspeakable suffering out of which this movement was born.

At about the same time as Hassidism—a faith to comfort the poor and ignorant—was beginning, another new type of Judaism was starting up for the intellectual and the progressive. This is what we now call Reform. Moses Mendelssohn laid the foundations for it when he wrote about the need to break away from sterile ritual and adapt to modern conditions. But long before, great Jewish sages of old, like Maimonides, had preached that Judaism must never become a fossil, embedded in rigid old laws after they had stopped being meaningful, but should be a living, growing faith, moving with the times. And so it had been, until the Middle Ages. Then it got stuck, because Jewish intellectuality had been held down, and the Jews' belief in themselves as active partners in human affairs had been ruthlessly crushed.

Only in a society where Jews could be free to think and participate could Reform Judaism flourish. And it was the French Revolution that really gave Reform the free soil it needed to grow in.

LETTER 7

Emancipation

I wish I could say that with the triumph of the French people against the king and the aristocracy, followed by Napoleon's conquest of Europe from 1798 to 1815, the ghetto walls came tumbling down forever and the Jews got the same "Liberty, Equality, Fraternity" that the French masses demanded for themselves. Alas, it was only true up to a point.

The ghettoes up and down Europe *were* broken open, just like the Bastille. The gates were torn down and Jews were greeted as fellow victims of the cruel oppressors, the rulers of Church and State. New laws were brought in everywhere Napoleon went, stating that all men had equal rights of citizenship and that there was to be no one religion dominating any others.

The Pope, Pius VI, fled from Rome, and a "Tree of Liberty" was planted in the Roman ghetto. As the eighteenth century turned into the nineteenth, it really looked as though a new, free era was at long last coming for the

Jews (at least those in Western Europe) to reward them for their 1,800 years of wandering and terror.

Their hopes were short-lived.

A mere twenty years after the revolutionaries had issued their Declaration of Human Rights, when the foremost Jews of France, Italy and Germany had just begun to make headway back into their rightful places in society, anti-Jewishness lifted its ugly head again.

Napoleon's laws had not been willingly accepted by the rulers of the states he conquered. Only in one place (Baden) had the Grand Duke lifted restrictions on the Jews of his own accord. And as soon as the Jews began to rise out of obscurity—as soon as they began to *succeed*—the old jealousies and hatreds flared.

For a while this backsliding into the old, barbaric attitudes was halted by Napoleon's advance towards the east. The King of Prussia had reluctantly freed his Jews, but not because of any real change of heart. He needed them to help fight Napoleon.

And strange as it seems, they did help. They were grateful for freedom, anxious to prove themselves loyal citizens of the country which had finally acknowledged them—and, perhaps, desperate to prove *to themselves* that they were men, and could fight for their country. The fact that they were fighting the man who had given legal equality to their fellow Jews in the wake of his victorious armies did not stop the Prussian Jews from fighting Napoleon like any Prussian patriots.

And how they fought! After centuries during which, along with every other insult, they had been told they were unfit to bear arms, they now showed they were true sons of Bar Kochba. Even some women fought, and of course Jewish doctors and nurses served the troops. Civilians gave money. The Jewish soldiers were decorated and promoted in every battle between 1813 and 1815 including Waterloo, where Napoleon was finally defeated.

How sure they must have felt, in this triumph of manhood and courage over centuries of deprivation and suppression, that they had now earned equality! No one could ever despise them again. Napoleon or no Napoleon, their futures as citizens of their own countries must now have seemed open and assured.

The Jews still had not learned that they *had* no country of their own.

As soon as the occupying French armies had been chased out, the royal rulers of Europe wanted nothing but a return to the old order, where the princes, not the people, held power. The Pope was brought back to Rome and at once renewed the Inquisition. The deadly partnership of Church and State was brought back too. It was called, if you can believe it, "the Holy Alliance," and by it all the despots and tyrants promised to come to each other's help if any revolutionaries dared to try to achieve democracy.

And the Jews, who had been promised freedom and who had fought so bravely? Well, they had served their turn. The war was over. So it turned out that, for them, their reward was to be a renewal of the cry, "Down with the Jews! Back with them into the ghetto!"

Some people cried for worse. An old Crusader battlecry —"Hep!"—arose again in Bavaria. It stood for Latin words meaning "Jerusalem is lost!" and mobs shouted it while rampaging through the streets, looting and killing. These ugly riots were put down by police, but governments used them as an excuse. "We can't give the Jews equality," they said. "The people obviously aren't ready for it."

The Jews couldn't believe in such treacherous promise-breaking. They appealed to every possible authority. The result was a tangle of laws and regulations—some for them, some against them; some ignored, some obeyed; new ones introduced, old ones canceled—so complex that the Jews could not tell where they stood, what rights they had, or what was going to happen to them next.

But they had tasted liberty. They had tasted, through fighting for the countries of their birth, the manhood and

people-hood they had been so proud of in the far past.
They were not about to trail tamely back into their sordid
ghettoes. They had bought their freedom; they now demanded what they had paid for. After all, this was the
nineteenth century!

They probably said those words to each other much as
Jews in Germany in the 1930s said, "It can't happen to us!
After all, this is the twentieth century." They meant, I suppose, that now, in a modern era, the conscience of
humanity was finally awake to the uselessness of repression,
the horrors of injustice, the barbarity, the absurdity and the
waste of religious oppression and strife. It would have been
more realistic if instead they had said, "Anything can happen. Human beings are still the same as ever. After all, it's
only the nineteenth, it's *only* the twentieth century."

I have heard today's Jews say, "It can't happen in England," "It can't happen in America," or even, "It will never
happen again. Humanity has learnt better now." History,
my sons, teaches us otherwise.

The nineteenth century, then, came in on a crest of new
hope, of enlightenment, of emancipation from Catholic
domination. This was true for everyone, including the Jews.
Despite all the broken promises and rescinded laws, they
struggled to keep that hope up. But their struggle was long
and hard, and it was not for decades to come that they
achieved what they wanted—or what they thought they
wanted. They had looked no further, at that time, than one
simple-seeming goal—equality with the Gentiles of their
own native countries.

It came at last, little by little.

England, which Napoleon had not influenced, was slow
to accept the new tolerance. It was not until 1839, after a
hard political fight, that the Jews got the right to vote, 1858
before they could take their seats in parliament. This was
in spite of Benjamin Disraeli, Queen Victoria's favorite
prime minister, who came to power in 1852. But he was a
convert, and so "didn't count."

Italy, as you would expect after the papacy had been re-established, banished the Jews back to the Roman ghetto and kept them there until 1847. At least that was the intention. But during those years when there were no civil rights for anyone in Italy, Jews joined with Christians in secret revolutionary movements to try to break the Church's stranglehold on progress. All these revolts were cruelly crushed, with the help of foreign armies (the "Holy Alliance"). It wasn't until a new royal dynasty—the Savoys— came in in the middle of the century that things improved for the Jews.

Austria freed her Jews in 1867.

In Germany it all dragged on even longer. It wasn't until 1869, when Bismarck and Wilhelm I signed a Tolerance Law, that the Jews there drew breath as free and equal German citizens. Two years later, a number of other states joined Germany in a union called the Reich, and a lot more Jews received their freedom.

Other European countries emancipated their Jews shortly after that. Holland had always stood fast by her Jews. France, the motherland of emancipation, was already reaping the benefits of a free Jewry.

And Spain? Spain was in a poor way without her Jews. So she invited them back. So did Portugal. A few went. I am thankful to say—I always cringe when I hear of Jews returning to the boot that kicked them—not very many. There are very few there today.

Spain has not recovered to this day from her crimes against the Jews. To Spain, perhaps more than any other country, we could apply the words of a German economist, who wrote, in 1911: "Israel [the Jews] passes over Europe like the sun. Where it shines, new life springs up; where it departs, everything that had previously flourished molders."

LETTER 8

Pogroms and a Return to the Dark

Anti-Jewishness is a strange force. It dies down in one place, only to spring up somewhere else. In the same way, whenever, in the strange pattern of Jewish history, we find the Jews happy in one part of the world, inevitably we find them wretched in another.

In America in the middle 1800s the Jews were well-off. Prejudice there was limited to a few clubs and universities, run by Americans who thought themselves "more equal than others," which did not admit Jews. Bad enough, you may think, but comparatively mild.

In Western Europe they had achieved freedom. Jews—some converted, but many still Jewish—were in positions of importance, and for the first time for generations were secure enough to help fellow Jews in other, less enlightened parts of the world.

What parts?

You noticed, perhaps, that I haven't mentioned the Middle East for some time. And when writing about enlightenment in Europe, I left out Poland and Russia.

Something very horrible happened in Damascus, Syria, in 1840. A monk and his servant suddenly disappeared, and the Jews were accused of murdering him. The motive was tied up with something I briefly mentioned before, which is usually called "the blood libel."

One of the basest lies which has ever been thought up to turn people against the Jews is that they need Christian blood to drink, as medicine, or to make matzot* at Passover. For God's sake don't laugh. You can't conceive how many people believed it, or how many Jews died for it, and if you say, "Well, but it must be a joke *now*," I must tell you that the blood libel was used by Hitler's propaganda experts to stir up modern, educated, scientific Germans, and that the same fantastic tale is being used today by corrupt South American governments to stir up hatred against the Jews.

So the monks of Damascus accused the Jews of the ritual murder of this Father Thomas. The Jewish quarter was searched, and several Jews, arrested at random, were tortured until one of them—a poor barber—accused some Jewish leaders of the crime. They were imprisoned and tortured. When they refused to confess, a number of Jewish children were taken and shut up without food or water. Even the parents, frantic though they were, would not admit to the crime. Such a thought was too horrible for orthodox Jews, who, as you know, will not even eat meat that has not been drained of as much blood as possible.

While the ordeal of the captured Jews continued, word of what was happening spread across Europe. There were newspapers by this time, and they were full of the story—and other, similar scandals which mysteriously cropped up in other parts of the Levant, like outbreaks of an old plague which the civilized Jews had hoped had been stamped out. But this time they were not helpless as before.

Among the important men of that time was a British Jew called Sir Moses Montefiore. He was rich, respected and

*Unleavened bread.

influential. With others, he traveled to Cairo to try to save
these poor unknown fellow-Jews, still suffering tortures in
a Damascus prison. By this time they had "confessed," but
of course Sir Moses knew—what every Jew raised as a Jew
knows—that there was not and could not be a word of truth
in their statements.

Sir Moses and his delegation so impressed the Governor
of Egypt and Syria that he ordered the wretched prisoners
(those who were still alive) to be released. But the delegation was not satisfied with this. They insisted that the accu-
sation should be publicly withdrawn, and a guarantee given
to all Jews in the Ottoman Empire of freedom and protection.

That Jews should have the power to save and relieve
other Jews, in faraway places, was a tremendous step forward. Sir Moses Montefiore was greeted as a hero by Jewish
communities all along his homeward journey.

He had made his first pilgrimages to Palestine quite early
in the century. I have a copy of the diary his wife kept
during their visit as early as 1827, full of interesting gossip
about their trip up the Nile and across the desert, and the
shock she and her husband experienced on finally reaching
the Holy Land and finding Jerusalem as it was then—a
neglected ruin, the Jewish life in it as poverty-stricken and
squalid as any ghetto.

Every inhabitant of the area then—and there were few
enough of them—lived inside the walls of the Old City:
Arabs, Jews, Turks, Christians of all shades of belief, all
lumped together in a warren of those same narrow alleys
where we used to do our shopping, and from which you
shrank because of the dirt and smells and the dark faces
which seemed to you so sinister. . . . They did not seem
sinister to Montefiore, only shockingly poor and degraded.
They lived in the meanest housing, huddled and scurrying
like rats in the ruins, with no means of earning a proper
living and no light in their lives except the eternal light of
their Torah.

But there was help at hand, whether they wanted it or not. Montefiore had money, plenty of it, and he longed to lavish it on them, his poor and despised brothers. I think he even despised them a little himself, for he saw that if someone did not drag them out into the light of day they would huddle and scurry in their alleys forever. He pitied them, and he was ashamed for them. He must act, and he did.

Unlike his namesake, Moses Mendelssohn, Montefiore's attack was not on their minds but on their physical way of life. He ordered the building of a row of houses, the first to be built outside the walls. He wanted to be fair towards both branches of Jewishness, so he allotted half of the homes for Sephardic Jews and half for Ashkenazim. Then he more or less bullied families from the "warren" into moving into these new, clean, and—by their standards— spacious and hygienic dwellings.

They obeyed and looked grateful. But as the sun set on their first day, a little procession of black figures could be seen hurrying back across the valley and through the Jaffa Gate, which shut behind them. They were afraid, and very rightly too, for the whole area of the Judean hills was in- fested with brigands who they were sure would murder them in their beds if they stayed a night outside the protect- ing walls.

When Montefiore found out, he mounted guards round these new houses. Was his project not called Mishkenot Sha'ananim—Peaceful Dwellings? Those he had chosen to live a better life there would find them peaceful or he would know the reason why! And to give them a livelihood he built a windmill to grind their wheat (but that never really worked), a print shop, and other places of trade to help them earn a sensible living. After a while, little by little, he ordered and coaxed and bullied them out of their dark lairs and into the first fringes of a wider world. And in doing that, wanting only to help poor Jews whose piety had brought them, without money or means of support, to their holy place, he also laid the first stones of the great modern city of Jerusalem.

I've been sidetracked by Montefiore because he was an example of the kind of philanthropic Jew—one who used his wealth to help others—who was a symbol to the Jews of Europe of a new era. From now on, they thought, it was not going to be so easy to slander and persecute Jews, for there were others strong enough to rise to the defense of the helpless.

Unfortunately all the new influence and enlightenment of the Jews of Western Europe, the freedom and confidence of those in the United States, were not equal to the dark powers ranged against the poor defenseless communities in the Eastern European countries, who were now about to undergo another terrible ordeal.

We left them just when Hassidism was spreading throughout the *shtetls* of Poland and the Eastern Russian provinces where Jews were allowed a bare existence under the tsars. An opposition to Hassidism had developed: Jews who believed in the possibility of improving their situation by study and effort and who despised all the mysticism and fatalistic acceptance preached by the Hassidim. They fought them fiercely, even excommunicating the whole Hassidic sect.

So the Jews, not for the first or last time, were split, although by the last quarter of the nineteenth century the bitter anger the two groups had felt for each other fifty years earlier had died down. This was chiefly because they sensed a threat from outside so serious that it was no longer worthwhile to fight among themselves.

I suppose you've heard the expression "beyond the pale." Everyone now used it to mean "what is not allowed," "going too far." But not everyone realizes its origin. The Pale was the limited area in Russia where Jews were allowed to live. To go beyond it was forbidden, except for a privileged few whom the Russian rulers wanted to make use of.

This was just one of the uncountable restrictions imposed on the Jews by the tsars. One of the worst things was compulsory service in the army for up to thirty-one years for each Jewish male (six years more than for ordinary Russians) starting from the age of twelve; but often boys as young as eight were hunted down and carried off in the most brutal way by Russian soldiers, and forced to march for miles to camps which many of them, of course, never reached. Eyewitness descriptions of these poor little conscripts "trudging towards the grave" are quite heartbreaking, but worse was coming.

In mid-century came a break in the Jews' misery. Alexander II, a new young tsar, came to the Russian throne, and immediately made reforms of all kinds, in keeping with the new spirit of freedom in Western Europe. Serfdom was abolished, freeing 40,000,000 poor Russian peasants from something close to slavery. Army service was reduced to five years. The Pale laws were relaxed, like those of the ghettoes, and the Jews—at least those who had some money and education—were allowed to go where they liked and take what jobs they could get. Those whose spirit and ambition had not been utterly crushed immediately followed the example of the Jews of the West, going in for medicine, banking, and all types of industry. True, the great majority stayed within the Pales. But at least they now lived in hopes of better times.

But it was a false dawn. In 1881, Alexander II "The Liberator" was assassinated, and only a few weeks later the most appalling anti-Jewish riots broke out. It's very doubtful if these were spontaneous; the attacks came in different parts of Russia all at the same time, so it seems probable that they were at least partly initiated by the authorities. Certainly the police stood and watched while howling mobs poured through the streets of towns and villages, murdering, raping, looting and burning. When the order came to the police to stop the attack, they did so easily; but it came only when the deaths and damage were incalculable, and the mobs had tasted blood. A new word had come into the awful dictionary of Jewish suffering: "pogrom," Russian for "devastation."

Pogroms broke out in every area which had been a Pale. The horror spread as far as Warsaw in Poland, and hardly a place where Jews lived was left unharmed. Once again the panic-stricken Jews fled here and there, their hopes, with their homes and lives, in ruins.

Why did the Russian masses turn so savagely upon the Jews? There was no question this time of the Jews having wronged their neighbors by siding with the landowners, because they had been so severely repressed for so long that it was impossible for them to gain any power over anybody.

The same question will arise soon about the Austrians and Germans and Roumanians and Poles when I come to the Second World War. You can only understand such sudden and seemingly reasonless violence if you understand something about the nature of anti-Jewishness. Its roots were different in different places and times; but in Russia in the 1880s its roots are not hard to see.

The Russian tsars (except Alexander II) had always tried to smooth out the irritating "bump" that the Jews, just by being different, made in the population. One tsar early in the century went so far as to order them to wear short coats and trim their beards, and you might have seen policemen chasing Jews about the streets waving shears with which to cut their clothes and hair forcibly to make them the same as other Russians! Another plot was to lure Jewish children into "Jewish" schools, where they would actually be turned into Christians. In other words, every effort was made to force or trick the Jews into assimilating. When they couldn't, or wouldn't, their distinctiveness was used by ruthless rulers to give the poorer people of Russia something to vent their anger on.

For years these Russian workers and peasants were fed

with lies about the Jews, who were blamed for whatever was wrong with the society and for all the people's miseries. This policy reached its climax when the head of the Russian church (a bit different from the Roman, but not in its attitude toward the Jews) recommended this solution to the Jewish problem: One-third should be physically done away with, one-third driven out of the country, and one-third forced to join the Russian church. With a background like that, it's not so hard to understand how easy it was to rouse the people to violence.

A famous French poet, Baudelaire, once explained his excitement during a revolution as "the desire for revenge —natural pleasure in destruction." And he was no bloodthirsty primitive peasant, close to an animal condition of nature, but a highly-educated and cultured man. In the same sort of way that your aggressive instincts lead you to fight and play war games, many grown men also like to run wild—to kill, loot and destroy—especially when the people they're attacking are defenseless. If someone in authority —their priest, or their leader—tells them that this or that group of "different looking" people are to blame for everything which makes them angry and discontented, they aren't likely to question the facts too closely before going to attack them. The trouble will be not setting them on, but stopping them. Mob passions are frightfully dangerous. Like a small flame set to the right tinder, the next thing you have is a raging, uncontrollable inferno. And that is exactly what happened all through the Pales of Russia, Poland and even Roumania.

News of the pogroms spread quickly to Western Europe and America. The reaction was one of righteous indignation and even horror, but there didn't seem to be anything that even the most influential people could do to stop it. It has always been difficult to interfere with what Russian governments inflict on their people, and it still is. The only marked difference between then and now, in that respect, is that it was possible at that time—just about possible, with

the help of money given by Jews in the West—for the persecuted to escape. And that is what thousands of them did.

No exodus in their history equaled, in numbers or in
terror, the masses of Jewish refugees who now abandoned
all their possessions and fled to the West. A great wave of
immigrants flooded the East End of London, and many
other capitals in Europe. Many more crossed the Atlantic,
heading for the legendary "New World" of equality, freedom and opportunity. Tens of thousands settled on the
East Side of New York alone. There, in a very short time,
their pale skinny bodies filled out, their bearing straightened, their eyes began to look straight into the eyes of
others. What the Bible calls "the cup of trembling" had
been taken out of their hands. And in gratitude and joy they
set about the wonderful task of making their contribution
to their new country as free men.

LETTER 9

The Birth of Zionism

The 1880s did not see the end of the pogroms. They came
and went in waves until the early years of our century, and
with each wave of persecution came a wave of emigrants,
fleeing Russia.

Several of these waves (well, it would be truer to call
them ripples, really) flowed south instead of west. Some of
the younger men had begun to conclude there was only one
place for Jews to be, and that was their ancient homeland.
They had finally learned the harsh lesson history had been
trying to teach them: that it was not enough for them to
want to be Germans, Russians, Roumanians or Poles. It
wasn't even enough to be given legal rights. The non-Jews
of those nations had to be ready to accept them. And they
weren't. Nothing the Jews themselves could do, some now
believed, would change that. So, for the first time, even
Jews whose families for generations had believed that only

the miracle of a Messiah could lead them back to Israel stopped waiting for that miracle.

Several Jewish thinkers and writers, who saw the matter clearly, had already begun writing books and pamphlets to rouse young Jews to action. Moses Hess was one. Hess was a follower of Spinoza. He was against orthodoxy, and for socialism. He knew Karl Marx, the Jew who is called "the father of communism." Hess also believed in nationalism, which was then a great force in Europe. It meant people having their own country, running it their own way, and feeling they belonged to it. It's unfashionable nowadays to be a nationalist because the wrong kind of nationalism—the intolerant, superior, greedy kind—has led to so much suffering. In my view you might just as well say that because family life has not always worked, and has caused a lot of misery through divorce, quarreling and so on, we should do away with families. The need for the identity and security of family life is as strong in most human beings as ever it was, and so is the need to know which country you belong to, to work to improve it and to be proud of it. Anyway, Moses Hess said that the Jews' country was Palestine and that they should be helped to go back there and recreate it.

Another Jew, Hirsh Kalischer, an orthodox rabbi oddly enough, agreed that there was no need to wait for the Messiah. He suggested agricultural colonies in Palestine, paid for by wealthy Jews. Since a lot of Russian-Jewish poets and writers had been writing about how much better it was to live off the land than in the towns, this suggestion of Kalischer's was welcomed by a lot more young men. Filled with idealism, they set off for the Holy Land.

By this time quite a lot of people were interested in the idea of a Jewish country. Even some Christians—and not just the ones who wanted to be rid of the Jews—took it up. A famous woman novelist, who called herself George Eliot, wrote a marvelous novel, *Daniel Deronda,* about a Jew who had a vision of a new life for the Jewish people in a reborn Israel, and this inspired Jews and non-Jews alike.

A society called Lovers of Zion started up in Russia to unite the Jews who wanted to go. One of its leaders was Leo Pinsker. He had believed assimilation was the best answer —until he saw a massacre of Jews during a pogrom. This forced him to change his mind. He wrote a pamphlet which said that Jews must free themselves by their own efforts— not efforts to blend in with others, but efforts to stand up for, and as, themselves. He reminded the Jews that Hillel, a famous rabbi in Roman times, had said, "If I am not for me, who is for me?"

This was the slogan that the young Jews of Russia had been thirsting for. What use, they asked, was all this endless praying? They got up off their knees and onto their feet. And once there, they walked. Many of them walked all the long, dangerous way down through Turkey and Syria into Palestine. They became what Israelis call the First Aliya. Aliya means "immigration." It also means "a going-up." Zionism—the movement of Jews back to Zion, or Israel— had begun.

But in the meantime something very important happened. People at the time didn't know it was important. All they knew was that it was a sensation all Europe was talking about. And it happened, not in backward Russia, not in Germany or Austria where anti-Jewishness had always been strong, but in the birthplace of European freedom: France.

Earlier on, I talked about assimilation. We saw how it didn't work in Spain. It didn't work in Russia—and perhaps I haven't made it clear that there were Jews there who tried hard to assimilate. It wasn't working even then in Germany, despite the fact that the Jews there completely identified themselves with their fellow-Germans, fought in their wars, and contributed all their skills to help their country. But in France it was supposed to be working. Or so Jewish intellectuals imagined. France was the most enlightened, toler-

ant, civilized nation in Europe. If a Jew wasn't equal in
France—if a French Jew was not treated the same as any
other Frenchman—what hope was there?

This was certainly the view of an Austrian Jew called
Theodore Herzl.*

I don't want these names—Hess, Kalischer, Pinsker,
Herzl—to be just names of streets in Tel Aviv to you. Some
children attending Jewish schools in Britain were recently
asked what they knew about Herzl, and a lot of them said
it was the name of a hill in Israel. So it is. Mount Herzl. I
took you there and we saw the big black box-tomb with the
name—four great gold Hebrew letters, nothing else—on
the top. The place, like many others in Israel, was named
for the man, because of a dream he dreamed which, with
his help, came true.

Theodore Herzl was Hungarian by birth but was brought
up in Vienna, the Austrian capital so famous for gaiety and
entertainment. It must have been a continual treat to live
there if one was rich, young and brilliant, as Herzl was. He
wasn't a very Jewish Jew. Many of his father's family had
converted. He thought of himself as a man of the world, a
cosmopolitan. He had charm and wit, and no small conceit;
he became a writer, tossing off clever articles and light
comedies for the stage. He was made aware of the "Jewish
problem" in his university days, but his early view was that
assimilation was the answer. He toyed with the idea of
baptizing his son; at one point he thought of a wild scheme
for mass conversions of Jews in exchange for the Pope's
help in fighting anti-Jewishness!

Then, while he was in Paris, the newspaper he was working for asked him to cover a big news story. It concerned
one of the few Jewish officers in the French army, a man
called Alfred Dreyfus, who was accused of spying for the
Germans. Dreyfus was tried and convicted. He was sen-
tenced to be publicly degraded—stripped of his army rank

*Try *Herzl*, a biography by Amos Elon.

and dismissed on his regimental parade ground, before being sent to prison on Devil's Island.

Herzl didn't expect to be particularly moved by this. On the face of it he thought Dreyfus was guilty. This humiliation was the normal punishment for spying in peacetime. But a profound shock awaited him.

In the life of every person who is destined to work for some great cause, there comes a turning point—a moment, an event, which wrenches them from their ordinariness and sets their mind on its new course. For Herzl, it was witnessing Dreyfus's disgrace: the insignia of his rank torn from his uniform and his officer's sword broken, while outside in the street a crowd bayed with hatred—not for anything he might have done, but for what he inescapably *was*. In the world's most civilized city, Herzl's heart turned cold when he actually heard the dread cry: "Death to the Jews!"

Herzl had long been troubled by the vulnerable position of Jews in Europe. But now it became clear to him that assimilation was no solution at all. If in France the poison of anti-Jewishness could bring about the ruin of an innocent man (and Dreyfus was innocent, as a five-year fight by his few brave supporters finally proved) then there was only one answer. The Jewish people must be taken out of their hostile surroundings altogether, and put somewhere where they could be safe, free, and beholden to nobody.

From then on, Herzl devoted himself heart and soul to securing a national home for his people. The first step was to convince others, so he wrote a slim book called *The Jewish State* into which he put all his conviction and all his new-found passion for his cause.

The response was very mixed. Rich philanthropists such as Baron de Rothschild and Baron von Hirsch were not interested: a few farming villages, a group of pilgrims or refugee-adventurers here and there, that was one thing, but a Jewish national home! That was a dream too fantastic to consider seriously. Those Jews who were still struggling to become invisible among the Gentiles thought Herzl's ideas would only draw attention to them, and orthodox rabbis considered the whole notion blasphemous.

But not all Jews were rich, assimilationist or bigoted. There were the masses in Eastern Europe, where the back-to-Palestine movement had started. They read Herzl's booklet and realized that here was the only "Messiah" they needed to lead them home. They hailed him with love as their leader.

Encouraged by all this excitement and enthusiasm among the ordinary people, Herzl called a congress—a meeting of representatives of Jewish communities all over the world. Nearly 200 of them came to Basel, in Switzerland. The year was 1897. At this first Zionist Congress, Herzl stood up and made a powerful speech. He said that if the Jewish people willed it strongly enough, a Jewish state need not be a dream. It could really happen, and Herzl prophesied it could become reality in fifty years. (He was exactly right. Fifty years from that year—well, fifty and a half—in May, 1948, Israel was born.)

More congresses followed, year by year. Between them, Herzl worked without rest. He used every advantage he had —his charm, his wit, his contacts, his commanding personality. He knocked on the doors of all the powerful men of Europe, and of the Middle East too. One of his ideas was to persuade the Sultan of Turkey to give him a charter allowing the Jews to colonize Palestine, which was then a Turkish province. The Sultan was quite interested, but he wanted money. It's ironic that at such a moment—with pogroms still going on, the Dreyfus case fresh in memory, a movement back to Palestine already started—rich Jews could not be found to support the scheme. Herzl's negotiations with the Sultan came to nothing.

The turn of the century saw the Zionist movement flourishing in every country, despite a lot of opposition. In 1903, Herzl, seeing the movement no nearer to achieving its goals, and with persecution in Russia still going on, grew so desperate he made a serious mistake.

The British government, whom he had approached for

help with his scheme, offered him part of Uganda, in Africa, for his Jewish homeland. His non-religious background had failed to teach him that there was only one place on earth which would inspire the Jews enough. At the sixth Zionist Congress, Herzl recommended the delegates to accept Uganda instead of Palestine, at least as a temporary refuge.

Uproar. Some of them called him a traitor. During the furious argument that followed, Herzl came to realize for the first time the depths of Jewish feeling for the land of their forefathers: he himself did not feel it and hadn't reckoned on it. The Russian delegates, who represented a community which had just gone through the hell of another pogrom, were the staunchest opponents of the Uganda scheme. It was to be "the real place" or nothing.

Herzl's final choice of Palestine as the most suitable location for a Jewish refuge was based not on an understanding of its vital importance to Jews raised more traditionally than himself, but on a tragically mistaken concept. *He thought it was empty.* Zionism, he had believed, was simply a matter of transportation—moving a people without a land to a land without people. He did not recognize the fact that there *were* people living there. This, not his opting for Uganda, was his greatest blunder, one into which, alas, a number of his successors were to follow him.

Now, however, faced with the absolute determination of his fellow Zionists, he gave way. He saw that he had awakened a force with deeper and more compulsive roots than even he had realized.

The following year, in the thick of his work for Zionism and aged only forty-four, he suddenly died. Golda Meir, in her autobiography,* tells how her family (then still in Russia) wept when they heard the news. Jews all over the world felt that their greatest hope had been snatched away from them. They might have been less miserable if they'd known that Zionism was now strong enough to move forward by its own power.

*Golda Meir, *My Life.*

LETTER 10

Meanwhile in Palestine

It's time now to have a look at what had been going on in that small area at the eastern end of the Mediterranean during all these centuries of Jewish dispersion.

Poor land! It too had had terrible trials. By the time the Russian Zionist pioneers began to arrive, late last century, it was many hundreds of years since it had been properly looked after.

After the Greeks came the Romans, as we saw, and after them the Persians. Then the Byzantines. Then, between A.D. 634 and 641, the Arab Moslems conquered and colonized it. They ruled it, and ruled it well enough may I add, for over 450 years.

During the early part of this first period of Arab rule, the land was not unduly neglected. There was plenty of agriculture. Dates, rice, sugarcane, cereals and citrus grew there, and even the Negev had settlements which it never had before and which the Israelis are only now rebuilding. The Jews farmed the land alongside the Arabs and it all worked

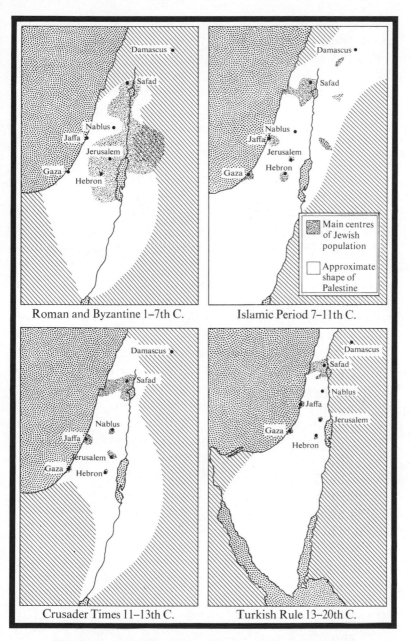

Roman and Byzantine 1–7th C.

Islamic Period 7–11th C.

Main centres of Jewish population

Approximate shape of Palestine

Crusader Times 11–13th C.

Turkish Rule 13–20th C.

Damascus
Safad
Nablus
Jaffa
Jerusalem
Gaza
Hebron

Variations in Boundaries and Jewish Areas

quite well. The whole area was a major trade-route at that time, which meant prosperity for all.

But then of course in barged the wretched Crusaders in 1099, and ruined everything. In the grim period when these foreign soldiers were laying waste to town after town, the Jewish population dwindled very quickly. The Crusader conquest of Jerusalem involved the massacre of practically every Jew and Arab in it, and Jews in many other cities (such as Haifa) didn't fare much better. Before long all the Jewish communities in the south had disappeared, their inhabitants either murdered, enslaved or fled.

But after about ten years, even the Crusaders' lust for bloodshed had been worn out, and they settled down to the duller tasks of occupying the country. The Moslems were still a majority of the population, so the Crusaders had no choice, if they didn't want uprisings, but to come to terms with them. They even accepted the Moslem toleration of the Jews. The massacres stopped. Things calmed down, and trade and other signs of normality reappeared.

But since the Crusaders had nothing to contribute to the country except forts, Christianity and desolation, the economy soon crumbled. Everybody grew poorer and poorer. Jewish artisans and craftsmen, farmers and traders, who had managed to survive, left their villages and came into the towns looking for work. So many rural areas which had had Jewish settlers until then were left empty. Only in one little village—Pek'in, in Galilee—is it possible to trace unbroken Jewish occupation.

Still, they had a hard time making a living. It was during this period that the first representatives were sent overseas to ask for money from Jewish communities abroad; there seemed no other way to keep Jews in the "Holy Land" from starving, or leaving. This dependence on funds from abroad grew as the land sank deeper into neglect and poverty over the coming centuries.

The Crusaders weren't content with ravishing the towns. They did irreparable harm to the countryside as well. It was during their rule that most of the trees which used to cover the hills of northern Palestine were cut down to build their ships and pay their costs. Little did they care that without trees the fertile top soil would be washed away, costing the country much of its agricultural land and many of its inhabitants. Still, it was not a steady downward trend. Under the next rulers—the Mamelukes—things improved just enough to encourage a steady trickle back of Jews whose forefathers had fled during the Crusader rule.

The Mamelukes, who were there for three centuries till 1560, were extraordinary people. They were white-skinned warriors from Egypt. Most of them were originally Circassian slave-boys, brought up to be fierce and splendidly dressed fighters. War and conquest were their whole destiny. Their children did not count as Mamelukes. When they needed to add to their numbers, they bought more Circassian slaves. The land, as land, meant nothing to them —all their instincts were for battle and spoils.

They did build some fine towers, bridges and other interesting bits of architecture which you can still see today, but they also destroyed the ports to spite the Crusaders. This harmed trade with Europe. Palestine ceased to be a world trade-route and became a backwater. It grew harder for the Jews to make a living. Nevertheless, persecutions in Europe, as well as the constant hope that the Messiah would soon come, brought quite a lot of Jews to Palestine. The *Yishuv,* which is the Hebrew word for the Jewish community in Israel, grew in numbers and strength.

Then, in 1516–1517, Palestine was conquered by the Turks and became part of the Ottoman Empire.

At first this seemed to be a blessing for the Jews. After the usual period of fighting and upheaval, the Ottomans established a firm rule, and for a short time there was a little golden age in which the roads were safe, agriculture improved, the population doubled and even the roaming Bedouin stopped raiding and took to breeding cattle and growing plants for medicine. The Jewish immigrants in

Safed started up a new industry—making and dyeing cloth, including silk. By the middle of the sixteenth century there was a thriving community of 10,000 Jews living in Safed, which was also an important religious center for them.

But at the end of that century, the brief golden age began to fade. The downward trend returned. Various Arab and Druze tribes took advantage of the weakening Turkish authority to start fighting among themselves, and the tides of war once again started disrupting the country.

As the Ottoman Empire went downhill over the next 200 years, the situation in their provinces—of which Palestine was a rather unimportant one—naturally grew worse and worse. When a power is beginning to lose its grip, it gets more despotic, unjust and greedy. So the Turks, feeling themselves slipping, parceled out control of their provinces to unscrupulous men and gave them orders to get money any way they could to pay for their privileges.

This meant, as usual, taxes and more taxes. One was a land tax, and because of it once again farmers, mostly Arab, left their land to come to the towns. Land abandoned in that climate rapidly goes back to desert, and it was because of this that travelers in the eighteenth and nineteenth centuries found the country so desolate; even fertile areas were not being properly worked, and most of the unfertile land of course had never been worked at all.

Everything slipped back as the Turks became weaker and lazier and more corrupt. Again it became a wild country where the Bedouin returned to being brigands, roaming unchecked over the underpopulated land, raiding even the towns. And in the towns was lawlessness of a different kind. The Turkish officials were no longer interested in justice or fair dealing, only in who offered them the biggest bribes.

The Yishuv was in trouble. Most of its members no longer had any way to earn a proper living, due to the general economy which was in a terrible state. But the taxes were demanded just the same, and these had to be paid out of money gotten from Jews abroad. If there was a delay in sending it, or it wasn't enough, there were punishments. Once when some Jews of Jerusalem got into debt with the local Arabs and couldn't pay, their synagogue was burned down and their quarter seized.

The general pattern of Yishuv (Jewish) life in Palestine during the 1800s was one of flux and upheaval. The picture is scarcely ever clear. At one point travelers would report communities and study centers in all the main towns and all the signs of a reasonably settled Jewish life. Then there'd be a war, an earthquake, a drought, a plague, locusts, a change of government; taxes would suddenly increase to a point where they simply couldn't be paid; a local administrator would launch a pogrom, for one of a dozen reasons; and quite abruptly—poof! that community would dwindle or even disappear.

But never for long. Conditions would change. A kinder or more tolerant ruler would take the place of the pogrom-maker; the economy would improve; the situation for the Jews of Europe would worsen, sending another ripple of refugees to bolster the numbers of the Yishuv. Now the travelers' tales would again speak of 30, 90, 150, 1,000 or 2,000 Jews in Safed, Hebron, Gaza, Tiberias and, of course, Jerusalem.

In the mid-nineteenth century our old friend Moses Montefiore organized a census—a head-count of Jews living in Palestine. He did this in order to be able to help them more efficiently. The census tells us that in 1840 there were nearly 3,000 Jews, most of them Sephardim, living in Jerusalem, and that this community, by far the largest in the country, amounted to a little under half the whole Yishuv, so there must have been around 6,000 Jews altogether. Not very many, and most of them living a life that the average Israeli of today would find contemptible—poverty-stricken, insecure, almost entirely dependent on money from abroad, and, worst of all, non-productive. This was the main thing Sir Moses longed to change.

1840, you remember, was also the year of the Damascus

Blood Libel case. That was the climax of Jewish persecution
in the Middle East in that century. From then on, better
communications—steamships, for one thing—and greater
awareness among Europeans that events outside Europe
mattered, meant that the Jews in these distant places could
have greater protection from the influential Jews in what we
now call "the West." And not only protection, in the sense
that the Turks now didn't feel so free to persecute any
minority group under their rule, but definite and practical
help.

Montefiore wasn't the only one who tried to raise the
standard of living, and especially of self-respect and self-
reliance, among the Yishuv. The leaders of the Yishuv
themselves realized how low they had sunk, and told Montefiore and others that what they wanted was not so much
funds as schools and training centers where Jewish young
people could learn useful trades. I must mention here that
the very first people who tried to help in this way were
Christian missionaries, who provided the first schools and
health centers, and did welfare work. But the Jews didn't
trust them, and in a way rightly so, for their main aim was
still the old one—the conversion of the Jews to Christianity.
The Jews were not prepared to have their children educated, or their poor helped, at that cost.

Most histories of modern Israel start in the year 1880. This
was indeed a turning point. It was where I meant to begin
this one, until I came to realize the importance of all that
had gone before. By that date, when what we now call the
First Aliya was about to travel to Israel, a great deal was
already going on there. The first agricultural school had
been opened eight years before, and 1,000 young Jews
were already working on the land. Jewish schools had been
open for over twenty years. Jewish quarters had been built
outside Jerusalem's city walls, the first of them being Yemin
Moshe, where we stayed. There were by this time expert
Jewish builders—a new trade for Jews. A Jew called Bak, had

introduced a printing press into Jerusalem, and newspapers, printed in Hebrew, came out regularly, as well as books and other writings, so that the cultural level had improved.

Things were not so thriving in other places. We hear a lot nowadays about resettling the "ancient Jewish towns" of Hebron and Nablus, or Shechem as the Jews call it. But the communities in these towns in the late nineteenth century were very small and their roots were not deep. These towns, together with Gaza and Safed, seemed to suffer worse from plague, earthquake and invasion than others, and by the turn of the century Shechem had no Jews at all, Gaza only about seventy-five, and the Hebron community was having great difficulty keeping its foothold.

Still, I can say that, in that turning-point year of 1880, the foundation stones of modern Israel had already been laid. They'd been laid chiefly by the poor Jews who had, never mind in what degraded conditions, hung on somehow through those fear-filled years of Ottoman rule, when even the forces of Nature had seemed to be against them; by philanthropists like Montefiore, who helped, with charity, new ideas and the power of his forceful personality, to give them a new start; and, let's not forget, by many of the Jews in the Diaspora who supplied, over the years, the funds without which the Yishuv would certainly have starved.

So that when in 1881 yet another appalling pogrom in Russia drove a wave (that really was a wave this time, and not a ripple) of pioneers to Palestine's shores, they did not have to start completely from scratch.

LETTER 11

The First Aliya— A Courageous Failure

In the film *Fiddler on the Roof* you saw, at the end, a thin stream of refugees leaving a Russian *shtetl,* Anatevka, which they loved despite its poverty because it had been all the home they had known. They were heading for—well, some of them had some idea, but most of them hadn't. They were just leaving, because the Russian government, and many of the Russians themselves, were making their lives impossible. Your own great-grandparents might have been among those pathetic uprooted wanderers.

In the early 1880s, more Jewish refugees fled from Russia even than had fled during the abominable times of the Cossacks. They piled up in vast numbers in little border towns where officials simply didn't know how to cope with them. If it had not been for other Jews, from America and Western Europe, coming to their aid, who knows what would have become of them?

But it was not so easy to know how to help them. It was not just a matter of money, though huge amounts of that were needed. The greatest need was for places to go. The well-established Jews of Europe, though willing to help, were not too keen to have their cities flooded with poverty-stricken Russian peasants—they were naturally (if not very heroically) afraid that the non-Jews would turn against the immigrant hordes and that this anti-Jewishness would affect them, too. So what they did was to wish the vast majority of them off on the New World, mostly the United States. Once they got there in their overcrowded immigrant ships, they chiefly went to the big cities.

Others finished up in England, but many of these only did so due to the dishonesty of various sea captains, who pocketed the money to sail them to America and then dumped them off at an English port and went back to Russia for more. Many a Jew who found himself in Liverpool thought he was in New York! And that just about shows the degree of helplessness of most of those poor people, depending wholly on the mercy of strangers of all sorts for the key not just to freedom, but to the new life they had to start living.

But there was another type of refugee, one who tried to take his destiny into his own hands. These were chiefly young men and women who, long before they were driven out of Russia, had a firm idea of what they wanted to do. They didn't want to go to yet another country where they would be a minority, at the mercy of non-Jews and their prejudices and laws. They wanted to go to the place they could think of as their own—even though it wasn't, yet— a place where they could have some hope of forging an independent *Jewish* life on their own soil.

They had been talking about this among themselves (very secretly, for such ideas were considered treasonable by the Russian police) for a long time. Now, inspired by men like Pinsker and Kalischer, they formed a new organization—BILU. Its name was taken from the four initial letters of the Hebrew rallying-cry of the biblical prophet Isaiah: "House of Jacob, come, let us go!"

In 1882, these "Biluim" began to arrive in Palestine,
which they, like others before them, called "Ha'aretz," The
Land, as if there were no other. There were very few of
them, but they were the leaders of that wave of immigrants
we now call the First Aliya. They arrived burning with hope
and idealism.

But their Land was not hospitable. It had many brutal
shocks in store for them. It was not merely the heat, the
strangeness, the hard conditions. They were coming to a
place worse in many ways than the horrors they had left
behind. Although there were no Russian police and angry
Russian peasants here to harass them, there were hostile
Arabs, corrupt and suspicious Turks, very little law and
order to protect them, and living conditions more primitive
than any they had known. There were also diseases, pests,
swamps and deserts, and—worse than any of these, as
things turned out—their own disastrous ignorance.

It was this ignorance as much as the hard life which was
to defeat many of them. They longed to redeem their Land
by farming it, but they didn't know how. Most of them had
never been farmers even in Russia, and farming here was
a total mystery to them. Full of passionate eagerness and
idealism as they were, they found that all the enthusiasm
and energy in the world wasn't enough.

They hoped their vision would help them through. They
believed with all their hearts in the destiny of the Jews in
a redeemed land of their own. And rich men in Europe
were ready to help them realize this dream, which others
laughed at and called insane. But even this much-needed
and much-appreciated help did not always come in the
right way.

As early as the late 1880s a rich French Jew called Baron
de Rothschild was already being called the Father of the
Yishuv. No doubt he liked the title. He certainly lived up
to it. He treated the Jews of Palestine as his children, and
rather naughty, irresponsible children at that. He was their
patron, but the word "patronizing" has two meanings. It

means financially helpful, but it also means a rather superior, patting-on-the-head, Father-knows-best sort of feeling. Both meanings applied to the Baron.

The system he followed was this: when a representative from the Yishuv, or from a group of would-be settlers, approached him for help, he would send his own representatives out to look over the site of the proposed village and if they approved, he—the Baron—would buy it and finance the group who wanted to settle on it.

Without this generosity, of course, many of the towns and villages we know in Israel today might never have got started. That much said, I must add that the Baron then at least partly spoiled this grand gesture by sending managers to Palestine to take charge of "his" villages, who were, for the most part, extremely overbearing, giving the settlers very little sense of independence.

In a way this may have seemed necessary, because, as I said, most of them really didn't know the first thing about local conditions or how to farm. But these dictatorial managers unfortunately made themselves (and through them the generous and well-meaning Baron) pretty unpopular. It's very often the way. When someone provides the cash for some project, he naturally wants to run it, or to make sure it's run his way. The Baron, living in some splendor in France, really did think he knew best what was good for the settlers. But they were grown men and women; they'd made enormous sacrifices; their whole idea had been to be independent on their own land.

Of course the Baron's handling was not the only cause of disillusionment. It would be unfair to put too much blame on him, when there were so many other, worse difficulties. Some of their troubles and the stories connected with them may give you an idea, a dim notion, of what those early pioneers faced. Then you won't blame those who couldn't take it, and left, many of them with broken hearts and broken spirits. Nor perhaps will you judge too harshly the ones who stayed, but lost their ideals and became

"colonialists" in the old, unpleasant sense, exploiting
cheap Arab labor and just trying to get what they could out
of the land for material reasons. At the same time I hope
you will realize the qualities needed to triumph over all the
odds, as some of them did, and survive everything to stay
on, and build, and till the soil themselves as they had originally intended.

I will pass briefly over the obvious obstacles which the
Biluim and their fellow pioneers must have known they
would have to face, such as the climate. You've had a good
taste of that now, but you may not remember the hot, dry
sandy winds which seem to dry out your very veins; or the
deluges of rain which can change unpaved roads, fields and
village streets to mud wallows, dry river-courses (wadis) to
raging uncrossable torrents, and clay or mud-brick huts to
the condition of a sandcastle after the first wave has washed
over it.

The pioneers knew that living conditions would be
primitive, but perhaps they hadn't realized that where they
did find an old abandoned stone building to shelter in they
would have to share it with snakes and scorpions. They may
not have expected to have to learn to cook like the Bedouin
you saw in Sinai, who baked flat bread for us on the back
of a curved iron pot over a fire of thistles between two
stones. Even to make flour was a most complicated and
time-consuming business—picking over the wheat grains
for pebbles, washing and drying the grains, and then either
carrying them to the nearest mill or grinding them themselves by some primitive method. Nor was the journey to
the mill a light matter.

Traveling at that time was a wearying occupation. The
roads were mere tracks, sometimes not even that. Either
one rode, usually on a donkey (or a horse if one were
lucky), or, if there was a lot to carry, a cart would be used
which jolted and bounced over the rocks, or sloshed
through the mud, or dragged through the sand, reducing
travelers sometimes to such a bruised state that when they
arrived they could not climb down without help.

The other method of getting from place to place—which most people used—was walking. It could take hours and days to get to the nearest town for supplies, or to carry essential messages; believe it or not, in some of the villages even water had to be brought from a distance until wells could be sunk. In such a situation the discovery of water, after weeks of digging, was the most exciting thing that could happen to the settlers. When the first successful well was sunk in Rishon Le Zion, the first pail of water to be hauled to the surface was greeted like a revelation from heaven, with tears, cheers, dancing and hugging. It meant the difference between the village's being able to struggle on, or having to be abandoned, as a number of them were.

But traveling was dangerous as well as tiring. So, indeed, was staying in one place, if it was not a well-protected town. The Turkish administration by that time had given up all real effort to make the country safe, and the marauding Bedouin had a free hand to hold up, rob and sometimes even murder people on lonely roads, or to launch night raids on outlying settlers. The local Arabs sometimes used to do this too, if they were not on good terms with the Jewish newcomers.

In most cases, with these Arab neighbors, it was not so much a matter of armed attacks, as harassment. For instance, the Arab shepherds used to purposely bring their flocks to graze on the settlers' newly sown fields, or steal any cattle or possessions that were left unguarded.

The Jews, who for generations had had to put up with harassment of every kind in their native countries, and who, there, had made a virtue of submission, now showed a very different temper. This was *their land*. The fields had been wrenched out of barrenness by the sweat of their brows, their very life's blood was in them, and when they saw goats munching their tender young crops they became men of fire and iron. They would leap onto their horses, catching up whatever weapons they had at hand (there were seldom more than a few firearms in a village, so they used farm implements or sticks) and rush out to drive off the intruders. In this way, ironically, many good relations were formed with the local villagers, because the Arabs respected the Jews' determination to defend their farms.

They also admired many of their more modern farming methods, and, even more, perhaps, their ingenuity and genius for improvisation. Once when some oxen were stolen, the Jews put a couple of camels into harness and made them pull a plough and a cart. The Arabs liked that. Sometimes there would be cooperation, and then (as ever) things worked well. In one place where Bedouin raids on a new well had become too much to bear, the Jews chased them and gave them a beating. Instead of bearing a grudge for their defeat, the Bedouin made peace, and there was a sensible agreement whereby they could use the Jews' well and the Jews could pasture their livestock on the Bedouins' land.

I should, incidentally, make it clear that these raids on the Jews' land were not, at that stage, political. It was only much later that the local Arabs began to fear and resent the Jews as intruders in any nationalistic way. All the land the Jews occupied at this time had been legally bought from Arab or Turkish landowners and this was not disputed (or even thought about) by the local peasant-farmers (who are usually called *fellahin*). The reason for the Bedouin raids was a simple one—they wanted plunder.

Not that the Jews had much. Their "wealth" was all in their land, in their crops and cattle. They lived in conditions of dire poverty. Once, when a new group of eight Biluim arrived at a settlement near Jaffa, a group of thirteen (twelve men and a girl) who were already there had to "move over" to make room for the new group in a house with two rooms and a porch. The table was made of planks resting on boxes, and there were no beds. Their celebration meal that night had two courses instead of the usual one: bean-and-potato soup, and rice pudding. They lived on almost no money at all.

Another great hardship was the work. I remember when

I first went to Israel I, too, was burning with zeal to do something "constructive" for the country, preferably farm work. I, like most of these newcomers, had never done any real physical labor before, and so I can well sympathize with their feelings of determination mixed with fear that they would not be able to live up to their intentions.

One of the Biluim, called Chaim Chissim, kept a diary, and this was his description of what he went through working (for a pittance) at the Agricultural School.

I have not written for ten days: I have been physically incapable of it. My hands are blistered and congested with blood, and I cannot straighten my fingers. When I was in Russia, I dreamed of working eight hours a day and devoting the rest of my time to things of the mind. But how can one's brain absorb anything when one's back is near to breaking and one is overcome by dreadful fatigue—when all one wants to do on returning from work is to bolt one's supper and fling oneself down and sleep?

On my first day of work I got up at five, the hour of sunrise, as work began at six. We did not drink tea in the morning. After arranging our bedding we grabbed a loaf of bread apiece. Although most of us could not eat so early, some arrived at our place of work with only a quarter of a loaf left . . .

We took our hoes, rolled up our sleeves and got down to work . . . We had to dig up the ground to a depth of about thirty centimeters and remove all weeds, together with their roots. We all stood in a row. I had not the faintest notion of what I was expected to do, or of what it was all about. Still, I raised my hoe and began bringing it down onto the earth at all angles. In a little while blisters developed. My hands started bleeding, and the pain was so excruciating that I had to lay down the hoe. But I immediately felt ashamed of myself. "Is this how you mean to show that the Jews are

capable of manual labor?" I asked myself. "Are you
really unable to come through this decisive test?" I
took new heart, picked up the hoe again, and despite
the stinging pain hoed for two solid hours, though it
nearly killed me. I then sat down exhausted. After that
I could do nothing for a whole day . . .

Oh, how I know that feeling! I well remember my first
day in the guava plantation at Ziqim—come to that, my last
day in the vineyards of Yasur . . . . The great spiritual
experience of manual toil can come to seem vastly over-
rated.

Exhaustion was not the only hardship Chissim and his
friends had to overcome. One becomes accustomed to hard
work if one can only keep at it. But there was a deprivation
that grew worse, not better, with time—that little matter of
"things of the mind."

Most of these young people had come from the kind of
Jewish background where learning and culture were vital
elements of their lives. When they broke away from their
past they had not expected that there would be no time,
energy or opportunity to keep up their studies or their love
of books and music. Once the appetite for these things has
been developed, a person soon begins to feel starved without them—even if his desire to prove himself a pioneer and
a farmer is being fully satisfied, he begins to experience a
gnawing dissatisfaction.

A few of the lucky ones found a piano-owner, and gathered round in the winter evenings to sing, recite and read
aloud to each other, for fear their intellects should wither
and die. But for many there was neither opportunity nor
strength, and they began to feel mere drudges, beasts of
burden, without minds or spirits—a truly terrible condition
which some could not endure.

Then there were the Turks.

Not only did they not do anything much to protect the
new settlers, they did all they could to hinder them. As early

as 1881, when the first wave of new settlers arrived, the Turkish governors grew alarmed by this influx of Jews and put a ban on all immigrants from Russia and Roumania. Of course the Jews came in anyway. Turkish port officials or border guards usually didn't try very hard to stop them if their fingers were closed over enough money. This sort of payment—which we call bribes—they called "baksheesh," and they were not ashamed of the word or the practice. It was by that time an entirely accepted method of getting around laws or regulations in all parts of the Turkish empire; in fact, it was not unknown for local administrators to invent regulations in order to collect more baksheesh from those who wanted to avoid them.

One of these maddening baksheesh-inviting laws was that no "permanent dwelling" could be built in Palestine without a permit from the Turkish authorities. What exactly was meant by "permanent" was something for the petty official on the spot to decide. A mud hut could be a "permanent dwelling" if he said so, and if he said so, you had to pay him to let you keep it up; if you didn't give him enough, a platoon of soldiers would be along to your village the next day and tear down your home.

On the other hand you could apply for a permit and do the thing legally. But that meant one of those endless journeys, often as far as Damascus, and when you got there if the governor didn't like your looks or the color of your money, or if he was inclined to take the new laws against Jewish settlement seriously, you wouldn't get your permit.

But there was a loophole in the law. A house with its roof on could not by law be pulled down. The Jews became very adept at building houses in the night, roofs and all. But houses built so quickly are apt not to outlast the first rains. The only truly permanent dwellings in that climate are of stone, and those take time to build. A lot of baksheesh changed hands wherever the Jews wanted to settle; but it wasn't always a solution.

So many of the settlers, such as the ones in Zikhron

Yaacov for instance, found themselves adopting native
methods of building as well as cooking. They cut reeds
from the marshes, and built reed huts. They soon learned
to make very good ones. The fleas also approved of them,
and moved in with the settlers—fleas "as large as flies."
They bit so mercilessly that on one hot night the poor
persecuted farmers rushed out of their huts and ran away,
scratching frantically as they ran. When they returned the
next day it was to find that their ploughing-oxen had been
pinched by the Bedouin in the night.

Fleas were not so bad, though. They didn't poison you.
And there was a worse pest even than the snake and scor-
pion, and that was the malarial mosquito. Malaria was a
terrible scourge in all hot countries, before medical science
found a cure for it. If you got it you just had to suffer, and
very often die, from the recurring bouts of delirium-induc-
ing fever. If you recovered, you knew that was probably not
the end of it—it was in your blood and you might be struck
down with it again at any moment, all the rest of your life.
Also you didn't have the luxury of a hospital or even a nice
comfortable bed while you alternately sweated and shiv-
ered. There were no hospitals and no beds. You lay on the
hard ground, with luck in the shade, and your comrades
looked after you as best they could (there was almost nothing anyone could do) until you got over it—or died.

Nor was this the only illness to be feared. There was
scarlet fever and dysentery, and an eye disease called tra-
choma. Even sunstroke carried off a number of them. In
that doctorless wilderness any illness was terrifying.

But those early settlers were determined optimists, and
this excellent quality made them also at times deaf to warn-
ings and blind to dangers. They refused to understand that
green ground in summer meant marshes, and that marshes
meant malaria. They simply wouldn't listen to advice, even
when they'd asked for it. One eager group took a Greek
doctor, with some real experience of the country, to the site
they'd chosen to settle in, close to the Yarkon River. They
asked if he thought it was safe and suitable. He climbed into

a ruined house and gazed at the sky. After a long time he came down again, and told them that there was one sure sign if a place was wholesome or unhealthy—did birds fly through the air above it? Here was a place full of attraction for birds, plenty of insects and seeds, yet no bird was to be seen. "This," he concluded, "is a deadly place."

And do you think they listened? Within five minutes of the doctor's verdict they were weeping on each other's necks in an ecstasy of joy—they had decided to ignore him and go ahead and buy it. That place turned into Petach Tikva, and a number of those same ecstatic men died finding out that the doctor had been right. Their village had to be abandoned.

There were other reasons why villages failed, and some that did so were not, like Petach Tikva, destined to be reborn later. One can see their ruins today, beautiful solid buildings raised with the Baron's money which now stand empty, memorials to broken dreams.

One reason I've mentioned already—insensitive and malicious administrators, whose attitude to the settlers killed all initiative and spirit in them. One of these, a man called Bloch, a Frenchman (and a Jew, alas), ruled like a despot over the private as well as the working lives of those under him, imposing punishments and fines on them for things like breaking Sabbath or dietary rules, though he was not observant himself.

And there were other "baddies" among the Jews. The inevitable property speculators who spring up like weeds wherever there are unsettled conditions and eager, inexperienced buyers, men who "sold" deeds to properties which didn't exist or were not for sale, or who cunningly pushed up land prices for their own profit.

The rabbis weren't exactly a help either. Some of them contented themselves with charging heavy tolls to travelers passing through their districts—this happened particularly in Safed, mainly to pilgrims, and didn't affect the pioneers much.

What did affect them was the obstructive conservatism

which led many rabbis to oppose every newcomer who was not prepared to join in the old order, in other words those who didn't want to live a religious life in the cities and "eat the bread of charity."

This opposition took different forms, from throwing stones at pioneer women who visited Jerusalem in European dress, to fighting, with every means in their power, the opening of trade schools or the establishment of self-supporting settlements. And this happened despite the fact that there were no really non-religious settlements then as there came to be later. Very often when a new village was starting, the Torah, which the settlers had carefully carried all the way from Russia, would be suitably housed before the settlers themselves! Yet as always, conservative religious forces stood four-square in the way of progress, independence and, indirectly, that greatest of all spiritual necessities, self-respect.

Then of course there was a traditional Jewish quality which caused its own chaos, as it always has and as it still does. It's that very quality which independence and freedom produces, and which lies at the root of every Jewish achievement and every Jewish failure, from the time of Moses to the present: the chronic inability of Jews to agree with each other, their stubborn insistence on "each man to his own way."

They know all about it, and make jokes: Take two Jews and you've got three political parties. When Jews get together to talk about peace, who needs any Arabs? Israel is a country of 3,000,000 prime ministers. Yet here were (and are) Jews striving to live together in small communities which could only be run cooperatively, on a basis of mutual agreement, and that always means some have to give way. Some did and do, and some couldn't and can't. So, promising groups quarreled, split up, reformed, or disintegrated forever, leaving those sad empty spaces in the hills or valleys. Others, as I mentioned before, stayed on in a very different spirit from the one they had started out with, as private farmers, shorn of their ideals of redemption through labor and given over to selfish interests.

But I mustn't end this letter about the First Aliya on a depressing note. There were successes as well as defeats. The memoirs written by some of those men are full of triumphs and moments of glory which are nothing short of inspiring.

One of the most impressive stories is that of an obsessive and eccentric Lithuanian called Eliezer Ben Yehudah. He immigrated to Palestine in 1881, bringing his young wife with him. He'd already made up his mind that his life's work should be reviving Hebrew as a spoken language; until that time it had been thought of as a language of prayer, and apart from that, was only spoken between men who had no other language in common, as a last resort, so to speak.

Charity, they say, begins at home, and Ben Yehudah decided to apply this principle to the rebirth of Hebrew as a colloquial language. As soon as he and his wife boarded the boat that was to take them to Palestine, he began speaking Hebrew to her, and from then on obliged her to give up speaking Russian. Needless to say she learned fast! At one point on the journey he excalimed *"Ma yafeh hamacom hazeh!"* ("How beautiful this place is!") and by that time she was able to answer, "It truly is a beautiful place," in Hebrew that sounds rather like mine after eight years in Israel, by which I mean, faulty but comprehensible.

At that time people were astonished to hear a woman speaking Hebrew at all, let alone talking to her husband in it. The couple made a great impression when they reached Jerusalem, where Ben Yehudah got work as a journalist and later as a schoolmaster. Through his work he pushed his ideas about a revival of the "national language," and went on practicing what he preached in his own family. When his wife had a son, Ben Yehudah could hardly wait to begin his greatest experiment—the raising of the first Jewish child for many generations to speak Hebrew as his native tongue. The dedicated father wouldn't even allow his sickly wife to employ any household help, for fear his child's ear should be contaminated with any other language.

Well, all fanatics are hard to live with and his poor little wife had some very difficult times. So did he, of course, because such a great enterprise as his heart was set on doesn't come about without struggles and setbacks. But as we know, he achieved it in the end, long before you, my little sabras* began to chatter in Hebrew before you could speak anything else.

*A native-born Israeli.

LETTER 12

The Second Aliya

Every generation, sooner or later, is apt to turn on its parents and cry accusingly: "Why did you (or didn't you) fight in this war, or for that cause? How could you let our world get into such a mess? *What happened to your ideals?*" The truthful answer to such questions is: "We were too busy getting on with our lives," but the more usual one is: "You kids don't realize what we were up against. Try fighting today's battles and see if you do any better."

No "generation" was ever more critical of the one before it that the Second Aliya was of the First. When this next wave of immigrants arrived, around 1907, they found a mess that horrified them—and they were as intolerant and critical as only untried idealists can be.

Most of them landed at Jaffa. Their first view of their dreamland shocked nearly all of them. Jaffa was nothing but a sordid, dirty little port-town, and most of the Jews in it were pretty sordid and dirty to match. Crowded into the narrow streets of tumbledown houses, members of the

Old Yishuv who had drifted off the land now lived in
squalor, ready to prey on newcomers in any way they could
—from putting them up at dingy, bug-ridden "hotels" to
fleecing them in dishonest land deals.

Finding no trace here of the inspiring new life they'd
come to seek, the youngsters often made their way hastily
to Jerusalem. There they came face to face with the pallid,
black-coated religious community who still lived their non-
productive lives in sunless hovels and study-halls, dependent on *Haluka* (money from abroad). These "praying Jews"
repelled the newcomers almost as much as the "preying
Jews" of Jaffa.

Still, the timeless beauty of Jerusalem, whose very air and
stones seemed to speak of Jewish antiquity, refreshed their
spirits and gave them new hope. In pairs or small groups
they set off on foot to the no-longer-new towns and settlements, established in the 1880s and 90s with Rothschild's
help or by independent groups—places like Petach Tikva,
Rishon Le Zion and Rehovot—hoping to find there the
foundations of the new Jewish independence on which they
could build with their own hands.

But a worse shock awaited them in these Jewish colonies
of the Old Yishuv. What did they find but Jewish farmers,
well settled and comfortably-off, living off the sweat of Arab
laborers. Jewish soil, bought with Jewish money and redeemed by Jewish courage and labor not a generation
before, now being tilled by *fellahin* for a miserable pittance,
while the owners sat back and played cards!

The young newcomers determined to replace these Arab
workers. They, as Jews, must do the hard work themselves,
as a step towards owning and working their own land. But
far from welcoming these young inheritors of their own
dream, the Old Yishuv farmers rejected them harshly. Perhaps they saw in these clear-eyed, reproachful faces a re-
flection of their own lost ideals. Assuredly they heard in
these strong, demanding voices terms for employment
which they considered would ruin them. Young Russian-

bred Jews, however many sacrifices they were prepared to make, were not able or willing to live at the level of Arab peasants.

At the same time one can imagine the Arab workers' reaction to this influx of Jewish would-be field workers. The Arabs regarded them as rivals and intruders, and the few Jews who did manage to get taken on in the orchards and fields soon found the atmosphere of hostility and hatred unbearable.

Rejected and disillusioned, the newcomers often re-treated back to their single rooms, rented or borrowed, in Jerusalem, and there sat on their straw mats endlessly drinking coffee and discussing ways of improving the whole situation. Some got work as teachers or in menial jobs to keep going; others stuck it out on the land, gritting their teeth and clinging to their dream of their own earth, their own homes and a chance to put their long-cherished plans for a new Jewish society into practice.

One young man called David Ben-Gurion wrote furious letters back to Russia, complaining not so much of the conditions in Palestine but of the lack of dedicated immi-grants. "This is Zion without Zionists!" he wrote. "These mummified diaspora Jews wouldn't emerge from their bog even if they heard the streets here were paved with gold! But the new Jew is proud and full of fight. He won't turn back."

He was wrong. Many did. Rachel Yanayit, who became the wife of Israel's second president, Yitzhak Ben-Zvi, and wrote a most beautiful and moving book* about her pion-eering days, tells how she arrived on the boat from Odessa to begin her new life, filled with hope and excitement. The first Jew she saw in Jaffa port was a man who rushed on board and at once began pleading with the sailors to take him back to Russia! Later he insisted on pouring out to her all his troubles—the sickness, the lack of work, the hope-

*Rachel Yanayit, *Coming Home.*

lessness of it all. She couldn't bear it and refused to listen.

Still, it was one view, and a realistic one, of the situation. Though Ben-Gurion and others roundly abused those who went home grizzling to Russia—"How I hate those slanderers!"—they said little about others who were so plunged in despair that they took their own lives. Fortunately there were, at that time, enough strongly motivated young people entering the country to make up for those who couldn't endure the tough conditions.

The ideals these young people arrived with—and which they steadfastly refused to compromise or give up—were similar to those of the Bilu, and the same, in fact, as those which activated your father and his Aliya, forty years later.

They believed with all their hearts in what they called "the conquest of labor"—that is, that Jews should, in their own land, become workers and producers. Not just in the country, as farmers working the soil themselves, but as factory-hands, fishermen, craftsmen and miners. In other words, that Jews should penetrate every branch of productive labor.

They wanted to change not only the Yishuv, but the whole image of the Jew. This drastic change could be summed up, perhaps, in the well-known words "do-it-yourself." This was the way of escape from the humiliating image of the *galut* (diaspora) Jew as a parasite, an exploiter or a victim. They wanted self-respect, and to get that they had to become entirely self-reliant. The key to all that was *work*.

Any kind of ease, soft living or self-interest was to be avoided like the plague. They were literally afraid of letting themselves slip into any kind of comfort, for fear they should go the way of the Old Yishuv. Rough, hard living was a matter of honor with them. They took pride in sleeping on planks, walking barefoot (they were called "the barefoot ones") wearing the oldest and plainest clothes, often topped by an Arab headdress, and eating the very minimum of simple food, usually pita (the Arab flat bread), olives, halva, and vegetable soup. The fruits of the land, such as apricots, oranges, dates and figs, they considered not only a treat for the tongue but for the soul, because they symbolized both the richness of the soil and the skill and hard work that had made them grow.

Those who crowded the rush mats in Jerusalem hovels did not sit there long. They were soon on the go again, tramping over rocky hill-paths or across desert land through heat and rain to any place where they might find the kind of work they longed for. One girl, called Sarah Malkin, summed up her dedication like this:

"There were two ideas which brought me to this country. One was that the object of Zionism is to live in Eretz Yisrael [the land of Israel]. The other was that everyone should work and create and not be a parasite, and that in Eretz Israel one should till the soil."*

By "one" she meant women as well as men. The few girls who had come with the young men wanted, and meant to get, something quite new—sexual equality. That meant equality of work, hardship, danger—and satisfaction.

Poor girls! Their "fancies and dreams," as Sarah called them, were soon brought up against hard reality. Incredibly, even their male comrades weren't willing to believe that women could work like them. At first no one would let Sarah "till the soil"—such a notion was unheard of. The old settlers, many of them (unlike the newcomers) still religious, thought Sarah and girls like her were downright wicked and immodest, especially when they were seen walking boldly all over the countryside in boys' clothes!

The utmost persistence was needed before Sarah was at last given a trial in the job she longed for—picking oranges. Eventually she became a skilled worker, earning good wages; but she was not content for long to be an employee. She, like the rest, thirsted for independence on their own

*This and much of the material for these chapters is taken from *The Goodly Heritage* by A. Yaari.

land, and eventually she was invited to join a group of boys
who were struggling to settle near the Sea of Galilee.

It was an area of uncultivated land inhabited by a particularly fierce Bedouin tribe. The boys were having a rough
time. They all lived in one stifling earth-floored, one-
roomed building, infested with venomous creatures. On
her first day, Sarah was left there alone to get on with the
cooking and cleaning. Out in the open over a few stones,
with no protection from the heat or from marauders, she
cooked for thirty men. Even when winter came and the rain
poured down, it was taken for granted by all, including
herself, that she would go on cooking outdoors somehow
or other—no one dreamed of building her a stove, let alone
a proper kitchen.

Interestingly enough, this hardy pioneer girl now cheerfully gave up her dream of being a field-worker and got on
uncomplainingly with her "women's work." Why was she
satisfied and happy? Undoubtedly because she had
achieved her basic aim. She and her comrades were free
and independent workers on their very own land.

One of the men wrote: "There are no police, no over-
seers, no one else to interfere. We are scattered over the
fields. A young woman is alone in the room. We bathe in
the lake. We all sleep on the flat roof. There is nothing to
trouble or annoy us. . . .

Malaria, hostile Arabs, snakes, scorpions, grinding hard
work in the sun and rain—are these nothing? Apparently
they are, when measured against spiritual fulfillment.

After only six weeks, the little settlement played host,
inviting all settlers for miles around to a memorial meeting
for the fourth anniversary of Theodore Herzl's death. They
built a small stage for the ceremony and arranged to serve
tea from their one-roomed house.

There were not many settlements in Galilee at that time.
Yet the new one, Kinneret, had been boycotted at first
(typical of the sort of pettiness that so often bedevils even
the finest endeavors) because their farm manager, a man
called Berman, had once hired Arab labor. But now the

boycott was forgotten. Hundreds of visitors came, on don-
keys, in carts and on foot. They were taken on a tour of the
newly ploughed fields which, a month before, had been
wasteland. Everyone was happy, proud and hopeful, and in
the end it was more of a party than a memorial.

Kinneret became one of the first kibbutzim quite soon
afterwards, when Berman left and they decided to run the
place themselves as a collective. By this time Degania,
nearby at the foot of the lake, was established too. It claims
the honor of being the first kibbutz, but Kinneret started
before it.

A number of famous men passed through Kinneret and
Degania during the next few years. One of them was Berl
Katznelson, whom Golda Meir described as one of the
finest men she'd ever known. He kept aloof from politics.
It seems strange that even in those early days the settlers
had already split up into two political factions—rivals! One
was the *Poalei Zion* (Zionist Workers) and the other was
Hapoel Hatzair (Young Workers). They argued endlessly
about which language to use, how to attract new immigrants, who was their real enemy—but actually the differences between them were so small that one wonders why
they bothered. Political splits seem to be the breath of life
to the Jews—there are now twenty-four parties in Israel!

But Katznelson refused to take sides. He was to play a
very important part in advising and sustaining Israel's leaders in later years; when he died, the whole country was
stunned, as the *galut* had been by the death of Herzl. But
that was years ahead.

Another visitor to Kinneret (though he loved Degania
best) was the poet A. D. Gordon. He was already nearly fifty
when he immigrated from Russia in 1906, so he found farm
work, which he'd never done in his life, even harder and
more tiring than the young people. But unlike so many, he
never lost his reverence for physical labor. He loved nature,
and believed that no Jew could hope for a fulfilled life who
didn't live close to the soil. Only if every individual first
improved himself through working close to nature could

the whole Jewish people be redeemed. Only work would give the Jews the right to their Land. So Gordon preached, and his beliefs influenced the whole workers' movement in Palestine. I've heard present-day kibbutz dwellers quote him with affection and respect.

One thing he abhorred was violence. When he was put in charge of guarding the settlement at night, he carried no more deadly weapon than a whistle. Other, younger men, however, saw it differently. While their saintly old comrade calmly circled the silent kibbutz with his whistle, they slept fitfully with their rifles by their heads.

Many settlements suffered attacks by Bedouin brigands, and also by local Arabs. Until the time of the Second Aliya, the Arabs had seen the Jews as bringers of work and prosperity. But ironically enough it was this new group's refusal to exploit them (or, from the Arab point of view, employ them) that made them resentful. There were, as well, Arab *effendis* (feudal landlords) who had fallen on hard times and sold their land to the Jews. Now they watched these strangers bringing the soil to productivity and they grew bitter. Sometimes they sent their sons or servants by night to steal, spoil crops or in more violent ways get their revenge for their sense of loss.

So a group of young Jews got together to form a professional defense-force. They called themselves *Hashomair* (The Watchman). Some of them had had experience of fighting in the Russian army before coming. They offered themselves for hire as guards to farms and settlements.

One such settlement was Sejera. Sejera had a better reputation than some places with the new Aliya because there the Jews did a lot of the work themselves. But they employed Arab or Circassian watchmen, mainly because they were cheap. *Hashomair* couldn't get anyone interested in them, until a Sejera farmer discovered his watchman was spending every night in his own warm bed! So he gave the *Shomrim,* watchmen, a chance.

As he feared, the local villagers were offended at the firing of their watchman, and for several weeks they kept

making night attacks. All of these were successfully beaten
off by the new Jewish guards. The attacks stopped.

After that, the reputation of the *Shomrim* spread. Soon
they were being hired by an increasing number of settlements. Of course they were well armed. The old, haphazard
night-chases with sticks and farm tools were a thing of the
past. Now it was a question of shooting to kill, and often
they did kill intruders. This led to reprisals, and a number
of the *Shomrim* also fell, heroes of the New Yishuv.

Yet not everyone was in favor of this new, vigorous defense system. A man called Zemach, a friend of Ben-
Gurion's, was strongly opposed. He argued that blood
begets blood; one death leads to many. His idea was to
prove that the Jews weren't hostile to the Arabs, with
whom, after all, they were to share the land. They should
refrain from killing or antagonizing them, and concentrate
on improving relations with them.

Hashomair's answer was simple. The Arabs were primitive. They had always shown that they best understood and
respected a firm show of force. They insulted the Jews by
calling them "children of death"—that is, non-men, cow-
ards. Besides, Jews for generations had been harassed and
driven because they had never organized their own defense. In this place, Jews would be harassed no more. Whoever would rob a Jew of his property or menace his life, *here*,
would pay for it.

Who can say who was right? Hashomair's methods were
effective. Their determined defense undoubtedly made settlements safer, and helped the spread of Jewish farming.
From these beginnings sprang the Haganah, which pre-
served the Yishuv during the period of British occupation;
the Palmach, which was in the vanguard during the War of
Independence; and today's Israeli Defense Forces which
for their size are the finest army in the world. *But.* It was in
those early days that the anger, the hatred, the feuds and
the bad blood between Jew and Arab had their roots. "He
who sows the wind reaps the whirlwind."

The myth of the Arabs only understanding force persists

to this day among vast numbers of Israelis. I've never faced them in battle, but your father has, and this is not his opinion. It is worth remembering that many young men and women in those early times traveled about the lonely roads on foot. Some of them were frightened or chased by Arabs on their way, but few were harmed. The Arabs are said to have admired them for traveling thus unarmed and unprotected, especially those who were inclined to smile at the Arabs they met and treat them with friendliness.

You really ought to read some of the memoirs written by these Second Aliya youngsters. Throughout all their disappointments and setbacks, their sorrows and fears and dilemmas, runs a thread of pure inspiration which makes their simply-written accounts read like lyric poetry. They reveled in hardship, and found a satisfaction amounting to ecstasy in merely living through the days in the Land that they loved. Their unpretentious accounts of their day-to-day doings are charged with the most moving descriptions of the effects on them of the special light, the fragrances, the feel of the earth and stones, the very air they breathed.

Their happiness came from working for a pure cause. True, it had been sullied by previous blunders; the way forward was blocked by obstacles, and they even quarreled among themselves. Yet these things did not basically alter their happiness. They were sure of what they were doing. They knew it was right, that their aims were wholly good, and that they were building something for the future of their people. Who needs more than that? I have no higher hope for you, my sons, than that you may experience that joy, some day soon—before you grow too old to believe that any cause is wholly good.

LETTER 13

The First World War

It's ironic to realize that Zionism probably helped to arouse the Arabs to their own kind of nationalism. The Arabs, who had lived under foreign rulers and in primitive feudalism for centuries, saw the Jews coming into their midst with new purpose, new ideas, new energy, transforming the land and their own communities, and this must have made them think: "If these Jews are a nation, and if feeling themselves to be one gives them such powers, then why not us?"

Of course it may well be that Arab nationalism would have been born anyway, with the downfall of imperialism. The fact is that around 1914, the Arab peoples began to feel that the very word "Arab" had an almost magical meaning, that it should unite all their countless tribes and groupings into a great nation, such as they had been in the glorious past when they led the world.

They dreamed a wilder and more fantastic dream than ever the Jews had—no less than an empire stretching from

the Atlantic to the Persian Gulf. Nowadays only the Jews of
Israel stand in the way of that dream; in those days Turkey,
Britain, France and other big powers made it look almost
impossible. But that didn't stop their wanting it.

From that time on, the two nationalisms gathered speed
and strength side by side, the existence of each spurring the
other on. The Jews had a head start, but the Arabs, with
their broader dream, their vastly greater numbers and their
enormous territories, were never far behind.

However, in 1914 only the first signs of this deadly race-
to-come were to be seen. Most eyes were on Europe, where
great events were brewing, events which were to bring
tragedy to the Jewish community of Palestine.

Theater people say that comedy is someone falling on a
banana peel—tragedy is someone falling off a cliff. In other
words, the higher the fall, the greater the drama.

The situation of the Yishuv in 1914 was a rising pinnacle
of achievement. No longer were the Jews of Palestine a
contemptible, poverty-stricken, backward community, depending on charity and sufferance. In less than thirty-five
years they had made themselves over into a thriving, hard-
working and self-respecting people with a language and
culture of their own. Most of them now earned their livings
in trade, crafts and industry, or on the land, much of which
had been redeemed through their efforts. Jews abroad who
had contributed money now had something to show for it,
and shared the satisfactions of achievement. And the Land
itself, cities, villages and farmland alike, showed the world
a face of pride and hope.

Then came the war.

The First Aliya, for all its achievements, ended in moral
failure. The Second Aliya, despite its difficulties, was a
moral, and practical, success.

Not only had the newcomers added a great deal to what
had been begun before, but they had held on to most of
their high principles. If it hadn't been for this moral and
material achievement, which gave the Yishuv as a whole

such strength, it is unlikely to have survived the ravages of that most wasteful and pointless of wars.*

Within twelve months of its outbreak, the numbers of the Yishuv, which had been steadily increasing, dropped by almost half. Those who were left faced famine. And the hard-won progress of many years was all but ruined.

It was the Turks' doing. They regarded Palestine as nothing more than a large field on which to prepare for battle against Egypt. Everything and everybody in it was either raw material for their army, or a dangerous nuisance to be pushed out of the way.

Jews with Turkish papers were drafted into the army. Jews with Russian papers were regarded as enemies and were deported, usually by ruthless force-marches inland towards Syria. Luckily a lot of these managed to filter off on the way, and were hidden in the Jewish settlements. Those who were neither "Turkish" nor "Russian" were hauled off to do forced labor—building roads or barracks or railways or whatever dirty work the Turks needed done. Whole settlements were stripped of men in this way.

One of them was Tel Aviv.

Tel Aviv, later the first all-Jewish city in the world, had been founded five years before the war by a group of Jews from Jaffa who had grown sick of the squalor and overcrowding there.

This enterprising group flattened some sand dunes north of Jaffa, marked off a main street with planks, and then, before even building homes, laid the foundation stone for a "gymnasium"—a high school, to which every ambitious Jewish parent in the region was soon to send his child. Then homes and gardens rose from the sands and by the time the war began it was a thriving and pretty little

---

*The propagandists for the present (Likud) Government of Israel are busy claiming that the true founders of the State were religious. This is only true if you think, which I don't, that the First Aliya contributed more to the foundation of Israel than the Second.

settlement. They were very proud of it, although they laughed heartily at the "prophet" who predicted that their new town would one day boast 100,000 inhabitants.

By 1915 it had no inhabitants at all. The Turks had evacuated it.

Their official excuse (not that they bothered about excuses much) was that it wasn't safe to leave civilians on the coast. But inland villages fared little better. Apart from taking away most of the able-bodied men, the Turks also commandeered everything that could be eaten or used by their army—foodstocks, tools, and of course draft- and farm-animals.

The four "holy cities"—Jerusalem, Hebron, Tiberias and Safed—where pious Jews had, for centuries, lived on handouts from abroad, were even worse off. No *haluka* was getting through. Nor were food supplies because there weren't any, and city dwellers had neither hidden stocks nor fields to grow more.

The situation of the whole Yishuv was desperate. Thousands fled—to America, to Europe, even to Egypt—anywhere where they thought they might find work and food.

You know the word "Aliya," meaning immigration, or "a going up." Now you must learn the opposite, "Yerida," emigration—a going down. And those who leave, or, as some think, *desert* the Land are called "yoredim."

This wave of yoredim suffered no less from shame and guilt than those before or those that were to follow, although they had mainly been forced to leave. Thousands collected in Alexandria, homesick and heartsick. Among them appeared Joseph Trumpeldor, a man with a strange record. He had been the only Jewish officer in the Russian army, and had lost an arm fighting against Japan for the tsar, the Jews' hated enemy! Yet here he was in Egypt, marshaling the despairing yoredim into a Jewish unit which would fight for Britain.

This first all-Jewish fighting unit of modern times, called the Zion Mule Corps, fought bravely at Gallipoli. Later,

Trumpeldor returned to Russia to try to organize a whole army of Jews to fight for the Allies in Palestine. The project fell through because, in 1917, came one of the most important events in modern European history—the Russian Revolution.

Perhaps you think this has no place in a book about Israel. But there *are* no modern history books in which Russia and Bolshevism have no place. Marx, Lenin and the Revolution changed the whole world for good. (Some would pun, "for bad.")

The non-Communist world, including Britain, was terrified of the Bolsheviks. They could envisage all the "workers of the world" rising up and overthrowing capitalism, murdering kings and "bosses," suppressing the western idea of freedom and individuality. One of the smaller steps Britain felt she could take was to try to win over the *Jews* of Russia at least, to the western (capitalist) camp.

This wasn't as easy as it sounds. Numbers of Jews were for the Revolution and they banded together in groups called the Bund. But the Zionists opposed them, because they couldn't see their future in a Bolshevik Russia any more than in a tsarist one. So Britain decided to woo the Zionists.

I should mention at this point that when the war had started, the Zionist movement in the diaspora just hadn't known which side to be on, the German or the English, if only because there were so many Jews in each country. They had to decide who was going to win the war, and/or which side was most likely to help the Jews to get their own homeland in Palestine when it was all over.

At around this time, some Zionists tried to contact Arab nationalists in an effort to make common cause with them against the Turks. But the Turks had started arresting people for nationalist activities. They even staged some public hangings as an example. Naturally every nationalist movement thrives on a few martyrs so the effect of their brutality was the opposite of what the Turks intended.

Two men who avoided hanging but were banished instead were David Ben-Gurion and Yitzhak Ben Zvi. *They* had both bet on the Turks to win the war and had actually urged the Yishuv to help the Turkish war-effort. They backed the wrong horse, and they soon discovered what an ugly horse it was when they found themselves arrested and exiled. They fled to New York, where they worked tirelessly for Zionism till the war was over and they were able to return and see just what the Turks had done to the Jews. They must have been very ashamed of their initial mistake.

A Zionist who backed the other horse, Britain, in the war race was the man who was to be Israel's first president, Dr. Chaim Weizmann. He was a brilliant scientist and a great admirer of all things English. He did everything he could to persuade Zionists everywhere to support the British in the war. He foresaw that the corrupt and decaying Ottoman Empire couldn't last much longer. He believed Britain would be likely to take over in Palestine.

The British government, for its part, returned Dr. Weizmann's admiration. It also needed his scientific skill. A cheap way of producing acetone (a chemical used in making explosives) was urgently required, and Dr. Weizmann's special interest was chemistry. It was strongly hinted to him that if he could solve this problem the British government would show their gratitude by helping the Jews.

He got to work at once, and before long had fulfilled his side of the bargain. With the formula for cheap acetone safely in their hands, the British government in 1917 issued a document which has been the subject of heated argument ever since. It took the form of a letter to Lord Rothschild, the banker, who had been as active as Dr. Weizmann in trying to get official British support for Zionism. (The second paragraph is the vital one to study. The italics are mine.)

Dear Lord Rothschild,
I have much pleasure in conveying to you, on behalf of

His Majesty's Government, the following declaration of sympathy with Jewish Zionist aspirations, which has been submitted to and approved by the Cabinet.

HM Government *view with favour* the establishment in Palestine of a *national home for the Jewish people,* and will use their best endeavours to facilitate the achievement of this object, it being clearly understood that *nothing shall be done which may prejudice the civil and religious rights of existing non-Jewish communities in Palestine,* or the rights and political status enjoyed by Jews in any other country.

I would be grateful if you would bring this declaration to the knowledge of the Zionist Federation.

Yours sincerely,
Arthur James Balfour

This, then, is the famous—or, to the Arabs, infamous—Balfour Declaration, named after the foreign secretary who signed it. Zionists everywhere greeted it with rapture. Herzl's prophecy must be on its way to coming true, if the greatest nation on earth (as Britain still was, then) came out openly in support of a Jewish—well, Balfour hadn't actually said "state," but surely "national home" meant the same thing?

As to the part about the "non-Jewish population," that is, the Arabs, not much notice was taken of that, for two reasons. One obviously was that the Jews were thinking chiefly of their own objectives and problems, as everybody does when faced with some great challenging vision. The other was that, truthfully, no Zionist at that time had the least idea of harming the Arabs or interfering with their rights. They bought land wherever it was for sale, chiefly from Arab landlords who lived abroad, and for every-increasing prices; they saw no wrong in that. It didn't occur to most of them until some years later that just by being there, they were bound to cut across Arab rights, or what they came to think of as their rights. It was a curious blindness of the kind which often comes before tragedies, and which, later on, people look back to and say, "But it was so obvious! What prevented them from seeing it?" The fact is, they didn't, perhaps because they didn't want to.

After the Balfour Declaration, there was no question of whose side most Jews—other than those in Germany and Austria—were on during the war. Jews all over America flocked to join special units to fight the Germans. Jewish money from the great bankers poured in to the war coffers. Jewish skill of all kinds was gladly put at the disposal of the Allies. What none of them realized was that another half-promise had been given, at around the same time—to the Arabs.

The war was not going so well in the Middle East. The Arabs, particularly the ferocious desert tribesmen, were wanted to fight the Turks. So the British government secretly authorized an Englishman called T. E. Lawrence, a crazy adventurer who had gained the Arabs' trust through his exploits in the desert, to tell the Arab and Bedouin rulers that if they fought the Turks and thus helped Britain win the war, Britain would give them independence from foreign rule and help unite them into a great Arab nation stretching all across the Middle East. Not unreasonably, the Arab rulers thought that included Palestine.

Well, the Arabs approved the bargain, and they, like the Jews, did their part. They were only too happy to give the Turks a trouncing anyway—they hated them. Led, according to his own rather boastful accounts, quite often, by Lawrence himself in flowing Arab robes, and armed with British weapons, they swept out of the desert onto Turkish camps, troop trains and even towns, slaughtering Turks left and right for the glory of the Arab empire which was to be their reward.

Meanwhile, in Palestine itself, the hungry, war-shattered remains of the Yishuv hung on grimly. Those who believed in God prayed to stay alive. Those who didn't, worked for the same end, and some did both.

Hashomair no longer thought merely of defending Jewish settlements against casual marauders, but saw it might have to be the Yishuv's fighting arm to keep off desperate, hungry mobs of Turkish deserters, fleeing as the war-front moved north. The Jews' struggles to get hold of weapons —any weapons—grew desperate. At the same time, the furious Turks, sensing that the days of their power in the region were numbered, became daily more savage and oppressive. And all the time, fear, hunger and disease increased.

Even before it became quite obvious that the British were going to win the war, however, some of the Jews in the Yishuv had opted to help them. There were two (at least) schools of thought about how best to do this. The bulk of the Poalei Zion, who were struggling to maintain a foothold on those villages and settlements which hadn't been forcibly cleared by the Turkish army or abandoned by their starving inhabitants in despair, were fired with the idea of forming a Jewish brigade to help the British fight for Palestine, when the time came. They did everything they could, trying to contact Dr. Weizmann and anyone else they could think of who could help them.

Long before this, however, there was a group of young people who went another way to work. They offered their services to the British as spies. Their group was code-named Nili, and was centered on an agricultural station in Zikhron Yaacov, privately run (using Arab workers, and so much disapproved of by Poalei Zion!) by a man called Aaron Aaronsohn. He was a world-famous botanist, having discovered the original strain of wild wheat from which all domestic wheat was developed. He and his sister Sarah, and two other men, called Avshalom Feinberg and Joseph Lishansky, directed the spy network. They noted all Turkish and German troop movements and relayed them to the British by signaling to warships passing the coast, or by carrier pigeons.

When rumors of this spy ring began to get about the rest of the Yishuv, Poalei Zion was deeply opposed to it. They thought spying was morally wrong, to begin with, also, they were afraid that if the Turks found out about Nili, they would deal the final death-blow to the Yishuv.

And find out they did, in the summer of 1917, when one wretched pigeon got lost and came down in the middle of a Turkish camp. The Turks went quite mad at this point. They had suspected there were spies among the Jews; now they suspected all the Jews of spying. No one in the Yishuv was safe, and every village crouched, caught between terror and defiance, waiting for the tramp of boots, the searches, the arrests.

All these happened, and worse besides. It was the lowest point to which the Yishuv fell, for on top of all their other miseries they now endured a reign of terror.

Scores of Jewish intellectuals, the cream of the nationalist movement, were dragged off to prison in chains. Others, including elderly people thought to be relatives of spies or to know where spies were hiding, were arrested and tortured.

By this time, Avshalom Feinberg was dead. Aaron Aaronsohn was abroad. Joseph Lishansky was hunted like an animal from village to village, endangering all who came in contact with him. He was given shelter unwillingly; his work for the British was despised by the settlers as underhand, and his own boastful and immature behavior made them angry and fearful. Eventually he was caught, taken to Damascus and hanged. He died bravely, cursing the Turks.

But before him died Sarah Aaronsohn.

She and Avshalom had been in love; perhaps his death had something to do with the fact that she refused to run or hide as the Turks closed in on her home in Zikhron Yaacov. Since childhood she had dreamed of Jewish heroes and martyrs of old; now it was almost as though she willed the same fate for herself.

For days she was subjected to the most brutal torture without revealing one name. They tortured her father and other old men of the village before her. What superhuman courage, or stubbornness, keeps a woman silent then? The Turks were well-known for their cruelty and ingenuity in the field of torture and they tried everything they knew on this indomitable woman. In the end they wanted to transfer her to their headquarters for further "questioning." Somehow she persuaded them to let her go alone to her room before leaving. There she had a gun hidden, and with it she was, mercifully, able to shoot herself.

It's reported that even her Turkish torturers followed her coffin with bowed heads during the funeral. There have been other cases of torturers and executioners in wartime not feeling ashamed to express admiration for their victims. How is it possible to ill-treat or kill a person you admire? I know the stock answer, but I doubt if many women could understand such a perversion of the word "duty."

Without offering a judgment on these two approaches to helping the British war effort, it's interesting to compare their effectiveness.

The blazing determination of the Poalei Zion boys—and girls—to form a regular force to fight the Turks and win their country honorably and openly, failed. It was not really their fault. By the time they'd persuaded the authorities to allow them to do it, argued hotly about their demands for their own flag, their own language, their own officers, by the time they'd been trained—it was too late.

The victorious British, following General Allenby's triumphant entry into Jerusalem in 1917, chased the Turks the rest of the way out before the Jewish Brigade could get there to help. Many of the fiery young would-be soldiers were brokenhearted.

On the other hand, Nili, it was uncovered, supplied such first-class information that the British High Command later credited them with having speeded the whole progress of the war.

There are many examples of that sort of bravery I could tell, but I'm not all that keen on these military exploits, no matter how necessary they are. To me, the most moving stories describe how ordinary settlers faced the terrible fears and hardships of those years; how they tried to grow vegetables in sand dunes; how the few nurses struggled to tend the sick, wounded and starving; how they helped each other, and bore starvation and grief without complaint. And the finest of all these stories to me is of another kind of heroism, called forth by another kind of disaster.

A man called Moshe Smilansky, whose pioneer diary reads like the most thrilling adventure-story, tells how, one baking *khamsin* day in 1916, he was working in his orange grove near Rehovot when he noticed a cloud, low, dense and humming, passing overhead. Soon some strange winged insects began settling on his trees.

He wasn't very worried at first, just cautious. He watched them alighting in the hundreds, then tens of thousands, till the ground seemed alive round his feet. The Arabs who worked for him (Smilansky was not Poalei Zion) ran about crying in alarm. "What are they?" he asked them, and they told him in dismay—"locusts."

No one had any experience with locusts except a South American zoologist who happened to be visiting Rehovot. He warned the farmers that the locusts themselves were not the worst menace, but that they would soon mate and lay eggs. When these eggs hatched, the grubs would do great damage, and the thing was to destroy the eggs by exposing them to the sun.

Easier said than done! With the ground so thick with the adult insects that you couldn't move without crushing hundreds of them, how could the eggs be found where the females had buried them? For several days, more swarms of locusts kept arriving and soon the air was full of the sound of their humming and rustling. Reports came in that the entire area southwest of the town was blanketed with them.

The settlers decided on a plan of warfare. Each farmer would get rid of the locusts on his own land. Moshe Smilansky was very doubtful, as well he might have been—even if he could demolish the millions on his own acreage of 3,000 trees, how could he stop more coming in from beyond his borders? Still, he got some workers to bang tins and shout in his grove, which scared most of the invaders away. It didn't kill them, however, and that night he found the first clusters of eggs on his land.

His fellow farmers were almost going out of their minds with helpless rage as the hated locusts rapidly destroyed the work of years. Smilansky saw one young man running up and down between his ruined vines furiously beating the ground. "Look what they've done! At least there's the satisfaction of vengeance." Others found consolation in pouring boiling water over their tormentors, even though it was too late to save their vegetables and fruit.

The locusts ate, bred and laid eggs for twelve days, then flew away. The farmers surveyed the wreckage and thought with horror of the billions of eggs, not only on their property but on all the land around, which would soon hatch into ravenous grubs. They began to plough, to turn up the eggs. The Turks had taken their draft animals, so they had to do it by hand, and where ploughs couldn't reach, they hoed. They destroyed a proportion of the eggs, but all the time the awful thought tormented them: what was the use of all their efforts, when the Arab villagers were doing next to nothing?

Next they dug trenches round their properties, obtained sprayers and prepared solutions of disinfectant and poison to fight the grubs when they appeared. The work itself kept them from complete despair—at least they were doing *something*. But even as they dug, the sun darkened. They looked up in dread, and there was another long cloud of the monsters, whirring overhead in an unending band. At first it seemed they might pass over, but then, as if they had spotted the ravaged remains left by the first wave, down they came . . .

Soon even the wheat stalks had been eaten to the roots. Helplessly the wretched settlers watched the whole process happening again, the eating, the mating, the laying of a new lot of the deadly eggs . . . and just as this latest invasion took off, and the ploughing began anew, the first lot of grubs began to hatch. White when they emerged, they soon darkened in the sun and became "as black as devils."

You would think the settlers would give up at this point, especially when they discovered that their sprays of poison were useless against the grubs. But they didn't. Every man, woman and child in every farm and settlement was mobilized to shovel, drive or throw the grubs into the trenches and fill them in.

In fifteen years they had never worked as they worked now from dawn till dusk. As fast as they disposed of one lot of grubs, new armies of them would appear, and soon they were climbing the trees and stripping them "in a twinkling" of every leaf and piece of fruit. It was a nightmare, made worse by the knowledge that even if they defeated this horde, there were more in the offing.

They were not long in coming. In the midst of the fight with the second lot of grubs, even more numerous than the first, the "hoppers," the mature locusts, which had developed from the unmolested grubs in the Arab areas, attacked the farms. There must have been a good deal still left to save, because Smilansky writes:

> The hoppers spread all over the fields of the fellahin. Not finding any food in their desolate fields, they streamed in their masses towards the Jewish settlements which were full of greenery and trees . . . They came in great armies from all sides. The yellowish hoppers were in the lead, and with them came grubs from the second invasion of locusts, the tiny black and gray insects jumping alongside their elder brothers

. . a sea of destroyers. Behind them, everything was consumed, a veritable wilderness. Before them lay a paradise . . . *

It was a Saturday. Typically, even in this crisis the old men and rabbis of the settlements tried to forbid the half-demented settlers to profane the sabbath by working. But for once they were ignored, and again every available person was mustered for the apparently hopeless task. The two armies marched to meet each other, the insect army fresh, uncountable and hungry, the human army "hoarse with shouting and shadows of their former selves." Three kilometers from Rehovot, they met.

Don't ask me exactly how they stopped them. Smilansky just says, "All day we worked . . . that day we halted the enemy's progress, and all the following week we destroyed him." A few more locusts flew overhead, but there was little below to tempt them, and before much longer the plague was over, the battle won.

Now listen to this:

It was dawn. The sun had not yet risen. I stood in my orange grove, leaning against the fence and contemplating the frightful devastation. I could not turn my eyes away from the terrible scene. The trees stood there like skeletons . . .

Suddenly I was aroused by an Arab speaking to me. "Don't worry, Khawaja, God will return it to you two-fold." It was an Arab from Ramle, astride a donkey with an empty fig-box on either side. He had a good-natured face, and both his gaze and his voice were soft . . . full of sympathy. I had never heard an Arab speak to a Jew in such a voice. My eyes filled with tears.

This Arab, too, had lost everything, and had to start again from his beginnings—a donkey, and two empty fig-boxes. Arab and Jew shared this disaster, and shared, too,

*Yaari, *The Goodly Heritage.*

the courage to start all over again. Encouraged, perhaps, by this timely sympathy, Smilansky began that very day to irrigate his devastated trees.

"Two months later," he writes, "the land, which had become a desolate wilderness, was a paradise once more. Sun, water and labor had returned it to its former glory."

That was in 1916. The worst of the ravages of war were still ahead for the Yishuv. But in the end, "sun, water and labor," plus boundless faith and courage and not a little ruthlessness, were to restore the Yishuv to its "former glory" in time to face a new and much more long-lasting challenge—the challenge of Arab hostility.

LETTER 14

Arab Anger

I want to take a few pages here to examine the question I mentioned earlier: Why did the majority of Zionists not realize that they must inevitably come up against the Arabs of Palestine sooner or later? Why didn't they act before the problem became too big, before it killed thousands and threatened world peace?

There was a certain sort of Zionist abroad, who worked, gave money, agitated and wrote books in support of Jewish settlement in Palestine. These men never set foot in the place themselves and had almost certainly never seen an Arab. They took their notion of Eretz Yisrael from travelers who had written about "empty and neglected lands." With pogroms in Russia still going on, it's not hard to see why, to such Jews, the Arabs were non-existent.

Other Zionist supporters took a fatherly view. One in particular (Ben Borochov) suggested that the Arabs, like any other "natives," would benefit from the higher culture

and better methods of the modern Jewish immigrants, and
that soon enough they would adopt a Jewish life-style and
be "absorbed." Not unreasonably, the sophisticated Jews
of Europe thought their ways much superior to those of the
primitive fellahin.

Patronizing as that sounds, there was a good deal of truth
in it. As soon as Jewish settlement really took hold, a whole
chain of benefits to the Arabs followed: better medical services, better farming methods, and much greater prosperity. This, don't forget, inevitably attracted into Palestine
from the surrounding countries a lot more Arabs, who had
never lived there before. The point is often made by Israelis that many of the so-called "Palestinians" who claim their
right to the "land of their forefathers" only arrived there
after the first or second wave of modern Jewish settlers.
This is quite true; but we are talking about the ones who
really had been there all the time.

What about the pioneers themselves? How did they regard their fellow Palestinians in those days?

Many of these young people were by no means blind to
the Arabs. Nor did they look down on them. In fact, in a
sense they admired them and even wanted to be like them.
One young Jew was proud to be nicknamed "Fellah," which
was the Arab word for peasant.

After all, weren't these fellahin rooted in the soil in the
only way the young pioneers of the Second Aliya recognized—through working it with their own hands and water-
ing it with their own sweat? Did they not live simply, only
on what they could produce themselves? Did that not make
them an integral part of the land?

This was exactly what the Second Aliya people were striving to achieve themselves. Most of them saw no basic conflict between the Arabs' interests and their own. As they
saw it, it was not Arab rights that were threatened. Did they,
the Jews, ever attack Arabs on their own land? No, it was
the other way round—the Arabs kept harassing *them*. If
asked why they thought the Arabs were so hostile, they

would no doubt have talked about the natural fear of strangers, resentment at seeing that the Jews farmed better, or just a desire for loot and a bit of excitement.

It is odd that they never thought: "If we believe (as our pioneer-poet A. D. Gordon told us) that laboring on the land earns us the right to it, why doesn't an Arab peasant have the same right to the land he farms, even though he may not be the legal owner? Why should he not be as attached to the soil he ploughs as we are? After all, our ancestors may have lived on this land; but the fellah was born here."*

From their own point of view, the Jews had every right to be there. Every dunam of land they used had been bought and paid for, either by themselves or by the Jewish National Fund, recently set up for the purpose. And in a very deep and fundamental way, these Jews considered the country to be their own. Not only because God promised it to Abraham (most of them didn't believe in God) but because it was the only true homeland their people had ever known. They were *returning* to it; and finding huge tracts of it empty, barren and neglected, they felt a tremendous desire to bring it back to life. This longing was so strong in them that there was little room for moral doubts.

There was room for unease, though, and some of the more farsighted did foresee trouble ahead with the Arabs. But like the prophets of old, they were not listened to. Even if they had been, probably no useful action would have been taken. The Yishuv has simply never, at any stage, been prepared to take risks which even might have resulted in their losing their foothold on the country. For this, considering their history, it's hard to blame them—unless of course you think that a risk at this early stage (or indeed at a number of later ones) would have been well worth taking,

---

*This question was asked, too late, by Amos Elon, an Israeli writer, in his marvelous book, *The Israelis, Founders and Sons.*

to avoid the horrors of ever-increasing hatred between the
two peoples.

The vast majority of the Yishuv took their lead from the
attitudes of their leaders. Dr. Weizmann, though he worked
hard over the years to establish good relations with the
surrounding Arab *countries,* didn't trouble to seek a common language with the Palestinians. As we'll see, he didn't
value even the more primitive *Jews* very highly, so it's possible he shared some of the contempt felt for the fellahin by
Aaron Aaronsohn (of the "Nili" spy ring), one of the makers of the Zionists' Arab policy in the early days, who dismissed them as "squalid, superstitious, ignorant."

But really Weizmann considered them more as obstacles
in the way of Zionism, though oddly he didn't regard them
as a *Jewish* problem. He was counting on the British somehow to remove these "rocks in our path." I'm sorry to say,
being an admirer of Dr. Weizmann, that when after the
1929 riots a British official suggested a transfer of population—sending the local Arabs off into neighboring countries to make room for more Jews—Weizmann was, shall we
say, not exactly opposed to the idea.

As for Ben-Gurion, he also looked down on the Arabs,
mainly because their style of nationalism was not like the
Jews'. The Arabs' was all "against"—against the Jews,
against the colonial countries. It did nothing to improve
the land or modernize their society. Ben-Gurion could not
understand why any but fanatical Moslems or feudal landlords would not welcome Jews as bringers of a new and
better order. As to *Palestinian* nationhood, he would not
recognize it, though all the signs, very like those the
Jews had shown when Zionism began in Europe, were
visible.

If Ben-Gurion was not always honest in his dealings with
the British—he believed in kowtowing to them while the
Yishuv was weak while fully intending to be independent of
them eventually—his attitude toward the Arabs was his
usual more blunt and open one: his first concern was for

the Jews, but he honestly thought that the Arabs would benefit by cooperating and accepting them. If they couldn't see this, well then, it would be just too bad for them.*

But the general attitude, and not only among the Jews, was one of simply ignoring the problems. As late as 1937 a British Royal Commission concluded blandly that if the Arab rulers got the big Arab state they wanted in the rest of the Middle East, "they would concede little Palestine to the Jews."

"Little Palestine," alas, was to prove not so little after all. As a bone of contention it was to grow to dinosaur proportions.

From the middle of the First World War, the Allies—Britain, France and Russia—had been politely jostling for chunks of the Middle East cake after victory. By 1916 they had more or less parceled out Palestine between them. The northern part, then known as Southern Syria, was to be France's chunk. The area around Haifa was to go to Britain for a naval base. The holy places—Jerusalem in particular —were to be jointly controlled by the three powers.

Naturally none of them was really satisfied with this "agreement" since what they each wanted was the whole cake. That was why Britain was eager to conquer Palestine from the Turks without French help. She thought that would give her a better claim on the whole country.

The Zionists, especially Chaim Weizmann, were pleased when this came about. They had feared that Palestine would be split up, and that then the Jews would never be able to get a "whole" homeland. Anyway, Dr. Weizmann trusted the British more than he did the French.

Looking back, it's easy to see that this trust in Britain— which he struggled to keep all his life, even when he was

---

*A great deal of fascinating, and disturbing, information about the roots of Arab-Jewish hostility has just been published by Israeli "peacenik" Simha Flapan in his book *Zionism and the Palestinians.*

forced to write sadly, "It was unrequited love"—was the root of great trouble which persists to this day.

If only Weizmann hadn't put British interests first, thinking that by that he could best help Zionism, he might have tried harder to establish a rapport with the only people on whom the Jews would ultimately depend for peace and happiness in their homeland—the Arabs they lived amongst. Even after Weizmann's policy of counting on Britain proved a failure, his successors—Ben-Gurion and all the later Israeli leaders—carried it on, only substituting the United States for England. The emphasis has been wrong all along. Dependence on a country, however powerful, far from the Middle East, cannot solve the Jews' problems. First Britain, later Russia and France, (and one day soon perhaps the United States) have abandoned the Jews, because, in the end, all any of the Big Power countries care about is their own national interests.

It later turned out, for example, that Britain had only issued the Balfour Declaration as a way of improving her claim to the area by securing Jewish support, so the Jews needn't have been so grateful. Britain as a nation cared not a straw for Jewish national hopes, or Arab ones for that matter (though some individual Britons had strong sympathies with both). The British government just wanted (a) to win the war, and afterwards (b) to get their hands on as much territory as possible.

Well, for a while it seemed as if British Palestine was going to be quite a large territory, but France who, to begin with, had only had her eye on Syria, turned nasty. British Palestine dwindled to an awkwardly shaped, lumpy area, not nearly as big as either Britain or Dr. Weizmann had hoped.

The war had not only done terrible damage to the Yishuv. The unhappy Jews of Eastern Europe had again suffered appallingly from the tides of war. Pogrom after pogrom had reduced them in numbers and spirit until a refuge for them seemed more urgent than ever.

In the summer of 1918 the British General, Allenby, who was holding on to Jerusalem by the skin of his teeth, fully expecting the Turks to "roll him back" at any time, suggested to Dr. Weizmann that he have a talk to Emir Feisal.

Feisal at that time was the most powerful and influential ruler in the Arab world, which, by the way, was not divided up into countries in the same way as it is now. Weizmann had to travel for ten days in blazing heat, by boat, car and camel, to seek him out where he was encamped on a hill above Akaba. They talked for two hours in his tent, drinking syrupy tea. Weizmann came away a happy man.

He had convinced Feisal that what he called "Jewish will, Jewish money, Jewish power and Jewish enthusiasm" could do nothing but good in the Middle East. All their know-how and energy would help the region to recover from centuries of misrule and sluggishness. Feisal believed the Jews and the Arabs were racial cousins. Later on he was to write in a letter: "We wish the Jews a most hearty welcome home . . . There is room for us both. Indeed, I think that neither can be a real success without the other." Ten years later, when he was King of Iraq and the entire Arab world had turned against Zionism, he denied every word. But at the time he was undoubtedly sincere, and Weizmann was surely justified in believing that he and this Arab prince together had achieved something of the greatest importance for the joint future of their two peoples. Arabists to this day often choose to ignore the fact that there were Arabs, high and low, who were in favor of Jewish settlement in Palestine.

The world war ended on a note of high hope for Zionism. They put their trust in the British and in the Balfour Declaration. Exiled Jews rushed home to Palestine, and other eager pioneers came too; the whole idea of Zionism had now been given a new sense of reality since the British had recognized its aims as legitimate.

Dr. Weizmann was of course in close touch with the British authorities. When the ordinary Zionist workers

came to him with their problems and hopes, they noticed
in alarm that he looked sad and anxious. He knew, long
before they did, that they were up against Britons who not
only never seemed to have heard of the Balfour Declaration, but gave every sign of being anti-Jewish.

Whether they were or not, most of them decidedly favored the Arabs, which was no small help to Arab nationalism. This movement, given encouragement by the British
promises to Lawrence of Arabia and the Arab chieftains,
was now smoldering away ready to burst into flames.

The British, having made two conflicting promises, took
a look to see which of the contending "nations" had most
to offer Britain. Clearly, then as now, the Arabs had. There
were a great many more of them, to begin with. Their
territory stretched over thousands of square miles, providing not only a vast area of influence but a land bridge to
Africa and the Far East. Then there was the matter of trade,
not to mention oil. The Arabs were capable (or so it
seemed then) of causing Britain a lot more trouble than the
Jews, and of bringing in many more benefits.

In any case, a lot of Britons had a very romantic idea
about the Arabs. It was loosely connected with their pic-
turesque robes, their nomadic life, their exotic customs—
even the savage reputation of the Bedouins seemed glamorous in British eyes. The Jews were not glamorous. True,
they were hard-working, cultured, dedicated, and rather
more inclined to be reliable. But their goodwill was not
very important.

At least, not in Palestine. In Europe it was different.
There, the great banking families like the Rothschilds held
some pursestrings, and their wishes couldn't be completely
ignored. But the Britons on the spot in Jerusalem had their
orders. If some of them *were* anti-Jewish, that only made it
easier to carry them out.

But Zionists abroad knew nothing of this. They firmly
believed that the Balfour Declaration was the final answer
to their hopes and prayers—a gateway flung open by the

mighty British government, through which all the Jews of
the world might enter their Promised Land and there create their Jewish state without interference from anyone.

Dr. Weizmann had the awful task of disillusioning these
overoptimistic Zionists. He had to convince them the Balfour Declaration was only a framework—if indeed it had
any real meaning at all.

The wretched Jews of Eastern Europe, who had endured
so much, didn't want to hear that more struggles lay between them and the safe haven they had thought the Balfour Declaration must mean, and Weizmann, in his travels,
often came up against a blank wall of sheer unwillingness
to face facts. For the first time he also tasted opposition and
unpopularity.

Still more horrible pogroms in the Ukraine in 1919—
60,000 Jews died in that year alone—drove a fresh wave of
immigrants into Palestine. The population of the Yishuv
was now growing by leaps and bounds and there were
exciting schemes afoot for more garden-cities like Tel Aviv,
a new university on Mount Scopus in Jerusalem (for which
Weizmann, greatly daring, had laid the foundation stone
before the war had even ended), new hospitals, schools and
settlements of all kinds. All these projects were surging
ahead without the Jews so much as glancing round them,
so to speak, at the glowering faces of the Arabs, who saw
all these indications of progress, expansion and perma-
nence as threats and outrages to their own nationalistic
dreams.

Up in the far northern corner of Galilee, where Syria, Lebanon and Israel now meet, the French were still trying to
edge forward to get more territory before borders were
finally drawn. The local Arabs were infuriated by this, as
much as by the few scattered Jewish colonies, and marauding bands were on the prowl, attacking French and Jewish
groups impartially.

A small settlement called Tel Hai—really no more than

a few farm buildings and fields—found itself in mortal danger. It was the northernmost Jewish outpost. If it fell, either to the French or to the Arab gangs, there would be no question of that area being included in any future state.

The man in charge was the same one-armed ex-Russian officer who had mustered the yoredim in Alexandria during the war—Joseph Trumpeldor. For days he and his small group of fellow pioneers, several of them girls, sent a series of urgent messages to defense headquarters in the south for help. None came. It didn't come, apparently, because there was none to send—no spare arms or men. But it's interesting to discover that of all the men on the committee which anxiously debated Trumpeldor's plight and the peril of Tel Hai, only one was in favor of giving the order to evacuate the settlement. This man's name was Vladimir Jabotinsky, who, ironically, had helped Trumpeldor to form the Zion Mule Corps.

I shall have more to say about him shortly, but his opposition, or indifference, to the future of a remote northern outpost-settlement is significant. The movement he founded, called the Revisionists, neither then nor later saw much point in settling the land at all. In all their history they never ploughed an acre of land or built a house or planted a tree. Their objective was political power, and their preferred method was battle.

However, Trumpeldor was not ordered to withdraw, and he probably wouldn't have obeyed if he had been. At last the Arabs arrived in the courtyard, demanding the right to search for the "French" officer they said was in charge. Trumpeldor, wanting to avoid a battle, let them in, but when one Arab tried to disarm one of the girls, she screamed, "He's taking my revolver!" At that, shooting broke out.

Six of the Jews died, including Trumpeldor; but he lived long enough (despite a horrifying stomach-wound) to direct the defense of the place and thus win the battle. You can see his memorial at Tel Hai—a stone lion. This suits

Trumpeldor in more ways than one, for he once wrote that
the sort of men who were needed as pioneers were men of
metal "that can be forged to whatever is needed for the
national machine." His words have a cold, inhuman ring;
he was a hero, yet I always feel glad there were not too
many who thought like him. You should always examine
your heroes before you begin to worship them, to make
sure you admire only the lion in them, and not the stone.

Defeats like Tel Hai did nothing to lessen Arab anger
against the Jews, which was becoming fanatical.

Just before Passover in the same year, 1920, Dr. Weizmann went to the British commander in Jerusalem and
warned him, as strongly as he could, that there were rumors
of trouble brewing among the Arabs and that it would
probably come during the festival. His warning was
laughed at. "The town," said the general, "is stiff with
troops. There can be no trouble."

On the eve of Passover, Jews who had witnessed pogroms in their native towns and villages in Russia looked
out of their windows in Jerusalem and were aghast to see
the hideously familiar sight of howling mobs chasing
women and children down alleyways, dragging old men
about by their beards and breaking down doors to get at
Jews who had shut themselves in.

The British troops, with which the streets were supposed
to be "stiff," were nowhere to be seen.

In one quarter of the Old City, a Jewish captain gathered
some young Jews together and tried to defend their streets
against the mob. At this point British soldiers did appear
—and arrested him. It was Jabotinsky, the man soon to
emerge as the Revisionist leader.

The death toll in this first riot was small, although many
were hurt. But the effect on the whole Jewish world, and
especially the Yishuv, was like a shock wave. They did not
use the words "riot" or "disturbance." It was a *pogrom*—a
pogrom in Jerusalem, and under the eyes of the British,

who only two years before had promised to help the Jews
to their own homeland. Had the horror of persecution,
which occurred while the authorities stood idly by, followed them even *here?* It was like seeing the devil run amok
in paradise.

For those who had believed they could trust the British,
and that the Balfour Declaration marked the final victory in
their political struggle—for those who had ignored the
Arab problem—for those who had deluded themselves that
The Land was a place where Jews could at last be safe—this
first riot was a tragic alarm-clock to wake them from their
dreams.

LETTER 15

The Start of Britain's Mandate

I have to deal now with a subject which hurts me to write about because it's connected with Britain, and British rule over Palestine. It was the period called "The Mandate," which lasted from 1918 to 1947. Nobody could call it a success.

Sometimes people like me, who have two nationalities, are asked (usually rather spitefully), "If your two countries were at war with each other, which would you support?" To me there can be only one honorable answer, and that is that I would try to support the one I thought was most in the right at the time.

By the same token, writing about the history of my two countries during the years when their destinies were so unhappily linked together, I must try to be honest about the rights and wrongs of it. At the same time my love for each side demands that I try to make excuses for the wrongs, and one important excuse that *can* be made for

145

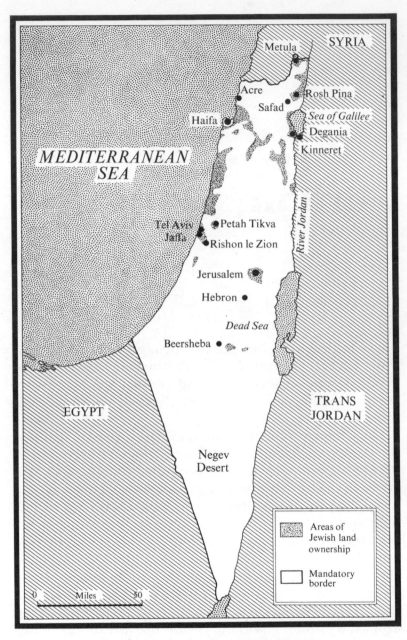

Area of British Mandate 1920-47

Britain in all her mistakes during her Mandate of Palestine is that she really did bite off far more than any nation in the world could have chewed. True, she didn't just have the task wished onto her, she actually asked for it. But I truly don't think any other nation could have managed it much better (or more humanely, in some ways) than she did, except for two or three really major blunders she made during those crucial years which I shall come to in their proper order, and for which I can make no excuse at all.

What is a mandate? Well, it's really an authority, usually given by some world body like the United Nations (or the League of Nations as it was then) to act as caretaker in a certain part of the world until it's reached the stage of being able to look after itself. This authority for Palestine was officially given to Britain in 1920.

Her first job was to cope with the wreckage, in all senses, left not only by the war, but by the centuries of Turkish misrule. This she did very well.

Unlike the Turks, the British officials were very fair and, within limits, efficient. They couldn't be bribed; they weren't lazy. They knew what they wanted to do and they got on with it. When the war ended, people were starving. So first of all, the British got water supplies to the villages; got food production under way again; improved medical services, and cleaned up the rubble and filth of centuries in the towns. The bulk of all these services were for the benefit of the Arabs, who had no real administration of their own. The Jews had, and were managing pretty well for themselves. Quite naturally, the British on the spot tended to become more interested in, and sympathetic towards, the people they did the most for—the Arabs.

In a remarkably short time the rot of centuries had been stopped. The effects of the war had been healed or cleared away. The economy picked up, and one might have thought a golden age was on the way. But in the midst of all these "good works," the British did one thing which was to have a lasting and deadly effect on the future of the country and the Jews.

The British High Commissioner, a man called Sir Herbert Samuel, happened to be a Jew. Perhaps to prove that he wasn't prejudiced, he appointed an anti-Jewish Arab called Amin El Husseini as the new Grand Mufti of Jerusalem.

This was a very influential post for an Arab leader. The one before had been friendly to the Jews. He had welcomed Dr. Weizmann into Jerusalem with the words, quoted from the Prophet Mohammed, "Our rights are your rights, and your duties are our duties." The new one was very different.

It was not so much that he was a religious or national fanatic. He was just wildly hungry for power. His way of achieving it was to fan the flames of Arab nationalism till they became a roaring inferno.

However, for the moment he bided his time.

Meanwhile the Third Aliya was in full swing.

This lot was mainly professionals, many of them German by birth, who came to the country full of idealism, ready to give up being doctors and professors and do whatever hard work was necessary to build the Jewish homeland. They were to be seen breaking rocks and building roads, their soft white hands callusing and their scholarly spectacles slipping down their sweating noses. In years to come, men who had worked in these road gangs were looked on as a sort of aristocracy in Israel, and many of them became leading politicians.

These were the German immigrants. But those staggering out of the pogrom-ridden Ukraine came barefooted and empty-handed after long and often terrible journeys. They brought only their survivors' strength and courage, and their desperate need.

Money! Money was needed—huge amounts of it. Land could no longer be bought for relatively small sums, such

as the great philanthropists had paid in the 1880s and
1890s. "We found," wrote Weizmann, "that we had to
cover the soil of Palestine with Jewish gold."* The absentee Arab landlords had learned what these stony fields and
marshes and stretches of barren sand meant to the Jews. As
fast as the old settlers made their lands productive and
green, so much faster did land values around them rise.

Against the advice of more cautious men, a Zionist
leader, Ussishkin, insisted upon buying the biggest tract of
land ever purchased in one piece till then—20,000 acres in
the Jezreel Valley. It cost a fortune, but it was worth it. It
gave the leaders at least a place to put the thousands of
land-hungry newcomers.

But of course land alone was only the beginning of their
needs. There was never, never enough money. How Dr.
Weizmann must have longed for a Baron de Rothschild
then, for all his patronizing ways! But for some odd reason
the Jewish millionaires, at this of all critical moments,
seemed to have lost interest.

So where did the "Jewish gold" come from? Some came
from "big givers" in lumps. But most of it came, in the form
of small coins and crumpled, grubby notes, out of thousands upon thousands of little blue boxes.

These were the collection boxes of the Jewish National
Fund. Nearly every Jewish home and shop and factory had
one. Few Jewish workers were too poor, or Jewish children
too selfish, to drop their dollar bills or sixpences or pennies
through the slot on Fridays. It was largely the Jewish poor
who, for the twenty-odd years between the wars, paid for
the purchases of land for the pioneers, who now became
known by a name which still has a magic ring—*chalutzim.*
They sang songs of vigor and hope:

> Who will build, will build
> A house in Tel Aviv?

*C. Weizmann, *Trial and Error.*

> We will, the *chalutzim*,
> We'll build in Tel Aviv!

"Build" was the watchword, and build they did, despite
the Arabs, in the teeth of their opposition. The Jews could
not stop to worry about whether the Arabs had a case,
whether what the *chalutzim* were doing was "right" or "fair"
from the Arab viewpoint. In spite of incredible difficulties,
lack of money, hindrance from the British authorities
rather than the help they had expected, Zionism was off the
ground and flying straight towards its target—a state, a
country of their own for the Jews for the first time in 2,000
years. What stood in the way of that goal must be pushed
aside, tunneled under, climbed over or, if that was impossible, "fought withal," as Shakespeare says.

A man called Arthur Ruppin was one of the first of the
old brigade to understand the scale of the Arab problem.
In 1921 he was already writing in his diary: "Without a
better understanding with the Arabs we shall face such
tremendous difficulties as will be almost unsurmountable.
But our Arab policy is nonexistent."*

He believed that Zionism was too nationalistic. He didn't
want the Jews to have just another nation-state. "The Jews
must merge with their blood-brothers, the Arabs," he
wrote. In other words, having chosen a territory which was
geographically part of the Arab Middle East, he thought (as
some enlightened Israelis still think today) it was vitally
important that the Jews should look east towards Arabia
instead of identifying themselves with Europe or America.
Without the agreement of the native population, the Jews
could never hope to be part of the region. They would be
like some foreign body, stuck on or implanted, bound to be
rejected. No matter how much support the Zionists might
get from the West, it would not make up for a failure to
integrate with the people they had to live among.

*A. Ruppin, *Memoirs and Diaries.*

I think it's a tragedy that Ruppin's early ideas were not listened to. Later on things got so much worse that even he changed his mind and decided it was hopeless trying to come to an arrangement with the Arabs. All through the 1920s attitudes were hardening as Arab nationalism strengthened, and the British seemed, at least to the Jews, to be more and more on the Arabs' side.

Oddly enough, the Arabs saw it quite differently. They grew frantic at the numbers of Jewish immigrants the British were allowing in. They were frightened that they'd be swamped by a more advanced, energetic and wealthy culture. The British took very little notice of the complaints of either side at first, but ploughed blandly on with their schemes for cleaning up the country and running it more efficiently.

Dr. Weizmann spent these years traveling between Jerusalem, America and the capital cities of Europe, trying to raise money and support for the builders and especially the farmers in Palestine.

Much of the time he was angry or disappointed. Jews in Europe were getting complacent. They were so sure they were safe. If they *were* Zionists, it was often so that the "rabble" from the East would have a place to go which was not France or Germany, where their poverty and lack of culture caused embarrassment to those Jews who considered themselves as French as the French, as German as the Germans. Many who could afford to give, wouldn't, or not what Dr. Weizmann thought was enough.

As for non-Jews, many powerful men opposed Zionism, and not just because they were sorry for the Arabs. For instance, Lord Northcliff, who owned *The Times* and several other important British newspapers, paid a visit to some of the kibbutzim in Palestine to "see for himself." What he saw was a lot of young people too busy working to take any notice of him. So he came home in a temper, convinced that Palestinian Jews were all a lot of rough, ill-mannered revolutionaries (or "Bolsheviks," as they were called then). It never helps to have newspaper owners against you, and he wasn't the only one. There was even a move in Parliament to cancel the Balfour Declaration altogether, but Winston Churchill, among others, scotched that. Still, there weren't many Zionists left who thought that that document was the gate at the end of the road. The end of the road wasn't even remotely in sight.

But Weizmann never despaired. He found his comfort in standing on a hill above the Jezreel Valley from time to time, watching, first, the land drying out as it was drained, and then the little clusters of houses which began to accumulate there, their red roofs just like those of kibbutzim today. At night he loved to watch the little lights "sparkle in the falling dusk like so many beacons on our long road home."

He was so convinced that the strength of the new Homeland lay in the *chalutzim* of the villages, that he was dismayed, every time he visited Tel Aviv, to see the growing sprawl of little businesses and shops, with their Yiddish-speaking owners from Poland and Roumania who had no notion of Weizmann's type of Zionism. It all had the smell of the ghetto to him. At heart I think he didn't really want just any and every Jew to come to Palestine—only the ones who were prepared to make themselves over into a new type of Jew, "proud, eager, upstanding, independent." To him, the Land was not just to be a place of refuge but of transformation and rebirth.

And while this great leader was working and thinking in this way, another, Ben-Gurion, was busy in another. *His* chief concern was the working people of the towns.

By the mid-1920s when funds were at their lowest, immigration at its highest (till then) and unemployment and unrest growing every day, Ben-Gurion managed to do something amazing. He actually brought the two workers' parties, Hapoel Hatzair and Poalei Zion, together. True, there was hardly any difference between their ideas that any outsider could detect, but their members had been at loggerheads for so long that to unite them was a miracle! He did it because the big workers' organization, the Histadrut, was about to collapse. This was because of strikes and quarrels and lack of money. The uniting of these two main labor parties into a single party, called Mapai, at least cheered everybody up at a time when they needed rather badly to be cheered.

It's interesting to realize that it was during these "bad years" that the two organizations which were to be such vital underpinnings of the state of Israel were really formed. They were the Jewish Agency, which was a sort of shadow-government, and the Haganah. The Haganah was a development of the old Hashomair. The meaning of its name is "Defense" and it was brought into being as a way of defending the Yishuv against attacks by the Arab gangs. It was not, to begin with, very effective because the British looked on it as the next worst thing to an underground army. They not only refused to arm or train its members, or cooperate with it in keeping law and order or protecting outlying settlers, they did all they could to suppress it. Their idea of self-defense for the settlers was one sealed case of shotguns per settlement, to be broken open only in an emergency.

The British did consent to recognize the Jewish Agency as leaders of the Jewish community, but they regarded them with some suspicion. They were not accustomed to dealing with "colonial" peoples who had a "government" of their own which behaved as if it expected to take over from the British before very long. It was this—the Jewish attitude of *equality* with their British administrators—that made the Jews unpopular.

One of the most important problems that Ben-Gurion, as head of the Jewish Agency, had to cope with was the question of Arab labor.

Ben-Gurion and many others were absolutely obsessed with Jewish "do-it-yourself." Of course this was a reaction away from the long diaspora tradition of the Jews as middlemen—buyers, sellers, lenders, fixers—hardly ever as makers, growers, producers.

Many Jews believed that here lay the roots of anti-Jewishness. Those sort of jobs, they said, were jobs for parasites —those who live off others' sweat. "Here in our own land, we'll do our own work. Then no one will hate or resent us," they said.

What they failed to realize was that work was important to the Arabs too, and not due to any high-flown ideals about it, but because if you didn't have any, you didn't eat. It was that simple. When the new, do-it-yourself Jews came along and refused to employ Arabs, the Arabs didn't care that this was a matter of principle with them: they thought the Jews were discriminating against them.

You remember Moshe Smilansky, of the locusts? Well, as I mentioned, he was never a believer in this creed of No Arab Labor. He had always employed Arabs in his fields. He saw things from both points of view. In the early 1920s he put forward a scheme whereby every factory and farm would employ a certain proportion of Arab labor. This, he said, would stop the Arabs from becoming resentful. But Ben-Gurion and his close friend, Berl Katznelson, turned their backs on the idea, which to my mind was a great pity.

Mark you, that was only one of the things the Arabs were resentful about. The plain fact was, *and still is,* that no matter what economic advantages the Jews brought to them, no matter what improvements there were in medical services or how much nicer the countryside looked now that it was splashed with green, the Arabs just did not want them there. The argument goes on till today, with the Jews saying, "Look how we've raised their standard of living! The Arabs of Israel are the envy of their fellow-Arabs." Maybe. But the fact is that the Arabs of Israel—even those who have been able to build themselves costly villas—are living, one and all, under a "foreign regime." They resent the Jews for occupying land they regard as theirs. They fear their influence and the changes they bring. From resentment and fear grows hatred—now, just as in the 1920s.

By 1929, then, the swelling bubble of anti-Jewish feeling was ready to burst. The Grand Mufti was crouched like an evil spider, awaiting his moment to strike. The usual account of how the bubble burst is that *he* burst it, with a lie which inflamed the Moslem masses into a religious frenzy. This he did; but it's only part of the story. Since the riots of 1929 were a vital turning-point, it's important to get the sequence of events right if possible.

It all started with a little screen made of wood and cloth.*

One day in August, shortly before the Jewish fast of Tisha B'av, a British official looked out of his office window. This happened to overlook the last remaining wall of the Temple destroyed by the Romans—the "Wailing" or Western Wall, holy of holies to the Jews. There was no giant piazza in front of it then; it was part of a narrow blind alley, where pious Jews came to pray and mourn the Temple's destruction.

Halfway down the alley he saw that someone had put up this little screen. It had been put there to divide men from women at prayer, but the official didn't know this. All he knew was how easily the slightest change to a holy site can start trouble in Jerusalem. So he got in a panic and ordered some soldiers to take it down. While they were doing this, some Jewish women began hitting them over the head with their sunshades.

Hearing the shouting, some Arabs came rushing along to join in the fight. The soldiers calmed everything down and no one was hurt. But evidently when the Mufti heard about it, he saw his chance.

He sent some Arab officials to the British. "That Wall is holy to us, too," they claimed (falsely, of course—the Arabs have no interest in the Wall). "We want the alley opened so that our people can use it as a thoroughfare."

The British, not wanting to set the Arab chiefs against

*Christopher Sykes, *Cross Roads to Israel.*

them, agreed. But when the Jewish religious authorities heard about this, they protested strongly, saying they would be disturbed at their prayers if the alley became a pathway. "It's our holy place!" they said. This was just what the Mufti had wanted.

It was now that he spread his rumor: What the Jews were really after was the whole area of the Temple Mount, in order to destroy the mosques on it and rebuild the Temple.

Now, was this all it took to enrage the Arab masses to the point of riot and mass murder? Not quite.

It didn't help matters that, a short time before, Vladimir Jabotinsky, by now an extremist Zionist leader, had made a very fiery and uncompromising speech—much quoted, and probably exaggerated, in the Arab press—in which he said that it was no use trying to calm Arab anxieties. What Zionism really meant, he said, was nothing less than a Jewish state with a Jewish majority *on both sides of the Jordan.*

This same Jabotinsky, who had a small but very aggressive young following, chose Tisha B'av to march to the Wall and there hold an anti-Arab demonstration, with noisy oath-takings and what-have-you. This naturally provoked the Moslem Arabs to anger, but on that occasion the police managed to calm things down.

Then there was a murder.

This was a real tragedy, because it was so senseless. Some Jewish boy kicked his football into an Arab garden. The Arabs were in such an excited state by that time that they attacked and killed him. At his funeral, the same extremists as before—Jabotinsky's party—made another demonstration. And the next thing was big crowds of Arabs coming into Jerusalem armed with clubs and knives.

The British Chief of Police noticed this. Very much worried, he hurried to the Grand Mufti and asked, "Why are your people armed?" "Recent events," smoothly replied the Arab, "have made them afraid of the Jews." The Chief of Police got some of his men and ordered them to disarm the crowd. They tried it, but failed. There just weren't enough of them and the reason for that was that the High Commissioner had recently cut down on the number of troops and police in the country to avoid provoking trouble.

Now the Grand Mufti called a mass meeting. It was really at *this* point that he burst the bubble. At the end of the meeting, the armed mob poured out into the streets and began attacking every Jew they could find.

What could the British do? There were fewer than 300 of them in the country. They sent an urgent message to the garrison in Cairo for reinforcements, and for the rest, they had to hope the Arab policemen would do their duty. But as their duty very soon turned out to be the shooting of fellow Arabs, it's not too surprising that they didn't do it.

The violence spread so rapidly that it must have been planned. Several Jewish settlements between Jerusalem and Haifa, and in the south, were wiped out, and there were Arab uprisings in various other towns. The worst happened in Hebron, where there was a massacre which is spoken of with rage and horror until today, and used to justify illegal settlements by Jewish religious extremists who say that Hebron is still a Jewish town. It had, indeed, been one of the four "holy cities" with a community of Talmudic scholars, for centuries. After the 1929 riot, in which sixty Hebron Jews, many of them old men, were hacked to death and as many others wounded, the rest of the Jews fled. Something similar happened in Safed, where children were killed with their parents.

In all, 133 Jews were killed and 339 wounded. Almost as many Arabs were killed, but, except for six killed in a Jewish counterattack, they were all killed by British troops who finally—after three days of rioting—put in an appearance.

The reports of these ghastly events are interesting.

The first report, issued in the heat of the moment by the High Commissioner (who no doubt felt rather ashamed of having been on leave at the time) spoke of "savage murders perpetrated upon defenseless members of the Jewish population." The Grand Mufti affected fury and indignation.

How could the Commissioner say that, before any real investigation had been made? To a fair-minded Englishman this seemed only right. He had been hasty. He backed down, almost apologizing to the Arabs, and hinting that there were probably faults on both sides.

Now, no matter what happened before the riots began, the Arabs alone were guilty of the bloodshed when they did. The High Commissioner may have been rash in his first statement, but it was the true one. In trying to be impartial later, he was, in fact, being completely unjust, and the Jews were justifiably very angry.

They were already convinced the British were pro-Arab, so they became anti-British. A sad sign of this was that none of the reports put out by the Jews mentioned the brave action of one young British officer called Raymond Cafferata, who held off the Hebron mob alone for hours till reinforcements came, probably saving hundreds of Jewish lives. Instead of praising this young hero, the Jews blamed him, just because he was British, for the deaths of the seventy he failed to save. That's how impossible it becomes to judge individuals fairly when national feelings become inflamed, and is one reason (and a good one) why many people hate nationalism.

Next came the Passfield Report. This was the result of the official inquiry made by the British government. It didn't restrict itself to the riots, but tried to go deeper, into their causes. One thing at any rate it got right, which was that the riots had arisen from Arab fears about a Jewish National Home in their midst. It made seven recommendations as to what the British government should do to restore peace. Five of them were pro-Arab and anti-Zionist.

The Yishuv grew more and more alarmed. These terrible events were happening at a particularly bad time. Seven thousand of them were out of work. Lots of immigrants were actually leaving again. Tel Aviv was full of half-finished buildings. Golda Meir writes: "It was as though a huge burst of energy had worn itself out." Morale was at its lowest ebb—and now the British were going to betray them.

The British assessment came out something like this:

"The Arabs are in the majority. They are justified in their fears—the Jews *are* expanding too fast. Anyway, there isn't enough farmland to absorb many more people. Jewish immigration and land-buying must be drastically cut."

This confirmed the Zionists' worst fears. Where was the Balfour Declaration now? The Jews were to be treated, not as people who have a right to be in their homeland, but as a minority—as they were in every other country. There was a terrific outcry, and Dr. Weizmann resigned from being president of the World Zionist Organization in protest.

That made the British sit up. Throughout history they've always had a bad name for breaking their word (which is what "perfidious Albion" means) so they are naturally sensitive when "promises" and "betrayal" are mentioned. They backed down a bit. "We didn't mean that you are not to *have* your National Home," they hastily and rather feebly said. "But we never said it would be a *state,* or that it would cover the whole of Palestine."

But at that, the Arabs flared up again. "The slightest Jewish pressure, and the British cave in!" was their cry. The British were insulted. They might be finding it hard to keep two conflicting promises, but let no one say they could be pushed around.

And from then on, until 1948 when the Mandate finally collapsed through sheer lack of will to carry it on, the British seemed to be guided by one principle above all others: the determination to prove that no matter what, at least Jewish pressure could not make them cave in.

LETTER 16

The Deadly Thirties

The 1930s were the years of my happy, protected childhood. How little I knew of what was going on in the world!
I doubt if in these days of television news any child could
be so ignorant as I was. I do remember my mother telling
me about the Spanish Civil War, and feeling some concern,
but not too much. In those days I believed that the right
side always won wars. As to what was happening in Poland,
Italy, Austria, Germany, I knew nothing at all about it.

The Poles have always been among the most anti-Jewish of
European people. A bad lead from a government in need
of scapegoats and the people of Poland have been quite
happy to turn against their Jews. This they did in the early
1930s.

  Thousands of Jews emigrated. The immigration figures
for Palestine, which had been stagnant for a long time,
began to rise.

In Italy, Mussolini came to power and began swinging his meaty fascist fist about in North Africa. (I remember hearing at school how the Italians took black Ethiopians up in airplanes and dropped them out for fun.) This new breed of conquering Italian wanted Arab support. They started broadcasting in Arabic, offering the Arabs all sorts of flattery and bribes. Later, Nazi Germany did this, too. These broadcasts fed the dark side of Arab nationalism—the racist side. As a fellow-gangster, the Grand Mufti of Jerusalem was a willing listener, and was soon converted to fascism.

But the real menace to the Jews, I need hardly tell you, lay in what was happening in Germany.

This is not the place to go into great detail about how Hitler came to power, but this much must be said. He was not just an aberration. Germany was *not* like a healthy human being who suddenly grows, say, an extra thumb, a gangrenous bit of freakery which spreads poison all through the system. Hitler was a symptom of a disease which already afflicted the whole body of Germany.

It was actually a mixture of several diseases. One was defeat, with its dangerous complications: humiliation, frustration and insecurity. Germany had taken a bad beating in the First World War, and the terms imposed on them by the victorious French and British at Versailles in 1919 were very harsh and bound to cause more trouble, because their effect was to put such a burden on the German people that they felt they could never get onto their feet again. Someone had to be blamed for this abject defeat, so people blamed the "revolutionaries," the "intellectuals," the "pacifists" who had "stabbed the army in the back." And who was behind these cowardly traitors? Some identifiable group had to be. Why not the Jews?

Inevitably, despite worldwide economic recession, some enterprising individuals, some of them Jews, managed to struggle upwards, and this gave rise to another "disease": a growing gap between rich and poor which caused bitter

Closed Gates

Legend:
- Area of Nazi occupation
- Countries effectively barred to Jews during World War II
- Places open to Jews

Shanghai

Spain

The Dominican Republic

envy. And this in turn led to a more dangerous infection: the increasing anger and fear of millions of little men—not the broad, strong back of the nation, and certainly not its brain, but what you might call its fingers and toes: the clerks, the shopkeepers, the semiskilled workers, who, because of the terrible economic situation (German inflation was so high that housewives went shopping with their baskets filled with all-but-valueless paper money) felt they were somehow being cheated and done in by everyone else.

And inflaming these national illnesses was the perpetual virus of anti-Jewishness which had been in the German bloodstream for centuries. And now at last there was not just the need for a scapegoat; there were excuses.

As far back as 1855 there had appeared the first racist document. It was written by a French count called Gobineau, who called it *"Essay on the Inequality of Human Races."* It claimed simply that the white races are fundamentally superior to yellow or black ones; but the Germans, having no colonial "natives" among them, had to transfer Gobineau's theories to the only visibly different group, the Jews, in order to have someone to despise and blame for their miseries.

Later the great German composer, Wagner, relishing Gobineau's ideas, wrote music which glorified the "pure German spirit." This music had the power to fill its hearers with passionate and unreasoning pride in their Teutonic, or Aryan, heritage, and the tall, fair-skinned, blond look that was supposed to typify it. From this, with the of writers, cartoonists and politicians seeking quick popularity, came a corresponding contempt for non-Aryans, chiefly the dark-skinned, small-boned, quick-witted Jews.

And thus anti-Semitism was born.

Born! you may exclaim. Born? So recently? And what do you call the horrors of prejudice that had gone before?

I've been careful to call all those manifestations of hatred "anti-Jewish" rather than anti-Semitic before about the mid-nineteenth century. True anti-Semitism is a modern phenomenon.*

We aren't dealing here with anything so rational as Christians hating Jews for denying Christ, or envious men hating Jews for being successful, or peasants hating Jews for being bailiffs. We're not even talking about people of any period who didn't like Jews for faults they may genuinely have found in them. We are dealing—for the first time in history—with an entirely irrational hatred, a hatred arising solely from the belief in superior and inferior races. Since there's no scientific evidence to support such beliefs, we must put it down to a warp—literally a disease peculiar to the mind of certain modern civilized people.

Nobody will admit to having this disease. Justifications of a sort have to be found. There were a number at hand in the late 1920s in Germany, for example a document which had been circulating since 1903 called *The Protocols of the Elders of Zion*. This had been cooked up with the help of the tsar's secret police, and purported to be details of a plot by the Jews to take over the world, no less. They were going to beggar the masses through playing around with the money market, allowing a few Jewish millionaires to seize total power. If this didn't work they were going to infect everyone with diseases. Though this nonsense had been exposed as a crude forgery, to the gullible German "little men" the notion of an ugly conspiracy summed up their fearful image of the Jew as an alien, a sinister, powerful and dangerous being who threatened their already tottering world.

The Germans of that period, hopeless, poor and embittered, craved a great leader. *Anyone* who had stood up and said, "You can be great again! I can lead you to greatness!

*This distinction, between anti-Jewishness and anti-Semitism, was made clear to me by Max Dimont in his gripping epic, *Jews, God & History*.

Germans shall be the masters of the world!" would have
been listened to. But just the same, how incredible that it
should have been not some Wagnerian hero, blond and
splendid, but a little, black-haired, rat-faced, ex-army cor-
poral.

And how ironic it is to remember that he actually wrote
a book, ten years before coming to power, telling anyone
who cared to read—and many did—exactly what he was
going to do! In *Mein Kampf* he set out in detail his entire
plan of campaign, how he would take power, how he would
use it, his violent hatred of the Jews and other minorities,
his intentions for them and for the rest of Europe. And
then, in 1933, it all began to come true, and *still* nobody
woke up; nobody, or almost nobody, realized the menace
or tried to stop him.

Hitler may have looked insignificant, but he touched the
right nerve at the right moment. He was also ruthless,
ambitious, cunning and a brilliant orator, full of a curious,
almost hypnotic charm. As the 1930s advanced, he and his
Nazis rose to ever more dizzy heights of power and prestige; "Der Führer" became, like Caligula, more than an
emperor, more than a dictator—almost a god to the German nation.

And he knew how to pick his men. Dr. Goebbels, who'd
already shown himself a master of the debased art of anti-
Jewish propaganda, was put in charge of focusing the Germans' anger and resentment upon the Jews in their midst.
No means were too foul, no myths too fantastic to be dug
up, dusted off and pressed into service. One cartoon, published in the grossly anti-Semitic magazine *Der Stürmer,*
even revived the old blood libel. It showed "clouds" of
blond, angelic children with holes in their throats spouting
blood into a ritual dish held by two hideous leering Jews.
This and a thousand other tales and images were dinned
into the Germans day after day, month after month. "If you
repeat a lie often enough," Goebbels cynically believed, "it
becomes true."

When those Jews who had told Weizmann they were
well-established and secure found themselves suddenly
singled out for discrimination and undeserved attacks, they
had to face an all-important question. Was Hitler to be
taken seriously? To cultured, rational men, he must have
seemed ridiculous, with his little toothbrush moustache
and his absurd rantings and ravings. Who could believe
that a whole country—one of the most civilized in the world
—would go mad at the orders of such an unlikely little
lunatic?

But as the madness grew and spread, the question
loomed larger. Those Jews who faced it and answered it
correctly, saved their lives. Many who refused to face it, or
answered it wrongly, or too late, paid with theirs. But that
was later. No one guessed *then* just how far the Nazis would
go.

Many Jews did leave, even before Hitler brought in the
infamous Nuremburg Laws in 1935 which altogether
banned Jews from important jobs, and forbade them to
marry other Germans, buy or own property or live like men
at all. (This is no exaggeration. The Nazis were instilling
into the minds of the Germans the belief that the Jews were
untermenschen—subhuman.) Those who acted quickly had
few problems about where to go. Many went to Palestine,
taking with them a great deal of money as well as technical
and professional skill. Their coming did wonders for the
Yishuv's economy.

Quite sharply, the slump of the 1920s in Palestine began to
turn into a boom. Buildings which had been started and
abandoned for lack of cash were now finished, and new
districts were built in Tel Aviv and Jerusalem to house the
newcomers. Everything expanded. There were new factories and businesses, new schools, hospitals, offices, and of
course the inevitable little shops and workshops. Unemployment went down. Prosperity went up.

Arabs in the surrounding areas were not slow to notice

what was happening. People talk sentimentally about how attached peasants are to their land, but throughout history they've abandoned it fast enough when there was more money to be earned in town.* Arab villagers now flocked to the towns to work for the Jews, many as stonemasons, builders and dockers. There were already some restrictions on immigration. If some of the Jewish immigrants were illegal, so also were some of the Arabs.

The new prosperity—the situation of Jews and Arabs working together in many enterprises, the general expansion and buoyancy in the economy—might well have brought a turning point for the better in Arab-Jewish relations. Alas, just the opposite happened.

Much like the country folk of Europe who migrated into the cities during the Industrial Revolution, these Arab workers flowing off the land discovered that the streets were not paved with gold. Their wages, though much more than they'd earned as peasant-farmers, were lower by far than the Jews'. This meant that they couldn't afford town housing. So shantytowns sprang up on the fringes of places like Haifa and Tel Aviv, where thousand of these uprooted people lived in dreadful conditions.

Nor could they go back to their land, much of which had been sold from under them by absentee landlords. The noble and farsighted efforts of a few Jews to bring in laws protecting tenant-farmers had failed—the Zionists were as greedy for land as the Arab effendis were for the price of it, and neither group wanted laws restricting land-buying.

When people's traditional pattern of life is destroyed, they often lose their values, their sense of who they are. They then become a prey to agitators and to violence. Ironically, it was in towns such as Haifa, where Jews and Arabs lived and worked side-by-side, that the seeds of Arab terrorism and revolt took root.

And Ben-Gurion must take his share of the blame. In

*James Parkes points this out in his admirable book, *Whose Land?*

1933, to back his determination to obtain "100 percent Jewish labor," he ordered the removal of Arab workers from Jewish enterprises—by force if necessary. You can imagine the ugly scenes that followed, and the incalculable harm to relations that was the inevitable result. This tragic blunder confirmed the local Arabs' worst fears, and a thick wedge was driven between the Jewish and Arab economies which, if they had been allowed to mingle on an equal footing, might have welded the two peoples together.

With the steep rise in Arab nationalism, and the violent forms it was taking, the dangerous split which had appeared among the Zionists in the twenties grew deeper. Jabotinsky's party, called the Revisionists, because they had revised the original ideas of Zionism, now began to fight openly against the socialist ethics and way of life of the old settlers.

Jabotinsky was a very important figure in Zionist history. He was, so to speak, the father of all the right-wing activists who came later—of whom one, Menachem Begin, is now Prime Minister of Israel.

Jabotinsky was the opposite, in a sense, of Weizmann, for Weizmann was a "moderate" and Jabotinsky was a "militant." Weizmann believed passionately that the Jewish state could only be built gradually, brick upon brick, tree beside tree, man after man, slow organic growth like the growth of animals and plants in nature, cell by cell.

Jabotinsky simply had no patience for this. He wanted the state. He wanted it big, he wanted it Jewish, and he wanted it *now*. His slogan was *"Koola Sheli"*—"All of it's mine." That meant fighting the Arabs *and* the British. It also meant fighting the Haganah's policy of self-restraint (about which I shall have more to say later), which infuriated him. If Arab gangs were going to terrorize Jewish settlements, Jews should form counter-terror gangs to attack the Arabs. Anyone who thought differently was a coward and a traitor (or a British agent!).

All earlier quarrels among the Zionists had been gentle-

manly differences of opinion compared to this. The depth
of the split, though, was not revealed until an evening in
1933, when something happened which marked the end of
a Zionist era.

A brilliant young man called Chaim Arlosoroff, a moderate like Weizmann and the bright hope of the socialist
leadership, was taking a stroll along the beach at Tel Aviv
with his wife. A stranger came up and asked him for a light.
Arlosoroff reached for some matches. The stranger pulled
out a gun and shot him.

If Arlosoroff had time to register the gun before he died,
his reaction was probably one of disbelief. Till that moment, no matter what angry quarrels had divided the Jews
of the Yishuv, they had all been, in a very deep sense,
brothers. No Palestinian Jew had ever deliberately killed
another. As news of the murder spread, the Yishuv went
into mourning. They mourned not just their lost leader,
but the loss of some quality—innocence, perhaps—in their
great movement which could never return. Cain had killed
Abel.

A young Revisionist called Stavsky was arrested and
tried, but released for lack of proof. Nevertheless, all the
leaders of the time believed him guilty. To many people,
the Revisionists and their political descendants—Irgun
Zvai Leumi, the Stern Gang, Herut and Likud—still carry
the mark of Cain: the taint of ruthlessness and fanaticism.

There was another fanatic at work—the Grand Mufti. He
recruited huge armed gangs, estimated at about 5,000 altogether, who lived in the hills and, at the word of command, swept down onto Jewish settlements. Many were
totally destroyed before help could come. Jews living
peacefully on land that was legally theirs found themselves
no safer than they had been in their *shtetls.* The Haganah
did its best; but the British, claiming that they could offer
all the protection needed, only with great reluctance allowed each settlement that one sealed crate of shotguns
(not even rifles) with which to defend itself. It really must

have seemed to the Jews that the British *wanted* the Arabs to demolish them.

But they were not to be demolished. Survivors of murderous raids would gather themselves together, and, with the help of their neighbors, set up whole new settlements —complete with prefabricated stockade, water tower, searchlight and tents—during the course of a single day, in order to be ready, the next night, to repel another attack. They bought new stock to replace their stolen herds, cleared and ploughed new fields and mounted stronger guard at night with whatever weapons they had. In time, widows married again, and had more children to replace those who had died.

The Arabs watched these stubborn new beginnings with a growing stubbornness of their own. They even began to turn against any of their own people who were friendly to the Jews. Gangs of the Mufti's hired killers took to murdering *Arabs,* among them village mukhtars (chiefs) often merely for refusing to contribute to guerrilla funds.

This may seem a strange moment to mention the activities of groups and individuals among the Jews who, around this time, were becoming more and more focused on the Arab problem.

It was late in the day—too late, as it turned out. But there were those among the Zionist leadership who, unlike Weizmann and Ben-Gurion, understood the dark heart of the situation. Men like Martin Buber, Ahad Ha'am, Dr. Nahum Goldmann and Dr. Judah Magnes repeatedly stressed that Jew and Arab must be reconciled. They put forward sensible suggestions, such as the integrating of Jewish and Arab workforces, opening up the Jewish economy, improving the social and living conditions of Arabs and having talks at all levels to try to find ways of bridging the growing gulf between the two peoples.

There were also movements, such as Hashomair Hatzair to which "our" kibbutz belongs, which wanted not a separate Jewish state but a bi-national one which Jews and Arabs would share. Despite being intensely occupied with the business of starting kibbutzim and settling the land, they found time and energy, over a long period, to make contacts with Arabs, to support them in their difficulties, and to argue at the highest level that cooperation and friendship were of prime importance.

Unfortunately these and other efforts ultimately failed. The mood of the times, the conflicting demands of the two nationalisms meant that hostility, not friendship, was the order of the day. It's only in very recent times that it has begun to be recognized—though still not widely enough— that men like Dr. Goldmann, now in his eighties and still campaigning for Arab-Jewish rapprochement, has had it right all along.*

Action against the Jews increased continually after the mid-thirties. What became known as the Arab Rebellion had begun. It became dangerous to travel—trains were being derailed, buses bombed and overturned. Every day there were black-bordered announcements in the Jewish press, and funerals winding through the streets. Any night, anywhere in the country, the sky could light up with the dreaded blaze of fired crops; any morning Jews might

---

*People who feel this are nowadays known as "peaceniks." One Jewish argument against us has been, "There's nobody listening." In other words, where are the Arab "peaceniks"? Of course they exist—they always have; but the more hatred and distrust builds up, the fewer people on either side have, until President Sadat's initiative in 1977, seen sense in reconciliation. To illustrate: A group I belong to, affiliated to the "peace" magazine *New Outlook*, originally had, together with Jewish and Gentile members, an Arab, once a PLO supporter but lately in favor of compromise. It was heartening to feel we were on the same side. But then Arab extremists murdered another Arab suspected of moderation, and our Arab colleague quietly dropped out. In these circumstances it's hard for Arab "peaceniks" to come into the open. And it also says something for the Zionists that none of *us* have been murdered for our willingness to compromise.

awake to the unbearable sight of hundreds of the trees they
had so lovingly planted, torn up by the roots.

Weizmann says that the ups and downs of Arab terror at
the time "reflected not so much the fortunes of war as the
fluctuations of British determination." In other words,
when the British were firm, as they were occasionally, terrorism died down. When their obsession with "fairness"
prevented them from dealing rigorously with the only side
of the quarrel which *at that time* was resorting to violence,
there was an upsurge of trouble from the Mufti's gangs.

In 1936 things got so serious that the Jews were allowed
to form police-squads to protect their outlying villages.
This helped, but despite it, the "unrest" (a favorite British
word for rioting and murder) kept getting worse. At last
there was a development which the British had to take
seriously. The great oil pipeline running from Iraq across
Palestine to Haifa came under attack by Arab commandos,
who would descend on it at night, wreck a section of it, and
disappear.

This was clearly a moment for the still-not-quite-legal
Haganah and the British to cooperate. And to their aid
came a man—a strange, brilliant figure—who served as a
bridge between British and Jews. His name was Orde Wingate. He was then a British major and also a very passionate
Zionist. The story of his meteoric career in various war-
zones is fascinating; what he learned in Palestine later
helped the British win the war in Burma.

First of all he formed motorcycle squads to patrol the
length of the pipeline, which severly discouraged the raiders. Then he explored the Palestine hills by himself (armed
to the teeth) until he had located the hideouts of the Mufti's
gangs, which were then commanded by a Syrian mercenary
called Kawakji; he was to prove a menace to the Yishuv only
a little smaller than the Mufti himself.

Next, Wingate barged into Haganah headquarters and,
having more or less bullied them into trusting him, hand-

picked some of their best men to form "night squads" of his own.

These groups he trained and led on sorties into the hills, where they would surround the raiders' lairs and chase them out. Many of them were killed; others fled back into Syria. For a while things quietened down. But not for long.

If those responsible for keeping law and order fail to do it, and fail to punish criminals, there will always be those who will take matters into their own hands. Preventing that is part of the law's duty. The British didn't do their duty in this case, so they are partly to blame for the rise of Jewish terrorism.

Jabotinsky's Revisionists were clamoring for action. Terror against terror was their answer. Give these Arabs a taste of their own medicine! And since violence makes a strong appeal to any people living under constant stress, there were a number—a growing number—who were ready to join him. It was these bad days, and British weakness, that spawned the Irgun Zvai Leumi, one of whose first gestures was to throw a bomb into a crowded Arab bus. The young man who did it was hanged by the British. At that point, one Israeli* claimed, "The place of every self-respecting, upright young Hebrew was in the Irgun."

The majority of the Yishuv, though, were in favor of self-restraint. It was basically a matter of morality. They didn't believe in shedding innocent blood by throwing bombs into Arab crowds or onto buses. Only those directly responsible for outrages must be punished.

To stick to this policy, considering the anger and provocation of the time, seems to me one of the finest—even one of the most heroic—aspects of Zionist history. Later it broke down; the pressures were too great. But looking

---

*Uri Avnery, *Israel Without Zionism*. The author has since changed his mind and become one of the most persistent advocates of peace and compromise with the Palestinian Arabs.

back, those leaders and others who stuck fast by it as long
as they could are proud of it and convinced it was right. Not
only was it very much in the spirit of Judaism, it was sound
practical sense too. After all, many thousands of Arabs were
not extremists. They lived and worked in friendly cooperation with the Jews. Wanton attacks against *these* could only
have bred more hatred and recruited more men for the
Mufti.

And there was another consideration. The Zionist leaders did not dare to forfeit anything that was left of British
goodwill towards them. They had already begun to realize
that what was happening in Europe would mean that, very
soon, the gates of Palestine would have to be opened as
wide as they would go, to admit, not just the thousands of
Jews who were pouring in now, but perhaps millions.

By 1938, three years after the introduction of the Nuremburg Laws, with the Germans already swallowing up
Austria and Czechoslovakia, the British government was
still finding it possible to treat Hitler as just another European leader—a little harsh and headstrong perhaps, but
that was Germany's concern.

Czechoslovakia, whom Britain had promised to help if
she were ever attacked, became "a faraway country of
which we know very little," not worth risking war to defend.
The British Prime Minister, Neville Chamberlain, rushed
off to Munich to sign a treaty with Hitler, and came back
waving it cheerfully and crying out that he'd bought "peace
in our time"—at the cost of Czechoslovakia's freedom and
Britain's honor. If he could bring himself to do *that,* the
Jewish leaders, Weizmann especially, realized that he
would not even let himself think about the fate of the Jews.

Dr. Weizmann tells an interesting story in his book.* He
was attending yet another conference, called in London at
the very end of 1938, at which Arabs and Jews were to sit

Trial and Error.

together and thrash things out. Naturally they did no such thing, since the Arabs would not even use the same entrance as the Jews, let alone sit with them, and the conference was a fiasco.

One day, Lord Halifax, the British Secretary for Foreign Affairs, came up to Weizmann. He told him he'd had a letter from a friend in Germany, giving shocking accounts of a concentration camp at a place Lord Halifax had never heard of. Weizmann soon realized he must be talking about Dachau. How could it be that a government minister, with responsibility for foreign affairs, had never heard of Dachau (whose name was known to every Zionist by that time) and was *just now* beginning to wonder whether these "tales" of Nazi atrocities against the Jews might have some truth in them? The fact was that the British government, among others, *did not want* to face the truth.

Leon Blum, the French Jewish leader, said to Weizmann at the time: "There is a wild hunger for physical safety which paralyzes the power of thought. People are ready to buy the illusion of security at any price, hoping against hope that something will happen to save their countries from invasion."

That was about the size of it. The Nazis had begun to seem like an army of soldier-ants. "March the other way!" was the prayer (though some braver spirits added, "At least till we're ready to fight").

For the Jews, it was the old, old story. They were expendable—just so many sacrifices laid in the path of that army, and nothing could save them but their own efforts. A conference called in 1938 by the American President, Franklin D. Roosevelt, to see what could be done to help the refugees flooding out of Germany, was attended by thirty-two nations, whose representatives stood up one by one and made smooth speeches about their deep regrets—alas, they wished they could take in more, etc, etc. Golda Meir, who attended as an observer, described it as a terrible experience. Once again the Jews were cast out, and nobody wanted them—except the Yishuv. *They* wanted them desperately. But the British government was already laying plans to cut off the only escape-route left for these poor doomed people.

First, however, they sent out yet another Commission to Palestine under Lord Peel, to see if they could come up with some solution.

The Arabs had started to attack the British now, and hundreds of British soldiers had been killed in raids. At last the Mufti had been arrested and jailed, but he escaped to Syria, from where he carried on directing terrorist operations. (Later he was to turn up in Berlin, an active Nazi.) The Jews were getting quite desperate, and Jabotinsky's Irgun was attracting more recruits. The situation was as bad as it could be, and it was this mess that the Peel Commission sincerely tried to come to grips with in its report.

This said that the situation couldn't be resolved by Britain, or, indeed, at all by anyone, as long as the two peoples were trying to live together in a territory they both regarded as theirs. They suggested partition as the only fair solution. The country should be divided, giving Jews and Arabs each a state of their own.

The report went on to suggest what bits should be given to whom. Roughly speaking, the Jews were to have the *best* bit, that is, Galilee and the most fertile part near the coast, and the Arabs were to have the *biggest* bit, which meant pretty well all the rest. The Mandate was to end—after a fashion; but the British wanted to keep Haifa as their Mediterranean port, and keep control over the holy places.

Dr. Weizmann's reaction was extraordinary. A man who had known him all through the difficult years and never seen him really show his emotions, now saw him almost weeping with happiness. He believed—for a short time—that his dream of Jewish statehood was about to come true. This was so wonderful to him that he hardly seemed to realize that the state would be too small to be able to absorb all the refugees that would need to come there. Ben-Gurion was also in favor of the plan, on the grounds that any state was better than none, but Jabotinsky of course opposed it —("All of it's mine!")—and so, more unexpectedly, did Berl Katznelson, who'd never trusted the British and considered the whole thing a hoax.

Golda Meir was also against it, but later she wrote that she was glad her view hadn't prevailed. "I couldn't have lived with myself if I had thought—in the light of what happened afterwards—that I was to blame for its collapse. If we had had even a tiny little mockery of a state only a year before the war broke out, hundreds of thousands of Jews . . . might have been saved from the ovens and gas chambers of the Nazis."*

Whether the British would ever have gone through with the plan, which involved giving up control, is doubtful. But they didn't have to make that decision because the Arabs flatly turned it down. For the Arabs at that time, it was all or nothing, an attitude they have continued to hold until very recently. There are many people who say it has not changed even yet, though it is now crystal clear—and it was clear even then to the members of the Peel Commission— that neither side could ever have hoped to get all they wanted and both would have to compromise.

So the partition plan fell through. But one suggestion that Lord Peel had made was snatched out of the wreck of the report, a suggestion which—taken out of context—was to result in the loss of an incalculable number of innocent Jewish lives. This suggestion was that *until* partition, the number of Jewish immigrants should be limited to 12,000 a year.

In 1939, the British government discarded the last of the reports and recommendations which various commissions had put forward, and issued a document which finally shattered even Dr. Weizmann's faith in British trustworthiness.

My Life.

It was called the White Paper on Palestine, and in effect it
promised to hand over control of the country to the Arabs
within ten years. In the meantime, land sales to Jews were
to be almost totally stopped; and immigration was to be cut
down to a maximum of 75,000 over the next five years, and
then stopped altogether, unless the Arabs agreed to it.
Seventy-five thousand sounds a lot, but consider that, in
the year before the Arab Rebellion (1935), over 60,000
Jews had come in in one year. Remember too, how desperate was the need of a refuge for *millions* of Jews in Europe
whom no other nation was prepared to accept. It then
becomes a paltry number. The Zionists felt it as the slam-
ming of an iron door in the face of Hitler's victims.

You remember that, in the fifteenth century, when the
Sephardim were expelled from Portugal, some of them
floated about the Mediterranean looking for a refuge until
many of them died of hunger, shipwreck or despair. Now
history repeated itself, and not for the last time. In 1939 as
the jackboots stamped and Europe cringed, the whole
world watched the "coffin boats," as they were called, sailing from port to port, helplessly seeking a way in to Palestine.

You can imagine the effect all these things had on the
Zionists. Worst of all were the stories that were coming out
of Germany about the sufferings of the Jews in concentration camps. Even though no one had any idea at the time
that the Germans would soon turn them into death camps,
the starvation, torture and slave labor that was going on
even then were enough to drive the Jews of Palestine frantic
in their efforts to save all they could.

The numbers of Jews who had been pouring in till the
gates were shut (or nearly so) by the White Paper do explain, in part, why the Arabs were so easily convinced by
their leaders that they were going to be swamped. It ex-
plains why Britain thought they were probably right. What
it doesn't explain is why the British turned their backs on
the Jews so completely. The White Paper set aside not only

the Balfour Declaration, but the great achievements of the
Yishuv which the British had witnessed for themselves.
They'd even benefited from them. Jewish money and energy had helped British administrators to bring the country
into the twentieth century and saved them a fortune in
doing it. They had even built Haifa port!

Why did the British ignore the desperate plight of the
Jews in order to appease the Arabs?

A man I spoke to recently, who was out there at the time,
said this, quite blandly: "Well, yes, looking back one can
see now that the Jewish need was greater than the Arab.
Jabotinsky was right in this, that it was one nation's appetite
against another's starvation. But at the time, you know, the
Arabs were making an awful fuss, and after all—well, it was
their country."

Was it? That is the ultimate question, the one every person who cares about Israel has to answer for himself. What
I don't believe is that the British ever thought that it was
so simple, or that they acted from such a straightforward
motive, as if they'd abruptly gone blind in one eye. Not one
of the many independent commissions that went out there
said, "It's the Arabs' country, the Jews have no right to be
there, and the Arabs must have all that they demand."

No doubt there were very valid claims on both sides. But
one argument you might consider is the one Berthold
Brecht uses in *The Caucasian Chalk Circle.* This play, you may
remember, ends with the words:

Take note of the meaning of the ancient song:
That what there is, shall belong to those who are good
     for it, thus:
The children to the maternal, that they thrive;
The carriages of good drivers, that they are driven well;
And the valley to the waterers, that it shall bear fruit.

So the question may be rephrased: not "Who owned it?"
but "Who was good for it? Who deserved it?" That's not
so hard to answer. But that answer, too, is too simple, and

begs too many questions, to put any thoughtful person's conscience completely at rest.

At all events, the British did what they did. As war came upon the world, and devastation upon the Jews, the Zionists moved heaven and earth to undo it. When they failed to change the laws, they broke them or evaded them in any way they could.

Whoever may blame them for other things, who that is sane and human shall blame them for that?

LETTER 17

The Holocaust

Now I must come to the Second World War.

This book so far has listed some of the terrible catastrophes that have overtaken the Jews down through the ages. The Egyptians, the Romans, the Mohammedans; the Catholics, the Protestants, the Inquisition; the Cossacks, the Tzars, the Bolsheviks; and many, many individual rulers or popes or regimes had done their worst. But it was reserved for a highly civilized, highly cultured European nation, in our own century, to show history that so far as persecuting the Jews was concerned, everything in the past was a mere rehearsal. Modern man with his technical skill and accumulated store of cruelty could achieve a "final solution" to the Jewish Question.

The German nation under the Nazis was not content merely to imprison or drive out groups of Jews, to revile them, destroy their works and take away the foundations of their lives. It was not even content with killing some of

181

them. The Nazi plan, entrusted by Hitler to a German
officer called Heidrich, was to make Europe *Judenrein*—Jew-
free. What that order may have meant to begin with, we
can't be sure. But what it came to mean was genocide—the
systematic murder of an entire race.

Are there words to describe this crime, and the way it was
carried out? Evidently there are, for there are by now hundreds of books about it. Some are mere catalogues of horror for the insensitive, the unimaginative or the perverted.
Some are scholarly studies, which try to make sense of this
monstrous episode in terms of history, psychology, politics,
what you will. There are books by survivors, and these are
the most unbearable to read; they can't be decently read
without deep feelings of guilt—if only because one *cannot*
share their sufferings. Even to share them in imagination
can bring me near to a kind of madness of horror and
anger.

To describe to you what the Germans did, what the peoples of other European countries allowed to be done, what
even those countries fighting Germany did little to stop, is
beyond my power. The bald facts are hard enough to state,
in their most simple, unemotional terms. Here they are.

Having decided to eliminate the Jews from Germany,
and, as the conquest of Europe went forward, from every
country they conquered, the Germans went about it sys-
tematically with the efficiency that has always characterized
them.

They began with laws degrading the Jews. Then they
made sure they could identify them, by issuing special papers, making them wear yellow Stars of David and so on.
Then when they were ready, they rounded them up, put
them into vehicles—usually sealed cattle cars on trains—
and transported them to camps in various parts of eastern
Europe. There they put them to forced labor, or used them
for medical experiments, or exploited them in any way that
suited them, until they had no more use for them or there
were too many of them. Then, in various ways, of which

starving, shooting and gasing were only the main ones, they killed them.

They disposed of their bodies at first by burying them in mass graves, but later, as they found more scientific ways to murder more of them at once, they burned their bodies in huge furnaces, specially built for the purpose. Not being a wasteful nation, the Germans first cut off any long hair, removed all clothes and shoes and jewelry they wore, and took out any gold that was in the dead people's teeth. All these things were put to use, and sometimes parts of the bodies were used, as the bodies of dead animals are.

By this time something terrible had happened to the minds and perceptions of the men who were carrying out this work. It was not a handful of sadists, or fanatics, remember, but thousands of ordinary soldiers and doctors and workers. What had happened was that they had been persuaded to think of these Jews as no better than danger-ous and repulsive animals. They used them, killed them, and disposed of their corpses much as you might deal with flies or rats. Jews were not even subhuman to those people by this time. The Nazi propaganda-machine had destroyed the morality of its followers to the extent that they could look at a Jew, of any age or condition, and see, not a fellow human being any longer, but a species of vermin.

That was the vilest crime of all, perhaps—what the Nazi ideology did to their own people.

The exact number of Jews who perished will never be known. It was in the millions. For those who doubt it, there is the Holocaust Museum at Auschwitz, where anyone brave enough to go can see, not only the gas chambers and the ovens, but long halls glassed-in at one side. Behind the glass are halls of relics. One hall is devoted to shoes of all sizes. Another contains nothing but uncountable pairs of glasses. The worst is the one which is heaped with human hair, mostly of course cut from the heads of women. Some of it is in plaits, with the ribbons still attached.

In one sense, though, numbers don't matter. Each person can only suffer so much. Except in the sense that he feels pain when his loved ones suffer and die, no one else's suffering can be added to his to make a greater sum.

One gaunt, white-faced little boy, with his hands up and his socks falling down, marching across Warsaw cobblestones to a train. One young girl, writing in her diary in an Amsterdam attic which she has not left for years, waiting for the door behind her to be broken down. One mother, standing before an open grave with her children thrust behind her, knowing that when she falls they will be exposed to the next burst of machine-gun fire. One old man like a skeleton, walking to the electrified wire at the camp-perimeter and putting his arms out to embrace it like a friend. . . . There *is* no more suffering in the world than this. Each of these alone indicts the Germans and blackens their name for ever and ever.

Nevertheless in two ways the total number *is* important.

The further we get from the events of the war, the more possible it becomes to distort them. It would have been unthinkable in the late forties, the fifties, or even the sixties to call into question the reality of the concentration camps, the massacres, or the evils inherent in Nazism. But now in the eighties, the War, the Holocaust, Hitler, German Fascism—they've all become "history," and history to some people is just another word for legend and propaganda—the "version of the victor" which anybody with a political ax to grind is free to dispute.

Thus we are getting books which—almost unbelievably to people who lived through the war—blandly deny that there ever were any death camps, or that more than a few thousand Jews were killed. The whole thing, these apologizers for the Nazis claim, was a myth dreamed up by the Zionists as a justification for Israel.

In short there are people and movements in the world today who are not so very much against what the Nazis did. Some of them appear to minimize the numbers, partly so that it won't sound so bad, and partly to discredit the Zionists who set the figure at 6,000,000.*

The second reason the number is important is because of the question which no one can keep from his mind. If there were so many as all that, why did they not resist?

When a terrible tragedy has happened, one tends to overlook all fault in the victims, but one mustn't if one is to understand. The questions must be asked.

Did the Jews somehow bring the tragedy on themselves? Did they do enough to prevent it or oppose it? Did they, perhaps, even make use of it in some ways?

These are, *for us*, more painful and important questions than the ones about who gave the orders, how many Germans were involved, how many Jews really died.

The first question is quickly answered. The Jews were innocent of any incitement to the crime against them. They were singled out this time, not because they refused to become Christians, not because they were grasping tax-collectors, not because they were unwilling to be assimilated. Not even because some of them were rich and powerful. The Nazis bothered with none of these previous "excuses." They wanted to wipe out the Jews for one reason and one alone—because they were Jews. Again I must stress that it was the first time in the history of Jewish persecution that it was based not on religion or superstition, or "the fear of the stranger," not on greed or envy, but on *race alone*.

Rich and poor, humble and powerful, educated and illiterate; assimilated, Orthodox, baptized Christians with a single suspected-Jewish grandparent; Gentiles married to Jews who would not give them up—they were all the same to the Nazis. All were marked for destruction. And this time

Guinness Book of Records underplays the Nazi massacres, first by giving those of left-wing regimes pride of place, but also by neglecting to supply numbers of those killed by the Nazis and by laying stress on Jewish "revenge" rather than on the causes for it.

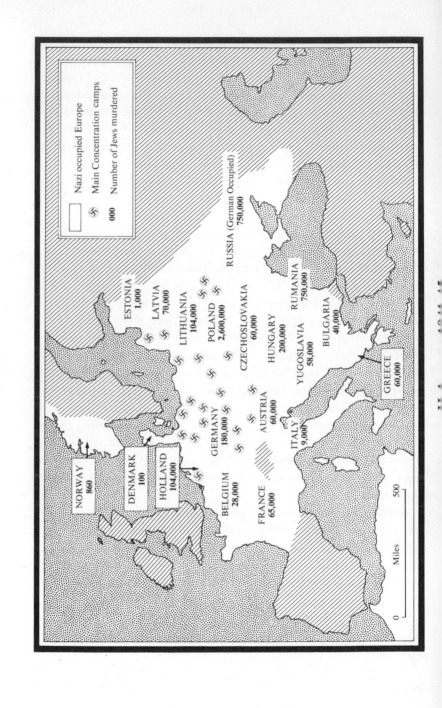

Legend:

Nazi occupied Europe

⑤ Main Concentration camps

000 Number of Jews murdered

NORWAY
860

DENMARK
100

HOLLAND
104,000

BELGIUM
28,000

FRANCE
65,000

GERMANY
180,000

AUSTRIA
60,000

ITALY
9,000

GREECE
60,000

ESTONIA
1,000

LATVIA
70,000

LITHUANIA
104,000

POLAND
2,600,000

CZECHOSLOVAKIA
60,000

HUNGARY
200,000

YUGOSLAVIA
58,000

RUMANIA
750,000

BULGARIA
40,000

RUSSIA (German Occupied)
750,000

Miles

0   500

no "out" was offered. Conversion could not save them. Nor could they, except in rare instances, buy their lives.

Did the Jews oppose their fate, and if not, why not?

The Israelis make much of such instances as there were of resistance. The uprising of the Warsaw ghetto, where the Jews held off the German might, much as the defenders of Jerusalem had held off the Romans, for over forty days until all was destroyed around them, was one most gallant and heroic episode. There were others in which Jews died fighting.

Apart from a number of other abortive rebellions in ghettoes, there were at least three uprisings in concentration camps, which, considering the condition of the prisoners and the odds against them, is astounding. There were about nine groups of Jewish partisans in German-occupied Europe who, by sabotage, did their best to resist.

The fact is, however, that most of the doomed Jews submitted. They walked into the gas chambers, naked and unresisting, some of them singing. There was, we are told, an air of pride, of dignity about them even in this terrible extremity. What was this—courage, or cowardice, or something else entirely?

The young Israelis know their answer. In an anguish of contempt they say, "Our people walked to death as sheep are herded to slaughter." The horror they feel at it may be part of what makes them such fierce fighters. Well, I don't think it was cowardice and I'll tell you why.

People can be what psychiatrists call "conditioned" to behave in a certain way. If, for example, a child grows up in a home where he is beaten for all sorts of things he doesn't understand, or for nothing except because his mother drinks and his father is a brute, then that child will grow up with many of his natural impulses crushed.

He will learn early that if he answers back, or hits back, he will be badly hurt by the powerful people he lives with. He will twist, and turn, and find subtle ways of surviving that don't involve direct resistance to his tormentors who have shown they can always defeat him.

If this can happen to an individual, why not to a whole people?

The Jews had become masters of survival techniques. It was many centuries since they had met aggression head-on. They had not been in a position to, since the time of Mohammed—a people without a country is a people without organized defense. A people without its own army is always more or less helpless against direct brutality.

During their long and dangerous history they had learned that there may not be *braver* ways of defying their destroyers than by throwing themselves into their fires, but there are cleverer ways. If they had not found these, they would have been snuffed out as a people long ago.

The ways they had learned were many. They could run or hide till trouble passed. They could camouflage themselves in various ways. They could live within the laws made for them, however restrictive, as best they could, waiting for better times. Or they could cooperate with their oppressors, reserving always in their secret souls the truth of what they were and what they believed in.

All these techniques, learned through the suffering of ages, were tried in the face of the Nazi war-machine, by a small minority. (Most Jews had no chance to "try" anything, after they had failed to escape in time.)

Some did offer money. Or denied their Jewishness. Or went into hiding. Some few, alas, did worse. Honesty compels me to tell you that there were some who helped the Germans to compile lists and round up their victims. They claimed to have done this not so much to save their own lives as to choose "the tainted wether of the flock, metest for death"—if some had to be sacrificed, better the old and useless, rather than the young and strong who might yet survive, as a remnant had always survived, to renew the Jewish people when the horror should be over. Later, there were to be Jews who, under threat of death, helped the Nazis even in the concentration camps.

I tell you this because you will read it anyway, and you

have to know that *nothing* is ever clear, simple, and one-sided. Terror breeds cowardice as well as courage. You must be able to distinguish between the rare acts of cowardice that there were (yet pity them, for we might all have done the same) and the *inability to resist* which was not cowardice at all, as I'm trying to explain.

When all the methods of survival that have been "conditioned" into a person have failed, he is helpless. He doesn't know another way—the way which seems to Israelis, born in freedom in their own land, the natural one—the way of battle and defiance. He becomes numb—paralyzed.

When the dreaded knock comes on the door, he goes quietly. When the soldiers push him and he stumbles, he gets up again and moves forward as if in a dream. On the long, terrible train journey he has time to think. He may tell himself that this cannot mean what it seems to mean. There cannot be so much evil in the world. At worst there will be a labor camp at the other end. All round him are men and women whose faces are frozen. He sees they cannot resist. Few men can resist as individuals when surrounded by others who are passive. He knows the hopelessness of it, deep down in his soul, because he is conditioned to know it. A single act of rebellion can only bring pain and death upon him at once, whereas if he waits quietly, who knows? They may never come. The history of his people has taught this typical Jewish victim that the only victory for a Jew is to go on living.

His simple inability to believe in the Nazis' true intentions was also a very important factor in his helplessness.

The more civilized, educated and humanitarian (or religious) the Jews were, the more impossible it was for them to believe that men—their fellow countrymen in the case of the Germans—could do these things. *It isn't possible*, they thought. Right till the last minute, in many cases, their minds refused to accept it. Some walked into the gas chambers still deluding themselves that they were going to be given a shower. It was, in a terrible way, a proof of the civilized quality of Jewish intellects that they became paralyzed with disbelief in the face of total barbarism.

Later on, those who did not die at once but were kept in the camps under the most awful conditions you can imagine could not deceive themselves any longer. They knew what was happening all right; perhaps they even realized that if every camp inmate were to rise up and attack the Germans, even with their bare hands, they could defeat them by sheer weight of numbers. The reason they did not do it then was not cowardice or self-deception but physical weakness. They were starved and brutalized. One look at the photographs that were taken when the camps were liberated shows the utter impossibility of a successful uprising. It takes only a few days to reduce a man to such a wretched condition of hunger, cold and terror that all his will power must be reserved for just keeping alive. After that he is not a danger to his captors. This is why uprisings like the one which took place in Sobibor camp in October 1943 are almost incredible in their courage.

There is something else I must mention, though it may be impossible for you to understand at this stage.

I sat next to a man at a dinner party one night recently and we were discussing Zionism. This man was against Israel although he was a Jew. When I asked him why, he replied, with a laugh which I found quite horrifying, "Well! All those people who hate the Jews can't be wrong. There must be something the matter with us. It's better for everyone concerned if we just disappear."

This unfortunate young man was another sort of victim of anti-Semitism. He had come to believe the lies. He thought that there was something wrong about being Jewish. He hated his Jewishness and wanted to escape from it.

If this well fed, safe young man felt this, what about the German Jews? The propaganda may have got to them. A man may submit to death because the upright quality in the human soul which proclaims "I have a right to be what I am, and to live!" has been gouged out of him.

The Nazis had far more to answer for than mass murder.

And was it only the Nazis? What about the other Gentiles of Europe, the conquered people of Austria, France, Belgium, Holland, Roumania, Poland, Czechoslovakia, Denmark, Norway—themselves victims of Nazism? What did they have to say about the yellow stars, the round-ups, the deportation and persecution of their Jewish fellow-citizens?

The punishments for hiding a Jew, even a child, or helping Jews to escape, were very severe. Until we personally have risked capture, torture for ourselves and our families, death or imprisonment, we can't know what it cost those brave few in every country who saved or protected Jews, often strangers to them, just on principle.

In view of what I've written earlier about the Catholic Church, it's only fair to say here that many of these saviors were priests, or nuns, who took Jewish children into their monasteries or convents and pretended they were Christian. To their eternal credit, some of these Catholics did not even try to convert the children, but respected their Jewishness and handed them over to Jewish families after the war. The people who did these sort of things are honored in Israel today and are called the Righteous Gentiles.* But the very fact that they *can* be honored individually is a terrible indication of how few of them there were.

As for the rest, the picture is black indeed.

Wherever anti-Semitism ran in the bloodstream of a nation, it now burst out again in response to the propaganda, threats and bribes of the Nazis.

The Austrians, Roumanians and Poles were probably the worst. They actually handed over their Jews and helped their conquerors to dispose of them. Many were eager to

*You can read about some of them in our friend Peter Hellman's book, *The Garden of Righteous Gentiles.*

take over a confiscated Jewish business or house in exchange for cooperating with the Nazis.

The French, although many were active in the Underground, were not much better regarding the Jews.

Holland had a fairly good reputation in this respect until recently, but then a Dutch journalist dug a little deeper into the matter and found out that it was Dutch collaborators (helpers of the enemy) who betrayed a lot of Jews in hiding, including Anne Frank. It was Dutchmen who manned the fatal trains which carried load after load of Dutch Jews to the camps. Nevertheless I personally know Dutchmen who sheltered Jews and I don't believe Holland's record was very bad on the whole.

Ironically Italy—itself a fascist state—had a comparatively good record. But few people remember this, due to the deeply disgraceful and cowardly behavior of the Catholic leadership. The Pope was so afraid of having his power removed by the fascists and of what might overtake the Catholic clergy scattered throughout conquered Europe that he refused to make any effective protest against Nazis, even when the Jews of Rome were being rounded up almost under the windows of the Vatican. Odd as it seems, many rank-and-file Nazis still called themselves Christians. A real outcry from the head of the Church would undoubtedly have made a difference; we now know that the Nazi leaders expected one and were vastly relieved when it didn't come. The Pope's shameful silence must be added to the long list of Catholic crimes against the Jewish people.

The only nation which came out with a clean slate is Denmark. The story of how the Danish king saved his Jewish subjects is famous (and, I hope, true). The day after the Nazis issued their usual order to all Jews in Denmark to wear the hated yellow star, the King himself appeared with it on his arm. He said he was proud to wear anything his Jewish subjects wore. At that, large numbers of non-Jewish Danes put on the armband. The Nazis, seeing themselves checkmated, withdrew the order and the Danish Jews suffered less than any others.

This wonderful action, and its result, has a tragic side. It
only goes to show how many Jews could have been saved
if only their fellow citizens in other countries had banded
together to support them against their common enemy.

But the Jews of Europe in general found themselves surrounded, not just by mortal enemies, but by hostile neighbors. It's not surprising that many felt despair. Once again
they thought they'd won an equal place in their various
societies. Once again assimilation had proved a myth, and
tolerance nothing but a thin plaster over the ugly sore of
anti-Semitism.

Even those very few who managed to escape hardly knew
where to go. It was not until late in the war, when the facts
about the "final solution" were at last getting through to
an unbelieving world, that the still-free countries of the
West began grudgingly to accept more than just a few of
them. I should mention that Britain took in about 10,000
German Jewish children, sent just before the war started,
by anguished and despairing parents. Even these had to be
sponsored by Jews in Britain. But adults were subject to a
"quota"—only a very few were allowed in. German-Jewish
men were actually put in prison camps as "enemy aliens"
at the beginning of the war, though they were released later
and allowed to fight.

The callousness of the free world all through the Jewish
terror is horrifying to think about now. Officially, nobody
wanted them. No nation cared, or acted, or reacted. Towards the end, the British could have bombed the concentration camps, destroying the gas chambers, the furnaces,
the railway tracks that, by 1944, were carrying daily loads
of Jews to annihilation. Earlier, there had been a time when
Jewish lives could have been bought—a "deal" was offered
by one corrupt German officer who wanted to swap thousands of trapped Jews for army trucks. At the least, Jewish

refugees could have been given sanctuary in the one country that was begging on its knees to be allowed to receive
them—Palestine. But the White Paper had shut the door,
and British officials were all too busy, too bureaucratic, or
too afraid of upsetting the Arabs to open it. Some were
undoubtedly motivated by anti-Semitism.

It was only Russia, oddly enough, who saved many Jewish
lives, by opening her front line as it advanced westward, to
let the fleeing refugees through, Jews and non-Jews alike.
Alas, this mercy was to be forgotten in the horror of Russian anti-Semitism after the war.

All these events and attitudes were having their effect on
the Zionists and the Yishuv, which I'll go into later.

In the meantime, the war ended. Germany and the Third
Reich lay in ruins. Hitler killed himself in an underground
bunker as the Russians advanced on the shattered remains
of Berlin, and his body was burned on his orders. The
victorious allied armies paused in their forward march to
liberate the concentration camps, where a telltale cluster of
broken wrecks of men and women still remained alive, despite the Nazis' frenzied last-minute efforts to wipe them,
and the extermination equipment, out of existence before
they fled. Cameras were raised by shocked and shaking
hands; the pictures and film were taken which finally convinced the world that the greatest evil in history had been
a reality and not just another atrocity story.

Jewish soldiers in the British and American armies (and
there were over 600,000 altogether who served during the
war, not to mention 500,000 in the Russian army and more
in other allied forces) broke regulations, stole trucks, commandeered medical equipment, and raced in every direction setting up centers where the survivors could be taken
and treated. Everywhere in Europe, Jews were desperately
searching for news of lost loved ones. A very few were
lucky. Some of the sufferers found new homes across the
Atlantic, or in Europe, and began life again.

And the rest? They were called, in the cold language of

the officials, "DPs"'—displaced persons. They had no one left to welcome them home, nowhere to go; their bodies, minds and souls had been badly damaged in many cases. Very many of them had only one longing left—to leave the slaughterhouse of Europe behind them forever and seek a country where they might heal their wounds and become (if such a thing were possible—who can blame them for doubting it?) *whole Jews* again. And that brings me to the last of my questions.

Did the Jews gain anything from the greatest cataclysm that had ever befallen them?

Fifteen years ago I would have felt able to write that the Holocaust had served the purpose of scotching anti-Semitism. It might still exist as a terrible warp in the minds of some people, but it could never (so I believed) be brought out in the open again. Knowing now what it could lead to, it—and fascism, of course—must have been forever discredited.

Fool that I was! As if *any* form of human failing ever totally dies out. I have learned better. Fascism is lifting its hideous head again, right here in Britain, never mind in Germany where it never really lay down. The National Front is not ashamed to use racist propaganda to rouse the very same little finger-and-toe people to see enemies in every black face; the Jews are only in second place as hate-objects because they are less easy to identify. Anti-Semitism is active in South America. In Russia, of course, it is government policy to wipe the Jews out—not physically, but culturally, by stifling all signs of Jewish religion, language, history—identity. Russian Jews who want to go to Israel are treated as traitors to Russia or as madmen.

Nevertheless, despite the persistence of the disease of anti-Semitism—despite the fascist sympathizers who try to minimize the Nazi crimes or even excuse Hitler—the world at large has learned some kind of lesson. Not just about the evils of anti-Semitism but about racism in general. There is a trend in the western world today to be more tolerant

of the stranger, the one who is different. There *are* those
who are against immigrants, especially when there seem to
be too many of them. But it is not "respectable." People
who feel this way have a defiant air if they come out with
it openly. Most educated men and women take pride in
judging every man on his merits and, if they feel prejudice,
they have the grace to be ashamed of it and to struggle to
defeat it within themselves.

This change of political and moral direction, this step
forward by the civilized conscience, may not be worth millions of Jewish lives. But it is something.

However, the surviving Jews did not do this—it's just
something that happened as a result of the Holocaust, a
lesson that humanity *in the main* has (I hope) at least begun
to learn.

Did the Jews themselves "use" the Holocaust in any way?

The Arab propagandists put it bluntly. "The Zionists
exploited the tragedy of their people to achieve their Jewish
state."

Well my boys, and so, in a way, they did. *And so they should.*
If it had not been "exploited" to some useful, constructive,
positive end, then those millions of dead bodies rotting in
lime pits, those tons of ashes and bone fragments silting the
topsoil around the campsites, those rivers of tears which
have not yet stopped flowing, would add up to the final
blasphemy—total and absolute waste.

LETTER 18

The Yishuv's War

As I mentioned, it took years before the Nazi treatment of the Jews "sank in" to the consciousness of officialdom everywhere. But the Jews of Palestine had not the least difficulty in believing the very first rumors.* Had they not good reason to believe in any horror concerning themselves? Had they not had proof, over two thousand years, that any atrocity against them was possible? They believed every rumor, and acted on it.

They were in a quandary, though. The Nazis were their mortal enemies. The British were enemies too, in a sense. Yet the British were their best hope for defeating Hitler. So how to help them in this, and at the same time defeat them in their blind determination to keep the refugees out of Palestine?

Each leader had his own answer, according to his own nature and character.

*Golda Meir, *My Life*.

Dr. Weizmann had been severely disillusioned, but he still believed the British would come to their senses after the war. A Jewish state in Palestine could, he believed, only be viable as part of the British Commonwealth. He spent this war, like the last, mainly out of Palestine, building up support for Zionism and getting promises of postwar help from important British and American leaders.

Both Winston Churchill and President Roosevelt gave such promises, and Weizmann was once more encouraged. He couldn't know that when the war ended Roosevelt would be dead and Churchill thrown out of power. But even if he had, he would not have despaired, at least about Britain, because nobody spoke up more strongly in favor of Zionism than the leaders of the Labor Party. Weizmann hardly had to ask them for assurances of support; they were offered freely. Weizmann had reason to be confident that, provided the "right side" won the war, the White Paper would be scrapped no matter which party got into power. So he felt free to urge the Jews to support Britain whole-heartedly.

Then there was Ben-Gurion. He was getting fed up with Weizmann's everlasting patience with Britain *and* with his "gradual" policies. This, Ben-Gurion believed, was no time for polite diplomatic methods. It was time for action to-wards a Jewish state, and had been ever since the White Paper came out.

"The Jewish people," he had announced just before the war, "will not submit to the conversion of the National Home into a ghetto."* He was prepared to oppose the restrictions on Jews' buying land (and did so by all sorts of roundabout methods such as buying land in the "forbidden areas" through obliging Arabs)† and especially on the halt to immigration, with at least half his strength. The other

---

*B. Litvinoff, *Ben-Gurion of Israel.*
  † Many of the "brokers" were later assassinated by the Mufti's hench-men.

half must be given to supporting the British war effort against Germany. He put this into words which became famous:

"We will fight the war as if there were no White Paper, and we will fight the White Paper as if there were no war."

That involved the Jewish Agency, under Ben-Gurion, in a policy of pressing every available Jew in the Yishuv into volunteering for service with the British. Not that many needed pressing. (Those who did need it, however, got it, and occasionally in a pretty rough way, but that was not Ben-Gurion's doing.)

The Revisionists took a different view, needless to say.

Jabotinsky died in 1940. But before that he had regrouped his followers, Irgun Zvai Leumi, sometimes called Etzel for short, which was still a terrorist organization, dedicated to getting Britain out and achieving their "biblical-sized" state. But for the time being even they were prepared to call a truce with Britain in the interest of beating the Germans.

There was another group, however, even more extreme, who were not satisfied with this policy. They broke away from the Irgun early on, under the leadership of a man called Abraham Stern. Stern was an out-and-out fanatic, so one-track-minded that he was even prepared to make a deal with the fascists if they would get Britain out of the Middle East! I'll have more to tell you about the Stern Gang later.

Whatever their differences of approach, on one thing the Yishuv leaders were united: the Jews of Europe must be rescued at all costs.

The Germans, at that stage, had not reached the decision to annihilate the Jews. Their main object at the beginning of the war was just to get rid of them. German officers with orders to do this were quite willing to take bribes to cooperate with the Haganah or the Jewish Agency. Between them they loaded up ships in Balkan ports with hundreds, or thousands, of refugees. The Germans, ever practical, took the trouble to forge the essential entry permits which

the poor Jews imagined would get them past the British
blockade and into Palestine.

This blockade is hardly a source of pride to anyone now.
In fact, the whole setup is mind-boggling. There were the
British, locked in a life-and-death struggle with the Nazis.
The Jews were supporting them in every conceivable way.
At the same time the British were blocking, with complete
ruthlessness, the entry of Jewish refugees into Palestine.
They did this in order to appease the Arabs—knowing full
well that many leading Arabs were supporting the Nazis!

So here were British soldiers and sailors, who presumably would have been much happier fighting the Germans,
lumbered with the horrendous task of preventing a large
number of overcrowded, unseaworthy old ships, which the
Haganah had somehow got hold of, from unloading their
thousands of terrified, exhausted, half-starved passengers
in the only country in the world where they were wanted
and where they might feel they belonged.

One wonders how these young men felt as the scoured
the coast off Haifa in British warships, looking for the lop-
sided old hulks chugging along on their ancient engines,
their rails lined with faces torn between despair and hope.
"Theirs not to reason why . . . " Duty came first. The
sailors would stop the ships, tow or escort them into the
port of Haifa, and there transfer the refugees (forcibly if
necessary) to a ship less likely to sink, and take them off to
the British island of Mauritius in the Indian Ocean, to wait
out the war in a sort of prison camp.

It may be hard to imagine what these young Britons felt
as they did this, but it's easy to imagine how the Jews of
Palestine felt as they watched it going on, knowing just
what the refugees were running away from and how badly
they were needed in Palestine. *Any* action, you might think,
would be justified to foil the British and bring the refugees
ashore.

Any action? Well. Consider the case of the *Patria.*

The *Patria* was one of the "safe ships" to which just such

a load of human derelicts were transferred, under the eyes of the angry Yishuv and despite the desperate appeals of the Jewish Agency to the British authorities. The scenes as the British soldiers forcibly removed the Jews from the two old tubs they had come on, to the *Patria,* must have been heartrending.

Suddenly a ship's siren shrieked a warning from the *Patria,* and the refugees were urged to jump into the harbor and swim to shore. A few minutes later there was an explosion on board. An hour and a quarter after that, the *Patria* sank. Two hundred and forty refugees and a dozen police were killed or drowned.

How did this tragedy happen?

The first explanation was that the refugees had scuttled the ship themselves in a desperate act of mass-suicide to advertise their plight.*

An inquiry the following year demonstrated that this was not the truth. What actually happened, it seemed, was that a determined group of Jews, working from the shore, had sabotaged the ship, without giving the people on board much choice. People who believed this naturally blamed Etzel, already well known for its aggressive and reckless actions. Gradually this "layer of truth" too was peeled off, and a deeper one revealed.

It was not Etzel at all, but the respectable (though still, from the British point of view, illegal) Haganah which was responsible, *and* with the connivance of the Jewish Agency! †

Of course they didn't intend to kill anyone, just to put the ship out of action so that it couldn't sail to Mauritius; this would have given the Jewish Agency more time to negotiate with the British—who, to be fair, had occasionally been known to give way in special cases and let refugees stay. (They did so this time with the survivors of the *Patria.*) But

*Arthur Koestler, *Promise and Fulfillment.*
†Christopher Sykes, *Cross Roads to Israel.*

something went wrong. Probably the engineer who had placed the bomb bungled it.

It's interesting to discover that when the survivors and relatives found out what had really happened, they weren't angry—not even with the bungling bomb-setter, who became an ordinary worker in Haifa Docks. Which only goes to show how much blind trust the Jews of Palestine (and later Israel) placed in the decisions of their leaders. Until very recently, the remark one always heard about any action or policy which seemed questionable was, "How can we know all the facts? They know what they're doing." Unfortunately this was not always the case, and doubts often proved justified. In general, the *Patria* episode is just another example of how complicated all these propaganda stories are, when you start to dig a little.

But that was only one ship. There were many others. Some sank on the way. Some ran the gauntlet successfully and were landed along the coast, their "cargoes" spirited off in darkness. Most were intercepted and their passengers sent off to prison camps far from their longed-for haven. And at least one was actually sent back to Germany. Questions were asked about that in the House of Commons, which did not save the lives of those on board.

Horrifying as all this undoubtedly is, you must realize that the British administration had no easy job. The area of Palestine was soon going to be needed as a vast military base—it might even become a war zone. Local trouble with the Arabs was the last thing they wanted.

Actually there was very little of that, partly perhaps because of the ruthless firmness with which the British stuck to the terms of the White Paper, partly because, for Arabs and Jews alike, it was hard to worry about local quarrels in the shadow of the huge world conflict. The Jews were preoccupied with the rescue operations. The Arabs were lying low. Many of them were no doubt glad of a breather after the Rebellion. Others (though not a majority) were hoping the Germans would win the war and solve the Jewish question in Palestine as in Europe. The Mufti, now in exile, worked actively for this result—he became an outright Nazi, and even helped in Germany to bring about the "final solution."

It was a time of some cooperation between Jews and Arabs. They simply had to work together sometimes. Again, if either side could have spared time or concentration *then* to work out a compromise, some solution might have been achieved.

The British certainly thought so. They seem to have hoped that the unnatural quiet might last forever if they just handled it right. Perhaps if Arabs and Jews could be brought to take part in the war effort side-by-side, they could overcome their distrust of one another. So a Palestinian army was started.

The idea was to recruit equal numbers, so there'd be no cause for resentment. This happy scheme came unstuck from the start, because the Jews volunteered in the tens of thousands and the Arabs in the hundreds. Also the Arabs had a tendency to enlist, grab a gun, and desert with it. For a while the British tried to keep Jewish numbers down and build Arab numbers up. They gave up in the end, so that the Palestine force was three-quarters Jewish.

But this was by no means what the Jews wanted anyway. Once again they clamored for their own army, under their own flag. Over and over again Weizmann, Ben-Gurion and others begged the British War Office to authorize the setting up of such a Jewish force. They wouldn't.

Why the years of delay? Why the bureaucratic obstacles, the broken promises, the deliberate refusal to let the Jews fight the Nazis *as Jews* (instead of just as ordinary members of the British forces) until it was almost too late?

Just the British being bloody-minded and anti-Semitic as usual? But there was more to it than that. Isn't there always, in this history, more to everything than meets the eye?

There were three reasons why the British didn't want a Jewish army. First, they must have thought, why bother?

Most of the Jews were already in theirs! Next, they felt that if they let the Jews help too much in the war, it would be that much more difficult afterwards to refuse their demands for a state. They would owe them more than it might be convenient to pay.

Also it was fairly obvious that the Zionists had a secondary motive for pressing for this army of their own. All the military training might well be useful, after the war, for purposes the British wouldn't approve of, like fighting the Arabs—or even themselves.

Personally I don't think it would have done Britain any harm at all, and probably great good in the long run, to let the Jews have their army. They were getting trained anyway, just through individual recruitment; and the goodwill Britain could have gained would have helped relations, whereas their blind refusals until nearly the end of the war caused intense anger and resentment. It caused worse—a deep feeling of frustration, growing out of the fear of annihilation, and nothing is more damaging than that.

This fear was very real. It came to a head in 1942, when Rommel's German desert army was rolling east along the shores of North Africa towards Palestine. The Yishuv well knew what their fate would be if Rommel were not stopped. They would go the way of their European brothers, and not only that, but all the love and labor they had put into their homeland would be devastated. In this darkest hour of the war, while the Yishuv passed through "the valley of the shadow of death," Weizmann wrote a moving letter of appeal to the British government: "Give us at least," he begged, "the elementary human right to go down fighting."*

The British refused to understand the fundamental difference between the Yishuv and their own troops in Palestine. To them, it was just another war-zone, which could be

---

*Dr. Weizmann, *Trial and Error.*

abandoned if the worse came to the worst. But for the Jews there could be no retreat. They would have to "go down fighting."

The question was, with what?

The increasing toughness of Jewish attitudes, and much of what others call their "intransigence" today, is rooted in that nightmare time before the tide of German victories turned. Many of their actions were based on the absolute need to build up a defense force of their own, separate from the British who might have to abandon them.

About 60 percent of the Jews in the Palestine army were also members of the Haganah, or, in some cases, the Irgun. The British feared (with reason) that these men had double loyalties, and that their loyalty to Haganah came before their loyalty to the British army.

This was soon confirmed when it was discovered that weapons were mysteriously disappearing from British depots and finding their way into secret arms-caches, hidden away in kibbutzim.

Most of these guns were bought from British soldiers. Others may have been stolen by the Jews themselves, but the Haganah denied this, on the grounds that since every Jew wanted the British to win the war it would be a crime to rob them of their weapons.*

Several Haganah men were caught and put on trial for gunrunning in 1943. At this trial a lot of British officers exposed their anti-Semitism very clearly. Some went so far as to say that the only reason Jews were joining up in such large numbers was to get their hands on guns for their own illegal organizations. Others tried to suggest that any Jew interested in Jewish self-defense was really a terrorist trying to stir up trouble for the Mandate.

Naturally these and other remarks infuriated the Jews, and so did the way settlements were searched for hidden

*Golda Meir, *My Life.*

arms. The British, then and later, conducted these searches
with great thoroughness and often brutality. They absolutely turned villages upside down, leaving chaos behind
them. Sometimes they did find what they were looking for.
The important question is, had the Jews good reason to
distrust British assurances that *they* would defend the settlements? Was it criminal, or was it wise and prudent, to make
sure, even by illegal means, that they wouldn't be dependent on the British as they had been in 1929 and in the
1930s when hundreds of Jews had died at Arab hands?

After the Arms Trials in 1943—in which Jews got heavy
prison sentences, whereas Arabs who had been stealing
weapons were let off lightly—relations between Britain and
the Jews got worse and worse. Zionist propaganda now
took on a hysterical tone. Everything and anything that
went wrong was blamed on the British. Reading this now,
it's hard to realize the very important fact that Weizmann
was by no means the only Zionist who actually didn't want
to get rid of the British but wanted to work with them. It
seems as if the press had been taken over by extremists,
whose sole aim and object was to get the British out of
Palestine at all costs.

Unlike the Irgun, the Stern Gang had been fairly active
until 1942, mainly assassinating fellow Jews who were moderates or who were working with the British. You can usually tell a true fanatic because he feels more hatred for his
own people who don't happen to agree with him than for
his real enemies.

The Stern Gang also made attacks on the British police,
who finally retaliated with a raid on Stern's home and found
him hiding in a cupboard. He died ingloriously; shot down
while trying to escape.

Only his immediate followers (who called him "The Il-
luminator," which doesn't sound quite so ludicrous in Hebrew) were particularly sorry. The rest of the Yishuv had
been appalled by him and his activities. But his gang
wouldn't lie down for long—too many things were stimu-
lating anger, hatred, vengeance and other violent emotions

that fanatics thrive on. In 1943, both the Irgun (which had been in hiding) and the Stern Gang became active again.

The most important thing to us now about this revival is the man who eventually took over the leadership of the Irgun. He was Menachem Begin, who at the time of writing this is Israel's prime minister.

There's a science-fiction story by Ray Bradbury about the perils of time travel. A big-game hunter goes back in a time machine to the primeval forests to shoot a dinosaur. He is warned not to kill anything else, or so much as step off an antigravitational track suspended above the jungle floor, for fear of altering the course of evolution (the dinosaur was due to die anyway). The hunter panics and steps off the path, crushing a butterfly. When he returns to his own time, he's appalled to find that the recent elections in his country have produced an extremist government, instead of the moderate one which had won before he left on his trip. The death of that single butterfly in prehistory had influenced the course of subsequent human history for the worse.

On the morning I learned that Menachem Begin had come to power, I remembered that story very vividly. Only it was no time-traveling hunter that distorted the course of Israel's evolution—it was Hitler, and also, I deeply regret to say, to a much lesser extent, British policy in Palestine.

Hitler's abominable deeds caused the Jewish people more suffering than humankind can bear. Those who passed through that time—not only survivors of the Holocaust itself, but *all* Jews who were adults in the 1930s and 1940s and a lot who were only children—carry a mark, a scar. No, that is not the word. It's not visible. It's more of an inner mutation. The terrible thing for someone like me is to realize that while the Jewish spirit was still (so to speak) molten from the fires of the Nazi rage, we, the British, twisted the shape again.

By a miracle, some Jews were actually mutated into greater moral strength, humanity, courage and fineness of soul. But others, as you have to expect, were warped.

If the results of the recent elections had been different,
I would only mention Begin in passing. His role in the years
between the war and Israel's independence, and later, is
not one I want to dwell on.

What sort of a man he is now, only time will tell. Men
change; maybe Begin has become more flexible. In the
1930s and 1940s he suffered from one of the most dangerous afflictions a politician can have—an utter inability to
see anyone else's point of view.

To believe in what you are doing is, of course, a great
asset to a political leader. But there is a vital difference
between that and an unshakable conviction that all right is
on your side and that therefore all other ways are wrong.
This is a disease. Begin had it then, when he led the Irgun.
It shows in every word of the book* he wrote about that
period. As I read it, the words of Oliver Cromwell were
constantly in my mind:

> I beseech you
> In the bowels of Christ, consider you might be wrong.

Begin never considered it when he was young. He believed in one way to statehood: the sword—that is, violence. Weizmann, on the other hand, believed only in the
plough—settlement. Ben-Gurion believed in both.† This
made him, at that time, the most balanced leader of the
three; but his willingness to adopt "the way of the sword"
—Begin's way—when the going got rough led him and the
Jewish Agency into great difficulties and trials of conscience.

By 1944, the Haganah was deeply involved with the British.
They had "lent" men to the British to take part in various

---

*Menachem Begin, *The Revolt.*
†This assessment is Barnet Litvinoff's from his excellent book, *Ben-
Gurion of Israel.*

daring raids (a young Haganah officer called Moshe Dayan
lost his eye in a British raid in Syria) and the British authorities knew all about the special commando-units the Haganah had trained, which were called Palmach. They'd even
used them when they needed to. But still there was no
official recognition of Haganah as the Jewish self-defense
force (which is what Haganah means). It was half recognized, half illegal, a very muddled situation in fact.

Irgun and the Sternists, of course, were totally illegal,
and were causing as many headaches to the Haganah and
the Jewish Agency as they were to the British. The Irgun
had called off their truce with the Mandate and declared
open war on it. But at least they confined their actions to
targets directly connected with the British administration.
Begin succeeded in fooling himself that this would not hurt
the war effort.

Meanwhile the hate-filled, vengeance-seeking youngsters of the new Stern Gang (nicknamed Lehi) were going
another way to work. Essentially, it was the Mufti's way,
based on the maxim, "Who is not for us, is against us." It
involved random terrorist attacks on civilians, Arab and
British, much bombthrowing, and a number of what they
called "symbolic" assassinations of Jewish officials. No
holds were barred; mercy was a weakness, compromise a
crime, sudden death the penalty for trying to find another
way to statehood. These young Jews were victims of Hitler
just as surely as were those who were still dying in the gas
chambers of Auschwitz, except that instead of being murdered they were twisted by hatred into murdering others.

The bulk of the Yishuv was revolted and shocked by all
this, but the problem of the moderate leaders was that they
didn't want to show the British that Zionists were seriously
divided. Because of this they failed, at this early stage when
the terror groups were just beginning to flex their muscles,
to stamp on them firmly.

Later that year, however, the Sternists pulled off an as-

sassination which forced the Jewish Agency to take a more
serious view. The victim was Lord Moyne, the British representative in Cairo.

Why did the Sternists think it worth the trouble of sending two young men to Cairo to kill this man? Their motives
are still not clear. Lord Moyne was said to be an anti-
Semite. Why? Because he had once said in Parliament that
Palestine was an Arab country? Or because it had once
been his duty to pass on a government decision not to form
a Jewish army?

More probably his "crime" was his part in a British
scheme to unite the Arabs in an organization called the
Arab League. This was dreamed up as a way to stop the
Arabs' fighting among themselves and to enable the British
to extend their influence throughout the Arab world. The
League still exists, and Arab unity still doesn't; but when it
was first formed, apparently it looked to the extremist Jews
like part of a Machiavellian plot against Zionism.

In fact, Lord Moyne was a typical British diplomat, no
worse than many others, and, I gather, more fair-minded
than some toward the Jews. But the Lehi was never too
fussy about individuals' deservings. The man was a servant
of the hated White Paper government. It was enough.

Two young Sternists went to Cairo and shot Moyne, and
also (by accident, one hopes) his chauffeur. They were
caught, tried and hanged.

Dr. Weizmann wrote a letter to Churchill: "I can hardly
find words adequate to express the deep moral indignation
and horror which I feel at the murder of Lord Moyne. I
know that these feelings are shared by Jewry throughout
the world . . . . The act illuminates the abyss to which
terrorism leads. Political crimes of this kind are an especial
abomination . . . they implicate whole communities in the
guilt of the few. I can assure you that Palestine Jewry will
. . . go to the utmost limit of its power to cut out, root and
branch, this evil from its midst."

This view no doubt did represent what the majority of

Jews felt about it at the time. They knew that the murder, and terror tactics generally, would never change British policy—on the contrary, it could only make matters worse. This it undoubtedly did.

For one thing, it infuriated Churchill enough to turn him against Zionism, just at the moment—the last moment—when he might have been able to help. It dashed all hopes of the British government, under Churchill or anyone else, reversing the White Paper. Begin, of course, believed there was no possibility of this anyway. What is sure is that this rash crime made new enemies and lost old friends.*

Following the Moyne assassination, Weizmann's promise that the terrorists would be cut out "root and branch" looked as if it might be kept. The Jewish Agency was sufficiently shocked to take the drastic step of cooperating with the British. The Haganah rounded up terrorists and handed them over.

The anguish, the rage, the torn consciences that followed this handing-over of Jews by Jews, when millions were still dying in Europe, was too much to bear. After that one gesture, the Jewish Agency fell back into a Hamlet-like state of indecision.

The British scarcely helped the moderates to make up their minds about terrorism by behaving, more and more, as if any act which might upset the Arabs had to be punished without mercy. The one-sidedness of the British administration (for instance, in matters like gunrunning),

*In 1976, a spectacular story broke in *The Times*. These two young assassins' bodies had been handed back to Israel after thirty-two years by the Egyptians and given heroes' burial with full military honors. The funerals were attended by high Israeli government officials. At the same time pamphlets were issued to schools, explaining that these men were freedom-fighters.

These actions by Israel caused an outcry abroad, especially in Britain. My own disapproval was based on one consideration: how can Israel protest against terrorist acts committed against her, yet glorify her own terrorists as heroes, to the point of "educating" children to applaud them?

caused such a sense of injustice in even the most moderate Jews that, in their secret hearts, many of them couldn't help sympathizing with at least some of the terrorists' actions.

The case of Lord Moyne was, in its way, another "crushed butterfly," which played its part in deflecting the development of Israel. But of course, not all crushed butterflies have *ill* effects. There are sacrifices which can have a lasting influence for good.

Towards the end of the war in Europe, the British found a new job for Jewish volunteers.

There were many Palestinian Jews, of course, who spoke European languages perfectly. The British put a deal to a number of them:

"We will train and equip you and drop you into occupied Europe by parachute. Your main job there will be to arrange for the escape of British pilots who have fallen behind enemy lines, and to act as spies to let us know about German troop movements. In return, you may try to rescue some Jews, or rally them to their own defense, while you're at it."

There are some fantastic stories of heroism connected with the young people (and a couple not so young) who undertook those daring missions. For Jews to go back into Nazi-controlled Europe once they were safely out, took enormous courage. To go as spies and agents, armed, and with portable radio transmitters which would mark them for death anyway if they were caught, made it even more dangerous.

Perhaps the most moving story concerns Hannah Senesh. She was a Hungarian girl who had come to Palestine at eighteen, leaving her widowed mother behind. She settled in a kibbutz, where she was immensely happy. She learned to do farmwork and in between she wrote poetry of great simplicity and deep feeling.

When she heard about the parachute scheme, she rushed to enlist, and was eventually dropped behind the German lines in Yugoslavia. After a long period of futile attempts to cross into Hungary, during which she and her companion worked with the local partisans, she finally couldn't wait any longer. With three young men whom she'd persuaded to join her, she crossed the border into occupied Hungary.

All this time she had been thinking, with anguish, of the million Jews of Hungary who were now at the Nazis' mercy. She burned to save as many of them as possible, but especially her mother, whom she adored. Alas, she was caught almost immediately. One of the boys she had recruited lost his nerve and shot himself when a German patrol questioned him, and then Hannah, who was hiding nearby, was betrayed by some local farmers. Her radio, which she'd hidden, was found. After that, the Germans' one objective was to force her to reveal the radio code she was to use to contact the British. Of course they wanted to use it to send false messages.

Like Sarah Aaronsohn before her, Hannah bore all that the Gestapo did to her, but not in silence. She told no secrets, but she spoke up for herself in a way that earned her interrogators' respect, if not their mercy. Unfortunately, she did reveal her name, and this led to the arrest of her beloved mother.

I'd like you to read the mother's account of their life together in prison.* It was here, I think, that Hannah's extraordinary character shows best. There were many Jews in prison for their Zionist sympathies, or just for being Jews, and Hannah, with her boundless enthusiasm for Palestine, found ways to "tell" them about The Land, teach them songs and even teach her mother Hebrew! She also made little gifts out of the scraps that were available, old tins, tissue paper, straws from her mattress . . . It seems as if the whole grim prison was given some measure of liveliness and hope because of this one girl.

As the allies advanced across Europe and it became clear that the Germans were losing the war, some prisons were

* *Hannah Senesh, Her Life and Diary.*

closed. Mrs. Senesh was released, but Hannah was taken to
another prison. The poor mother was in despair. She
managed to see her once, for ten minutes. Hannah told her
she was going to be tried, and asked her to arrange for a
lawyer. Shortly after that, a Hungarian "puppet" government replaced the German Nazis, but hideous to relate,
they turned out to be even more violently anti-Jewish. Almost the last remnant of Hungarian Jewry perished in a
blood bath, and those few who were left, who had some
influence to protect them, were restricted so greatly that
Hannah's mother could scarcely get out of her house to go
to the trial. There were heavy air-raids going on too.

Utter confusion reigned in Budapest as fascists began to
flee before the advancing Russians. Mrs. Senesh could find
out nothing, not even what sentence Hannah had received.
At last she made her way to one of the police barracks, and
found the army lawyer who was responsible for Hannah's
case. In a most harrowing conversation, this fascist officer
—a Hungarian himself—at first denied knowing anything
about Hannah's fate. But gradually it came out that, contrary to everything Mrs. Senesh had been led to expect,
Hannah had been taken out and shot that very morning.

What shall be said of *this* crushed butterfly? Her mission
failed. Did she die for nothing? Did her death distort the
evolution of her people, or tilt it in a more healthy direction?

There was not one person who saw her, even through a
cell window, while she was in prison (and that includes the
man who was responsible for her illegal execution) who did
not carry away a memory of a kind of Jew whom no anti-
Semite, Hungarian or German, could bear to contemplate.
"She seemed," said her official murderer to her stricken
mother in tones of wonder, "proud of being Jewish." Perhaps that was why she was killed, so needlessly, so savagely,
right at the end. Why ever it was, she died for the honor
of her people.

When the war ended in 1945, the world seemed to slump back, numb with weariness, shock and sorrow. But the Jews of Palestine couldn't afford to slump. Europe still contained the remnant of the Jews—ill, starved, brutalized, but alive. The "War for Civilization" had been won, partly due to Britain's courage and endurance. But now those same qualities were about to be used to the disadvantage of that stricken remnant, whose chief longing was to come to Palestine.

The Jews' war wasn't over. It hadn't even begun.

LETTER 19

"Labor Pains" and the Hundred Thousand

I remember very well the shock among "people like us" at the results of the 1945 general election.

No sooner had Winston Churchill won the war for us than he was pushed out of office by a huge majority, and replaced by a nondescript-looking little man called Clement Attlee. It was a case of out with the Tory bulldog and in with the Labor whippet! The working people and returning soldiers of Britain, whose mass votes had done the deed, cheered long and loud. Conservatives like my parents—professional people—shook in their shoes, with indignation and with anxiety for their future.

The Zionists had no doubts about how *they* felt at the change. Weren't they socialists too? Hadn't they listened for years to fulsome speeches of support and praise, and above all promises, from out-of-office Labor leaders?

"The working people of Britain," Ben-Gurion had once remarked confidently, "will understand what we are trying to do."

Weizmann knew better than most that what men say when they are not in power doesn't always correspond to the things they do when they are. Nevertheless he hoped for great things from Labor, and he and most of the Zionist leaders sent ecstatic telegrams of congratulation to Mr. Attlee.

Alas for their hopes.

A mere ten days after Labor took office, Ben-Gurion came to see the new foreign secretary, a fat, bespectacled trade unionist called Ernest Bevin. He asked no favors. He demanded, on the basis of Labor's past promises, a Jewish state. He also said that meanwhile 100,000 Jewish survivors of Hitler's camps should be admitted at once to Palestine.

Mr. Bevin didn't like his manner. He wasn't too keen on Jews at the best of times. He thought them pushy and troublesome, and had thought so ever since he'd had to make peace between Jewish and Catholic trade unionists in London's East End before the war.*

In any case he was very new to his job, and in fact extremely ignorant about the whole setup in the Middle East. As he saw it, his task was straightforward. He had to make sure the British stayed in Palestine, which was vital to Britain's interests. To do that, he had to keep in with the Arabs. Arab nationalism—Jewish nationalism—the recent history of the region—all such background information was a closed book to him. For guidance, he relied on the permanent staff of the Middle East Department of the Foreign Office.

Now the Foreign Office, as you may know, is staffed by people who don't change as governments rise and fall. The same crew were running that ship after the 1945 election as before. I won't say they were pro-Arab to a man, but there was a definite tendency that way.

They confirmed Bevin's rough notion of the situation. Of

*Richard Crossman, *A Nation Reborn.*

course it was very sad about the Jewish refugees, but if
100,000 of them were admitted to Palestine there'd be hell
to pay. The British administrators and troops out there had
their hands full enough, without inflaming the Arabs by
flooding the country with more Jews.

Besides, there were the Russians to consider.

Russia had been on Germany's side at the beginning of
the war, Stalin having signed a pact with Hitler. Then all of
a sudden in 1941 Hitler invaded Russia, which thus became
"our gallant ally."*

But before the war had been over a few months, it began
to be clear that gratitude was not the only feeling we should
have for "our gallant ally," but also a healthy alarm as to
what she would get up to next. What the British Foreign
Office thought she might well get up to was a Middle East
takeover.

Bevin and Attlee were obsessed with the idea that, since
many of the Yishuv came originally from Russia, they must
be secretly conspiring with Stalin against Britain! In vain
people who knew better tried to convince them that these
ex-Russian Jews hated the Russians and were only "plot-
ting" for themselves and their own future as an independent nation.

This seemed great nonsense to Bevin, who was convinced that the Jews were no more than a religious group.
Let them sit in Palestine by all means, preferably quietly in

*Oh, how we all loved the Russians during the last part of the war!
So much did we owe them that some people never got over it. One day
quite recently I was picketing outside a London theater, where the Bol-
shoi Ballet was appearing. We were picketing in support of two Russian
ballet-dancers who were being prevented from dancing, or emigrating,
by the Russian government. Suddenly a little old Jew rushed up to me,
snarling: "You leave the Russians alone! They saved our bloomin' hides
in 1944! They beat 'Itler for us! If it wasn't for the Russians, all us Jews
in England would've been done for!" I mentioned that a great many Jews
in Russia had been "done for" in the meantime, but he wouldn't listen.
The sense of relief when the might of the Russian army (not to mention
the cold of a Russian winter) was turned on Hitler seemed to have
stopped the clock for that little East Ender.

their synagogues, and the British would protect them and
run the country for them, and for that they should damn
well be grateful.

Meanwhile Britain must also protect her own interests
against any possible threat from Russia, by turning Palestine into one big armed camp. The poor old Arabs (who
clearly were not half as advanced as the Jews, due to not
being so pushy, presumably) would be given help by means
of irrigation and other schemes for improving their agriculture.

Of course the money couldn't come out of the British
purse, which hardly contained any. Never mind. The Jewish
areas around the towns seemed well-off, and there were all
those funds from Jews in America . . . Let some of that
money be hived off to pay for the welfare schemes for the
Arabs.

As for the 100,000 camp survivors, it was just too bad
about them. Oh, a few could come in—1,500 a month, say
—enough so that nobody could accuse the British of inhumanity, but not enough to irritate the Arabs.

Ben-Gurion and the whole Jewish world reeled from the
shock of this "generous" offer. What price their Jewish
National Home now? Was the Balfour Declaration totally
forgotten?

The Irgun and the Sternists were almost triumphant.
"We told you so! Britain is the arch-enemy! We've fought
them from the beginning. Now you see that even a socialist
government betrays us, you must join in the battle."

The Jewish Agency, the Haganah, the whole Zionist leadership, were stunned with disappointment and dismay. Had
the Irgun been right all the time? Was it a case of "perfidious Albion," or simply that an abominable stroke of ill luck
had brought the worst possible men into power at this
critical moment?

Weizmann and Ben-Gurion tried to keep a sense of proportion. In other ways, the Labor government was doing
truly great, truly socialist things. They were bringing in the

welfare state at home. In their colonies in Africa and the West Indies, and especially in India, they were behaving nobly. While the terrorists begged for action, the leadership still hesitated. Surely this betrayal was a blunder, a temporary aberration! It was too soon to despair and turn to violence.

But while they hesitated on that issue, there was another on which all Jews were united. Illegal immigration, outside the miserly "quota," must be gotten under way immediately to bring in as many refugees as possible.

Of course they didn't regard it as illegal. They called it *Aliya Bet,* and Jews all over the world helped. Even organizations which till then had tried to stay within the law, now gave money and aid to that secret branch of the Haganah which was straining every nerve to bring in those whom Hitler had not managed to kill.

As fast as the British forces discharged them, Haganah members joined the team in Europe. Many of them were battle hardened veterans who had spent the war driving trucks. A kibbutznik called Arazi organized an escape network (nicknamed *Bricha**) which ran right down through Europe, from Poland to the Italian ports. They hung on to their uniforms and masqueraded as British transport units. They bamboozled, coaxed, bullied and bribed their way through dozens of staging-points, always having to dodge and outwit the British, who were ruthlessly determined to keep them from achieving their goal—to get the weary refugees over the Alps, down through Italy, and onto a war-worn fleet of old troop-carriers they had bought, begged and borrowed to try to run the British blockade and reach the coast of Palestine.

Yes, the same blockade. Only worse this time—far worse. There was not one man, woman or child aboard those rusty

*For exciting details of Bricha, read *The Story of Israel* by Meyer Levin.

old tubs who had not suffered beyond imagination. Again the British troops had the terrible job of intercepting the boats, towing them into Haifa harbor, and then dragging their weeping, screaming passengers off to detention camps in Cyprus, looking all too terribly like the camps they had thought only the Nazis knew how to build.

Of the sixty-three ships that set off in hope from Italy in the three years between the end of the war and 1948, no fewer than fifty-seven were intercepted, after desperate voyages. The scenes in Haifa shocked the world. They maddened the Jews. The most humane, the most patient, the most anti-violent and pro-British, could stand no more. At this point, who can blame them? Bevin and his obstinacy was largely responsible for the spiral of terror and counter-terror that followed.

The Haganah declared war at last on the White Paper government. It stopped its efforts to suppress the terrorist groups, and joined with them instead—on condition that they would obey Haganah orders. Irgun and even Lehi agreed, but they made a condition too. They were not willing to give up their separate identities. Haganah had fought them once. Things could change again. Meanwhile, for the first time, all the Jewish fighters were on the same side. Bevin had united them. They called themselves the Jewish Resistance Force.

The first thing they did was to make a blunder.

They sent telegrams to the Zionist headquarters in London to tell of a planned joint operation against British installations. The telegrams were intercepted by British intelligence and brought to Bevin. They were all he needed.

Next time Weizmann came to see him, he waved the decoded telegrams at him, shouting: "If you want a fight, you can have it!" The messages, which spoke of plans for "a single serious incident," confirmed Bevin's conviction that every Jew in the Yishuv was a terrorist, bent on driving the British out of Palestine. How dared they oppose their will to his? How could they be so ungrateful? Bevin began to hate the Jews with absolutely obsessive viciousness.

The "incident" took place at the end of October. The Palmach (Haganah's striking force) sank three British patrol boats and blew up railway lines in fifty different places. The Irgun attacked Lydda railway station. Lehi's target was the Haifa oil-works.

All these operations were carried out with great skill and almost no loss of life, thanks to the Haganah's strict orders to avoid bloodshed.

There were two immediate results. The British public woke up to the Palestine problem. And Bevin grew more determined than ever not to give way.

Thus the name of Bevin became almost as hated in the Yishuv as Hitler's. And the British soldiers who were there to do Bevin's bidding—ordinary decent boys, most of them, though the spiral of violence was soon to turn some into brutes—began to be looked on as "oppressors," "tyrants," "the enemy." Jewish children swore and spat at them in the streets, as Irish children do today (and, let's not forget, as Arab children did to Israeli troops in the West Bank after it was captured in 1967).

Bevin poured more and more troops into Palestine in an obstinate determination to fulfill his policy. The more troops, arms and camps there were, of course, the easier it was for the Jewish Resistance Force to pick targets. In joint operations over nine months, they blew up police stations, staged arms raids on camps and trains, destroyed observation and radar emplacements, and bombed offices, railways, boats and (Haganah's speciality) bridges. In one operation Haganah blew up all eleven bridges linking Palestine with the neighboring states.

How did they get on together, these three groups who had been so divided in their aims and methods?

Haganah, like most of the Yishuv, had learned to hate the Irgun, and even more the ruthless Sternists. Now they were united under one command, it was like holding a tiger by the tail.

The Irgun, for their part, thought the Haganah rather lacking in daring and enterprise.* They chafed at the restrictions on actions of their own, especially those that might result in capturing weapons, of which there were never enough. The Irgun had always believed that war with the Arabs was inevitable, and were eager to stockpile arms. Every gun—especially mortars—they could lay their hands on was a cause for rejoicing. They resented the Haganah, who seemed to them to be keeping the lion's share of any booty for themselves.

Lehi despised both for their scruples against murder, and bided their time, only waiting for an excuse to get back to their old methods.

With violence increasing week by week, a challenge was thrown at the new American President, Truman. Bevin and Attlee were heartily sick of Truman at this time. He had blandly urged that the 100,000 should be let in, but what he hadn't done was offer any American troops to help keep order when they arrived, or any dollars to pay for their settlement. So now, said Bevin and Attlee, let's see what you Americans have to offer apart from sanctimonious advice. Let America and Britain each supply six members of yet another Commission to see if a solution can't be reached.

Bevin said two things before the twelve-man Anglo American Commission started its work. If they presented their report unanimously, he would put their recommendations into practice. If they couldn't agree, Britain would turn to the United Nations—the new international organization which had replaced the failed League of Nations—and hand the wet, squalling, monster-baby of Palestine over to them.

*Menachem Begin, *The Revolt.*

So this latest group of well-meaning men set off on their Mission Impossible.

They were very conscientious. They traveled all over Europe first of all, listening, looking, learning. They found out there really were about 100,000 refugees who were set, heart and soul, on going to Palestine and to nowhere else. How could they be expected to live in Europe any more? Who could they look in the face with trust, where could they turn and not see ghosts and graveyards, gas chambers, lime pits, ovens, and the shadows of black SS uniforms? By the time the commission arrived in the Middle East itself, they were convinced to a man that, whatever other recommendations they made, these poor people must be given permission to come in.

But then they began to meet Arabs.

The Arabs had, from the beginning, flatly refused to agree to even the 1,500 a month that Bevin had suggested. "It's not our fault that the Nazis killed the Jews," they said (and have gone on saying ever since). "Why should *we* pay for it? Let the Europeans, who did the harm, look after the refugees. We don't want them here." The Commission began to see things differently. They began to realize that the British troops would have to hold down the Arabs of Palestine if thousands of Jews were to be poured in to swell the Yishuv. This was not such a simple matter, after all. Who was right? Whose country was it, anyway?

They began to interview the men on the spot. Ben-Gurion, when his turn to give evidence before the Commission came, was unusually cagey. He pretended not to know what "Haganah" was! His main emphasis was on accusing the British government. Begin, who was still a wanted man, didn't come forward to testify. It was left to Weizmann to give some straight answers.

"This is not a choice," he said, as he had often said before "between a right and a wrong as far as the Jews and Arabs are concerned. It is a choice between a greater and a lesser injustice."

What did he mean? It's important to know, because what he meant is still true.

Both peoples claimed the region. Both had some title to it. Both needed it. But since it was impossible to satisfy both, then the *degree* of need must be the deciding factor.

The need of the 100,000 was obviously the greater. These Jews—in fact, the whole remains of the Jewish people—must have a homeland. The Holocaust had been the final proof that no other solution was possible. To do a great right, therefore, Weizmann urged the British to do a little wrong. After all, before they came to power Labor leaders had even talked of encouraging the Arabs to move out as the Jews moved in. How could these same leaders turn around now and refuse these desperate people what they *had* to have?

"Give those 100,000 a refuge," begged Weizmann. "Give us the remnant of our people, and we may reconsider our demand for statehood." (Weizmann, don't forget, had always seen the future of the Jewish homeland as part of the British Commonwealth.)

But to Ben-Gurion, this was akin to treachery. The whole of the Yishuv now strained after statehood. Better a state without the 100,000 than the 100,000 without a state.

The Commission heard conflicting testimony from all sides, for months. Then they wrestled for a solution they could all agree to, trusting Bevin to keep his promise. Eventually they managed it.

The country, they said, could neither be turned over to the Arabs nor to the Jews. Nor was partition the answer. Somehow (they didn't say how, exactly) the Jews and Arabs must be made to run it *together.*

For the rest, the 100,000 must come in at once, and the White Paper restrictions on Jewish immigration and land-buying must cease.

What they called "private armies" (meaning the Irgun and Lehi, presumably) should be disbanded.

And dancing by British troops at cafés by the Sea of Galilee should stop because it was a holy site.

This last was the only suggestion Bevin acted on. It wasn't the sheer impracticability of the rest that drove him, and Attlee, into a fury. They saw the whole report as a sell-out to the Jews. When President Truman enthusiastically backed it, that put the lid on things. A look of implacable anger and stubbornness settled over the fat features of Ernest Bevin. What Churchill was to call the "squalid war" between him and the Jews had begun.

LETTER 20

Terror: "Only Thus"?

Attlee made a speech in the House of Commons in May 1946, shortly after the Anglo-American Commission had made its report. Before anything could be done about implementing its proposals, he said, all the "illegal armies" in the region would have to disband.

When he said this, he did not mean just the terrorist organizations. He meant the Haganah. The Haganah, which had, in an undercover sort of way, worked with the British on and off for years, which had helped to fight terrorism, whose men had been employed during the world war on all sorts of dangerous missions. But the British had been careful never to recognize the Haganah officially. Now they demanded that the Yishuv strip itself naked of all defense, except what the British themselves had to offer. The Yishuv and the Jewish Agency were dumbfounded.

The Sternists reacted first. Dodging out from under the umbrella of the Jewish Resistance command, they attacked a British patrol guarding a parking lot of no strategic importance. They killed seven out of the eight soldiers.

At that, the British troops began to lose their patience.
A group of them broke into a Jewish settlement and went
on a rampage, beating up the Jews and damaging property. It was the first act of British counter-terror, but it was
not to be the last. The British public became convinced that
Zionism equaled terrorism, and a cry was raised to pull the
troops out of Palestine.

But Ernest Bevin wasn't beaten yet. He ordered every
prominent Zionist in Palestine to be arrested and interned
in a prison camp at Latrun. The harassed British administrators on the spot were delighted to oblige. In a mighty
swoop they rounded up some 2,600 prominent Jews and
put them under lock and key at Latrun. Only a few, Ben-
Gurion among them, got wind of the purge in advance and
slipped through the net to Paris.

Of all the stupid things the administration ever did, this
was surely one of the maddest. They had locked up some
of Britain's best friends among the Jews, including those
who for years had been counseling moderation and restraint. Now restraint was, for the time, abandoned. The
biggest and (from the point of view of casualties) blackest
operation in the history of Jewish underground resistance
was mounted: the blowing up of the King David Hotel.

For years afterwards there were conflicting accounts of
the background of this attack, and where the responsibili-
ties for it really lay. The Irgun never denied—in fact they
boasted—that they had done the deed; but they said that
they had done it in cooperation with the Haganah. The
Haganah denied all responsibility at first. It's now pretty
clear, however, that the Haganah was involved. What seems
to have happened was this:

During the British swoop on the Jewish Agency headquarters, a number of secret papers had been taken which
implicated the Agency leaders in a number of operations
against the British. The Haganah was anxious that these
should be destroyed. So together with the Irgun commanders, they planned the destruction of one wing of the hotel,

which was the headquarters of the British Administration.

The policy of the Haganah was always to avoid blood-shed. The original plan was that the explosion should take place during the long lunch break, between one and three, when the offices would be largely empty. A warning would be given fifteen minutes beforehand to give everyone a chance to evacuate the hotel completely.

But several things went wrong. First of all it proved in-convenient for the Irgun to place the bomb during the lunch break, probably because they would have been more conspicuous then, even in their disguise (they loved dress-ing up) as milkmen—the explosives were hidden in churns. So they decided to time the explosion for 12:30 when the building would be full. At that point the Haganah drew back, and ordered the Irgun to stop the operation. Mena-chem Begin and his operational leader, a man called Gideon Paglin, decided to go ahead anyway.

A warning was telephoned to the hotel, and to other places too. Why wasn't it taken? Legend has it that the British officer in charge at the King David remarked, "We are here to give orders to the Jews, not to take them," and refused to order the hotel evacuated. Whatever happened, the explosion destroyed the whole southwest wing of the Hotel and killed and injured nearly 200—British, Jewish and Arab.

The world let out a roar of outrage. The Irgun looked with genuine dismay at the devastating casualty figures, and turned to the Haganah to share the responsibility. The Haganah refused. The Jewish Agency reacted with holy horror to the affair. Indeed with most of its top men in jail, it was able to claim innocence. Its members knew better, however, and were appalled at the violence and intrigue they had enmeshed themselves in. Though they now shared with the Irgun the aim of opposing British policy in Palestine, the terrorists' methods smote their consciences. There must, even now, be a less bloody road to statehood than this!

The truce between the "legal" and the "illegal" fighters was broken off.

Bevin was now getting desperate. Up ahead he saw the end of the Mandate, which, for him, spelled DEFEAT in large letters.

The camps in Cyprus were overflowing with refugees intercepted on their way to Haifa. Children were dying there. But still they kept coming. The camp in Latrun was full of Zionists. But still the terrorists kept attacking. Many British installations had to be turned into fortresses, stiff with rolls of barbed wire and searchlights and guns—the Yishuv mockingly called them "Bevingrad," after Stalingrad, the Russian fortress town which barricaded itself against the German army. Sabotage and murder were the order of the day for Irgun and Lehi, loosed from Haganah restraint. The Yishuv was torn between horror at the repression brought down on them by terrorist actions, and a reluctant sympathy. It was hard not to rejoice when the ever-more-hated British were thrown into confusion by some daring raid on an airport, a prison or an arms depot.

The rejoicing stopped when counter-terror squads were formed by some British units, which, in their turn, terrorized Jewish settlements. Arms searches grew really rough at this time. Again kibbutzim were turned upside down, and some British soldiers, infuriated by the terrorists' hit-and-run tactics, so far forgot decency as to write things like "Hitler should have finished the job" on the walls of kibbutz buildings before they left.

Soon there were terrorists in all the main prisons, some wearing the red uniform of those condemned to death.* But for a long time, despite everything, there was no actual execution.

---

* About ten years later, your father happened to be in Acre one day when the film *Exodus* was being made, and ran into the film unit shooting scenes of the famous Acre Prison break. He was invited to be an extra and was sent to be fitted with his costume. This turned out to be the dark

But nonetheless, 1947 was a year of desperate measures. Bevin had staked his political career on forcing the Jews to submit to his will for them. He came down on them with sledgehammer blows after every terrorist attack, and every blow was answered with more bombs, more murders, more terror all round. Then the administration did a very ugly and stupid thing. They decided to try an old colonial remedy: flogging.

They announced that they would flog two young men of the Irgun as a punishment. The Irgun said that if they did it, two British officers would be kidnapped and flogged in return. The British carried out their threat. The Irgun carried out theirs. The floggings stopped. But the executions started. An Irgun fighter called Dov Gruner was hanged in Acre Prison.

The Irgun kidnapped—not officers this time, because they were too hard to catch, but two British sergeants. When these two young men were hanged in retaliation for the hanging of three men of the Irgun, the uproar in Britain forced the government to realize that the Mandate could not be carried on much longer.

The terrorists were achieving what they had wanted— getting the British out of Palestine. Did that justify their actions, as they still claim to this day?

The answering of flogging with flogging and hanging with hanging would, I believe, have been a sort of rough justice if the flogged officers, and the hanged sergeants, had had any personal responsibility for the punishments given to the Irgun men. But the killing or torturing of hostages taken at random can never be right. Whatever it seems to "achieve" is only achieved at the cost of what Weizmann called "profound moral deterioration." As he

---

red prison uniform worn by the condemned. When he emerged in this sinister outfit, other extras who knew its significance, and people in the town, reacted with horror, almost shrinking away from him. That's why he is not in the film—he refused to come back the next day.

said, terrorism was "tragic, futile, unJewish . . . an unmitigated curse."

To inspire *fear,* which the terrorists certainly did, is not the same as inspiring *respect,* which is what they wanted. Their experiences, as individuals and as inheritors of Jewish history, had made them desperate to prove to Britain— to the whole world—that Jews can fight back, that here in their "own place" they would not be treated as British colonialists were used to treating the natives of Africa and India, deciding what was best for them and punishing those who dared to rebel. In doing this, they made it inevitable that they *would* be punished, and incidentally that the entire Yishuv would suffer. They took a sort of self-defeating pleasure in courting capture and even death, regarding themselves as martyrs to the cause of Jewish national pride. In actual fact, they were self-sacrifices to Jewish shame. Begin says that "Jewish backs everywhere straightened" as a result of Irgun actions. The only Jewish backs that stayed straight after the first, superficial thrill caused by Jewish militancy were those of men like Ben Hecht, an American-Jewish writer who publicly proclaimed that every time a British soldier was killed in Palestine he had "a little holiday in (his) heart." Such Jews were the victims, though unmarked physically, of Hitler and all the other persecutors of the past. They were the spiritual non-survivors.

The Irgun badge showed a fist, gripping a rifle with a fixed bayonet. The motto below was Jabotinsky's: "Only Thus."

They believed then, and most of those who are still around believe now, that "only thus"—by the gun and the knife, through blood and fire—could Israel be reborn.

All questions of higher morality, you may one day say to me, must wait upon this question: Was it "only thus"? Was Irgun's way, ultimately, right?

To answer that, I must explain the Jewish Agency's way, the way that opposed terrorism most of the time, though sometimes circumstances grew so bad that they were forced to deviate from their policy of self-restraint.

This policy is called in Hebrew *havlagah*. The fighting arm of the Jewish Agency had followed it as closely as possible since the thirties, and, considering the tremendous provocation offered by the Arabs and, just before and just after the World War, by the British, it is something of which Israelis may be extremely proud.

What exactly did *havlagah* involve? Basically it meant that the Haganah rejected counter-terror, or anything more than self-defense in the face of Arab assaults or British provocation. They refused to throw bombs into crowded Arab markets or buses, as the Irgun did. They stood firm and did their best to defend what was theirs, but they tried to avoid shedding innocent blood.

The terror gangs, trying to goad the "regular" Jewish forces into joining them in their policy of random reprisals, retaliations and attacks, openly scoffed at the policy of *havlagah* as weak, cowardly, treacherous. But it was none of these.

It was, instead, the policy by which the official Jewish leadership not only retained its moral authority but gave itself time to create the foundations for the State of Israel.

If they had, at an earlier stage, joined the Irgun in its shortsighted policy of get-the-British-out-at-any-cost, one of two things would have happened. The British *would* have pulled out, before the Jewish leaders were in any sense ready to take over authority and face the Arab threat. Or —and this was always a dread possibility, right to the end of the Mandate—Bevin could have given orders to his 100,000 troops on the spot, plus a squadron of RAF bombers, to smash the Yishuv altogether.

The cooperativeness, responsibility and moderation of the official Jewish leaders (in general—there were lapses, of course) made it impossible for the British to take such drastic action. As one British politician laconically remarked, "I doubt if the world would stand by and watch another massacre of the Jews." The Irgun, on the other hand, simply invited retaliation, and, I suspect, rather glo-

ried in trials and jailings and punishments in its eagerness
for martyrdom.

In Begin's melodramatic account, every terrorist operation becomes a death-defying act of heroism, every plan a
stroke of military genius, every Irgun soldier a candidate
for sainthood. In all this highly-colored prose, the essence
of what the Irgun was doing tends to be lost.

What they were actually doing was risking the whole
Yishuv. It must be said that if any nation *except* the British
had held the Mandate—the French, say, or the Russians—
there would have been a catastrophe. The Israelis themselves admit this. *The Irgun, while mocking the self-restraint of
the official Jewish leaders, was absolutely counting on the same quality in the British.* If it hadn't existed (again, with lapses) the
whole Yishuv would have been doomed by the rash acts of
Irgun and the Sternists.

They could see no further than getting Britain out. They
had no long-term aims. They never built a hospital or a
school, or even a house. They didn't drain a single dunam
of land or plant a tree. The Revisionists were never interested in settlement, never saw the point of it. They wanted
Jewish independence, but beyond fighting for it they did
nothing at all to secure it. The fact that nationhood means
farms, factories, food supplies, trade, education, services,
and day-to-day existence, never entered Irgun's calcula-
tions. All the time they were blindly hurling themselves
(very often abortively) against the British, mainstream
Zionism was quietly building up the whole superstructure
of the future state.

They were also building up their moral authority, which
later enabled them to take over the administration of every
section of the Yishuv, from the armed forces to the trade
unions, from the transportation system to the education
and health services. If they had not done that, no Jewish
state could have come into existence, because nothing is
more certain than that the Revisionists, led by Mr. Begin,
were in no position to do it.

LETTER 21

The Mandate's Violent End

The reprisal murder of the two British sergeants happened at the same time as the episode of the real-life *Exodus,* the refugee ship on which Leon Uris based his book and the film of that name.

Neither the book nor the film was much like the actual story, which had anything but a triumphant end. The *Exodus,* after the usual hair-raising journey, was sent back to France. The French agreed to receive the refugees, but only if they would disembark willingly. They refused. Your father, who was then in Port de Bouc, near Marseilles, waiting to set off on his own illegal immigration, saw the *Exodus* sitting for days in the harbor while negotiations went on. In the end, almost unbelievably, the British government decided to ship the refugees back where they had started from—Germany.* Amid horrifying scenes of vio-

---

*It's been suggested they would have been brought to England but for the strong anti-Jewish feeling caused there by the hanging of the two sergeants, which had caused ugly demonstrations against Jews in several English towns.

lent resistance, watched by a shocked world, the refugees were dragged ashore at Hamburg and reinterned in the same camp they had left many weeks before.

One of the most amazing aspects of this disgraceful affair was the fact that the British let it happen just when the last of *nineteen* Commissions had come to Palestine to collect evidence to submit to the United Nations. Britain had at last turned to them, in February of 1947, for help in finding a solution to the problem of Palestine. If none were found, the British said, they were leaving. They had had enough.

The Commission, called UNSCOP,* witnessed not only the scenes on the *Exodus* which forced them to acknowledge the urgency of the refugees' plight and the intransigence of the British. They were also "shown" by the Irgun how a minority of Jews reacted. A detail Mr. Begin omits from his account of the episode of the sergeants was that the body of one of the men was booby-trapped, a vicious act of spite hardly calculated to inspire the men of the UNSCOP with hope for a peaceful future in the area, whatever they should decide.

Their recommendations were published in early September 1947.

Basically these were: an end to the Mandate as soon as possible, but in any case not later than August 1, 1948 (about eleven months later). And the partition of Palestine into two states, one Jewish, one Arab.

They drew a map which divided the country in such a complex way one can scarcely work out who was to get what. An earlier partition map had been described as "consisting of three segments, entwined in an inimical embrace like two fighting serpents." This one's six segments were even more so.

The Jews were to have the eastern and western parts of Galilee, the coastal plain including one wholly Arab town

*United Nations Special Commission on Palestine.

(Jaffa) but excluding another (Acre). They were also to get most of the Negev Desert. The Arabs were to get the rest of the Negev, a large central slice of Galilee, and the whole of what we now know as the West Bank of the Jordan, except Jerusalem, which was not to belong to either side. It was to be a neutral international zone.

The Jews were not what you'd call satisfied with their allotment, but they accepted the plan gladly. Hadn't Weizmann said that Jews should accept even if their part was only the size of a tablecloth? Anything to have a state of their own into which, at long last, they could freely bring the refugees.

The Arab governments, one and all, rejected the proposals. A chunk here and a lump here did not interest them. Like Jabotinsky, their watchword was: "It's all ours."

Meanwhile the British announced that although they didn't like the plan, they accepted the part about ending the Mandate. They would leave as soon as they reasonably could, they hoped in the coming May.

Well and good. But there was a difficulty. *Nobody believed they meant it.* Who had ever heard of a great nation abandoning a territory where it had an interest and a responsibility, leaving such a mess behind? Surely they wouldn't really go! No one was less certain that they would than the British government themselves. What, lose Haifa, lose their vast army bases in the Eastern Mediterranean? Leave the field open for France or Russia? Announcing their departure was a dramatic gesture. But actually leaving!

Meanwhile the twin announcements of (possible) partition and (possible) British withdrawal had a number of effects. Whether they were really going to happen or not, the interested parties had to plan as if they were.

The first question to consider was, would the UN vote in favor of partition? No one could answer this, but most people reckoned that, since the U.S. and Russia never, ever agreed about anything, one or other of them would scotch the plan. Britain was certain of this. The Jews, who desper-

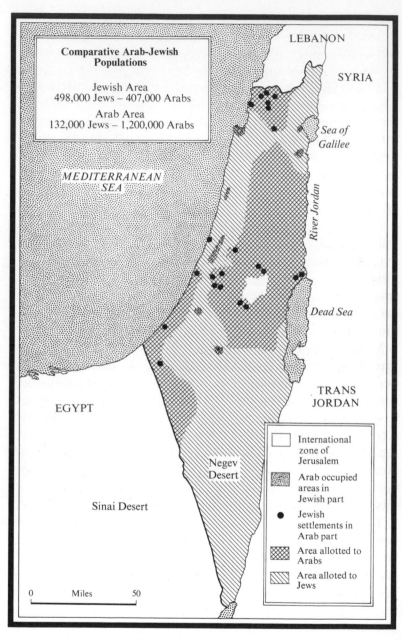

Comparative Arab-Jewish Populations

Jewish Area
498,000 Jews – 407,000 Arabs

Arab Area
132,000 Jews – 1,200,000 Arabs

LEBANON

SYRIA

Sea of Galilee

MEDITERRANEAN SEA

River Jordan

Dead Sea

TRANS JORDAN

EGYPT

Negev Desert

Sinai Desert

International zone of Jerusalem

Arab occupied areas in Jewish part

Jewish settlements in Arab part

Area allotted to Arabs

Area alloted to Jews

0   Miles   50

U.N. Partition Plan

ately wanted world recognition of their right to a state, had to hope and pray. The Arabs didn't voice an opinion. They were busy answering the second question: if and when the British left, would there be a war?

The Jewish Agency leaders, on the whole, thought not. The Yishuv in general thought not. How they deluded themselves, when many Arab spokesmen were issuing loud threats, is hard to understand. Perhaps they were just too overjoyed at the prospect of becoming a sovereign nation again after 2,000 years. The problems and possibilities of statehood, absorbing the refugees and so on, left them with little slack.

Ben-Gurion, however, was more clear-sighted. He saw war as an inevitability. *His* chief concern at that time was to get the Haganah in shape to defend the new state. He fought to raise money for arms, to find ways of buying and smuggling them in; he insisted on training and organizing every able-bodied man and woman in the Yishuv, so far as the British allowed—which, as I shall explain, wasn't far.

Meanwhile, the Arab leaders weren't keen on all-out war with the Jews. They didn't yet realize that they'd got their people so inflamed with hate-propaganda against Zionism that they would be forced to go to war whether they wanted to or not. But they didn't want to be left out of any land-scramble that followed British departure. So they made separate plans, each country for itself—regardless of the fact that in theory they were all (except Transjordan) members of the new Arab league, created by the British, which was supposed to bring them all together in happy union.

The Syrians and the Lebanese wanted chunks of Northern Palestine. The Transjordanians, under Hussein's grandfather, King Abdullah, wanted the whole of the Arab part of Palestine. The Egyptians weren't about to let him get away with that—they had their eye on the Negev at least, if not Tel Aviv. The Saudis and the Iraqis made plenty of saber-rattling noises for fear of being left out, while the Mufti, Amin El Husseini, together with his terror gangs,

sprang back into action in an open determination to drive
the Jews out completely and take over the whole of Palestine himself.

Abdullah of Transjordan held a number of secret meet-
ings, not only with the British but with the Zionists—represented by Golda Meir. To her he said that he welcomed a
Jewish community in the region and would not attack a
Jewish state, nor would he stand by and watch Syria, Iraq
or any other country annex any part of the Arab area. He
wanted peace. Therefore he would, with his own Arab Legion (the finest army in the Arab world, officered and
trained by Britons) fill the gap left by the withdrawing British. He promised not to join the Arab League, which would
certainly commit him to action against the Jews.

To the British he told a different tale. He hinted that the
Jews would try to grab more than their alloted share of
Palestine when the British withdrew, and for that reason he
had better send troops in to protect the interests of the
Palestinian Arabs. Bevin said that seemed sensible, so long
as he didn't invade the Jewish area. It's now fairly clear,
though, that the British anticipated some fighting, and were
expecting (if not hoping) that it would result in the Arabs
finishing up with more territory than the UN had allotted
to them. That could leave the Jews cowering in a little
mini-state which would be impossible to defend or run
economically, and if *that* happened they would have to beg
the British to return and run it for them. That way, with the
Jews dependent and submissive and Jordan already a British ally, the British wouldn't lose their influence in the
region by withdrawing after all. They could even look forward to a quick and permanent recovery of Haifa, their only
Eastern Mediterranean port.

With these Machiavellian considerations in mind, the
British became firmer about their intention to pull out.

In the last quarter of 1947, there were two important
developments. As early as September, there began to be
skirmishes, as irregular Arab fighters (many of them the

Mufti's men) infiltrated across the borders and started harassing the Jews. These disorders (to use the favorite British euphemism) increased in seriousness, with the British doing very little about them, till November 29. This is a very important date in Jewish history. It was the day on which the United Nations Assembly voted on the resolution to partition Palestine into two sovereign states.

In Palestine every Jew crouched over his radio, pencil and paper in hand, marking down the votes as they were announced. As each "no" vote came through there was a groan, each "yes" vote being greeted by a cheer. Toward the end the cheers became wilder, the groans deeper, for "the hopes and fears of all the years" were indeed met in the UN that night. If the required two-thirds of the member nations approved, the Jews would have their own state, not imposed by force but accorded, as of right, by a majority of the world community.

The greatest surprise was that both Russia and America voted *for* partition. So did thirty-one other governments. Thirteen, including all the Arab nations, voted against. The rest—including Britain—abstained from voting at all.

But no matter. Thirty-three votes was enough. Partition was approved. The Jews were to have their state, and so, of course, were the Palestinian Arabs, if they were prepared to act on the UN decision. But unfortunately they weren't. Unlike the Zionists they had made no preparations for statehood, and were not, *at that time,* a coherent national group in any sense.

The first thing Britain did after the vote was to announce that, for her part, she would do nothing to enforce any solution which did not have the approval of both Arabs and Jews. Since the Arabs had made it abundantly clear that the only solution they could approve would be the removal of the Jews, or at least the handing over of all authority to an Arab regime, and since the Jews were not likely to go along with *that,* what the British were really saying was this: We don't recognize any solution; we will not cooperate with

any other power. We are in a ghastly mess and must pull
out of it but in the meantime nobody else is going to step
in and make us look foolish.

The most shocking period of the entire Mandate now
began.

Almost the moment the UN vote was announced, the
Arab irregulars launched attacks on Jews everywhere in the
Middle East. In Palestine itself, members of the self-styled
Arab Liberation Army (not to be confused with Abdullah's
Arab Legion, which was holding its hand till the British got
out) began entering the country in large battalions.

The boldness they showed, with the British still there in
force, is astonishing. There's no doubt that the British
could have seen off these Arab invaders in short order, and
many Arab commanders beyond the borders expected
them to do so. When they didn't, more and more Arab
irregulars entered the country, and pretty soon the "disorders" had reached a state of war, though it wasn't yet called
that.

These Arabs laid firm hold on the roads, especially the
vital one leading from Tel Aviv to Jerusalem. Buses were
overturned, cars set on fire, convoys ambushed. Towns and
villages were attacked; there were orgies of murder, arson
and looting. The enormous force of British soldiers and
police, whose one clear duty was to keep order, did very
little, except in one or two places where they managed to
arrive in time; on these occasions they easily drove the
Arabs off.

This one-sided behavior on the part of the British forces
goaded the Jewish terrorist forces to more and more extreme lengths. Sabotage and murder by the Irgun and the
Lehi in turn made the ordinary British soldiers more and
more angry.

From Westminster, the British government watched as
you might watch a scene of growing chaos in a dream—
knowing you should act, but somehow lacking the will to do
so effectively. British officers and administrators on the

spot were left without clear guidance. They knew they were supposed to wind up the Mandate and get ready to move out. They were under orders* not to get embroiled on either side in the mounting conflict. But how? What *was* British policy? It seems she hadn't one. What would happen in Palestine after the British left was never even discussed by the Labor cabinet. The whole burden of day-to-day decisions fell on the troops on the spot. And they were largely pro-Arab.

It was reckoned that no matter what men's views were when they arrived in Palestine, after serving there a short time seventy-five percent of them became anti-Jewish and pro-Arab. Why? One officer gave a lot away when he remarked, "It's because the Arab is below your level. If he were educated and your equal, you mightn't like him so much."† In other words, your average Briton tends to favor the underdog and also likes to feel superior to the people he is responsible for. The Jews denied him that. This caused a basic dislike. In addition the terrorist campaign, spread over years but now reaching its climax, was reaping its harvest of hatred. Inflamed by the Irgun and Sternist atrocities, the troops were quite ready to see the Jews paid out by the Arab bands of the Mufti. Only some of the officers sometimes stepped in and tried to keep discipline and "fair play."

Historians of all opinions have been bewildered ever since by the blend of obstinacy and ineffectiveness with which the British Government handled this crisis. You might compare it to people who are moving out of a house where they have had nothing but trouble. It's already in a state of chronic disrepair; now, having sold it recklessly into the hands of two feuding families, they are packing up to go, caring nothing about maintenance or structural repair,

---

*Issued, ironically, by a Jew—the Minister of Defense, Emmanuel Shinwell.
†R. Crossman, *Palestine Mission.*

let alone cleaning the place. What does it matter if the roof falls in or the rats run riot? They are leaving.

In vain the UN begged to be allowed to come in before the British left and try to prepare for the birth of the two new states. Had not Britain turned to the UN for help in solving the problem? Why would she not now allow some-one else to implement the solution, even if she was unwill-ing to do so herself? But no. "We can cope, leave us alone!" was the general message the UN got. With 100,000 soldiers, *one for every five Jews,* and 2,000 policemen in the area, it would have been a disgrace to admit that in fact, coping was just what the British could not do.

The last months were a disgrace indeed, a fitting end to the chaos and confusion of the last years of the Mandate. Like a cumbersome truck rolling downhill with no driver to apply its brakes, the British army in Palestine went blindly on, ferreting out arms, dragging immigrants off to Cyprus, frustrating the legitimate efforts of the Agency and the Haganah to prepare for British departure. It was just as if there had been no UN decision, as if there were not going to be a Jewish state, needing to be peopled and defended, in a very short while.

Though much of this idiocy can be put down to a lack of direction from London, one firm order they did get was to disarm both sides to discourage fighting. Both Arabs and Jews claim that this was done unfairly, to favor the other; but considering that the sea blockade was effectively pre-venting the Jews from bringing in arms, while meantime the British government was busy making massive deals to supply Egypt, Jordan and Iraq with weapons, there isn't much doubt which side was really being favored.

Armed Arab bands were still entering and roaming the country unchecked; and as the date of British withdrawal—May 14, 1948—drew near, the Jews saw that the British were handing over most of their major strongholds to the Arabs. These included the so-called Teggart Forts, built as police stations but almost impregnable, and the huge army base of Sarafand. The strategic points in several mixed towns such as Safed (where the Jews had already suffered terribly from Arab attacks) were also put into Arab hands, virtually dooming the remaining Jews. Perhaps worst of all, the strongholds overlooking the Jerusalem–Tel Aviv road were put, or left, in Arab hands, effectively cutting off the Jewish community in Jerusalem (which formed a supposedly neutral island in the hostile sea of the Arab area) and leaving them defenseless and without supplies.

The situation in the country had reached the point not just of chaos, but of a kind of schizophrenic madness. The British officials went on with their day-to-day lives, going to their offices, proceeding with the work of winding up the Mandate. The administration buildings were now so heavily guarded and fortified that they were effectively cut off from the life of the people they were supposed to be responsible for. And meanwhile, all over the country, undeclared civil war was raging with scarcely any action being taken to stop it.

To return to my metaphor of the house, the new joint owners, the feuding families, were already in possession and were murdering each other in every room, while the outgoing family was barricaded into a couple of the lavatories finishing their packing and only worried about whether they were going to get out alive. The ground landlords (the UN) kept offering to send in the police, but the outgoing owners repeatedly said that there was no need and that anyway, they'd still got the keys and they wouldn't let the police in.

On May 14, Sir Alan Cunningham, the last British Commissioner to Palestine, boarded a British naval vessel in Haifa and, with the remnant of his staff, sailed away. He must have been a very unhappy man. Twenty-seven years of British occupation, which at the beginning had done a great deal for the country, lay behind him in ruins.

That same afternoon, David Ben-Gurion stood up in a small stuffy hall in the Tel Aviv Museum. It was packed with leaders of the Yishuv, 200 men and women who had striven for years to bring this moment about.

The proclamation Ben-Gurion read was fairly brief. It outlined the history of Jewish separation from, and faithfulness to, the Land. It reviewed the legal title the Jews now claimed—the Balfour Declaration, ratified by the League of Nations and the United Nations. And the moral title: the need, proved by the Holocaust, for an independent national home which they could defend themselves, and the fact that by their contributions to the allied war-effort the Jews had earned their right to join the family of nations. Furthermore: "It is the natural right of the Jewish people to lead, as do all other nations, an independent existence in its sovereign State."

The unanswerable claim.

Ben-Gurion then proclaimed the establishment of a Jewish state in Palestine, to be called the State of Israel.

He appointed a thirteen-member provisional government.

He declared the new state open to immigration for Jews all over the world.

He said Israel would be based on the principles of liberty, justice and peace and all its citizens would be equal. There would be freedom of religion, conscience, education and culture.

He appealed to the United Nations to admit Israel as a member.

He called on the Arabs within the new borders to join peacefully in the development of the state, on a basis of equal citizenship, and he offered "the hand of peace and neighborliness" to the Arab states.

He sent out a call to Jews everywhere to support the "great struggle for the fulfillment of the dream of generations for the redemption of Israel."

At last he called some thirty members of the audience to sign the Scroll of Independence.* As these privileged few stepped forward one by one, they must all have been aware that it was the most dramatic and important moment in Jewish history since the day the Romans destroyed the Second Temple and scattered the Jews abroad into two millenia of exile. Some were numb with emotion, some exultant, some openly crying as they signed their names.

They were not just moved by the triumph of rebirth. They knew that their action was partly one of defiance. The UN, in the six troubled months since the November vote for partition, had had second thoughts, and were at that very moment urgently discussing some alternative solution. The world was standing back, watching, expecting a new cataclysm for the Jews. And the Arabs had declared quite openly that if the Jews declared their State, there would be "a war of extermination and a momentous massacre which will be spoken of like the Mongol massacres and the Crusades."†

So Israel emerged from the Mandate's inhospitable womb into the unwelcoming arms of the UN midwife; and behind her stood the Arab nations, a giant with an upraised sword. Luckily for the infant state, it was born with armor on its back.

I say armor. God knows—and Ben-Gurion knew—how pitifully thin that armor was. There couldn't have been a single man or woman in that stuffy little hall in Tel Aviv without a deep and proper feeling of fear underlying his

*Dr. Weizmann was not one of them. Ben-Gurion had cunningly stipulated that no one who was out of the country at the time might sign; but the fact was, Weizmann was not invited. He was at that moment in America, making sure that Truman would recognize the new State as soon as it was declared—a diplomatic feat he managed almost single-handed. Although he was made Israel's first President, he was pushed out of the real leadership by Ben-Gurion. Several people close to him, including his wife, told me he never got over it.

†Azzam Pasha, secretary-general of the Arab League.

elation, and very mixed feelings as they filed out through exultantly cheering crowds. (For security reasons, the time and place of the Declaration of Statehood was supposed to be a deadly secret, which, as it turned out, only everybody knew.)

"You see?" said Ben-Gurion in boyish triumph to a British reporter outside the museum. "We did it!" But he was under no illusions. It's one thing to stand up and make history with a declaration. It's quite another to face the immediate and—everyone knew it now—inevitable consequence.

War.

LETTER 22

Liberation and Catastrophe

That first war—which the Jews call The War of Liberation and the Arabs call The Catastrophe—was both a triumph and a tragedy. And I don't mean just a triumph for the Jews and a tragedy for the Arabs, because I believe that that, and every Jewish victory since, has been, in a way, Pyrrhic—that's to say that it's cost too much, not only in lost lives. Every one of those wars (five altogether if you count the War of Attrition in 1968–69) has taken the Jews a step further into isolation from their neighbors, and lately, from the world.

This is not to say that the Arab states were justified in launching their assault on the new-fledged Jewish state in 1948, or that any of the wars since then could have been avoided by the Israelis—not, that is, if you judge by the situation immediately before battle commenced. Each war, although undoubtedly forced on Israel by its hostile neighbors, was built like a flight of steps upon the war before and all the chances lost by both sides in between.

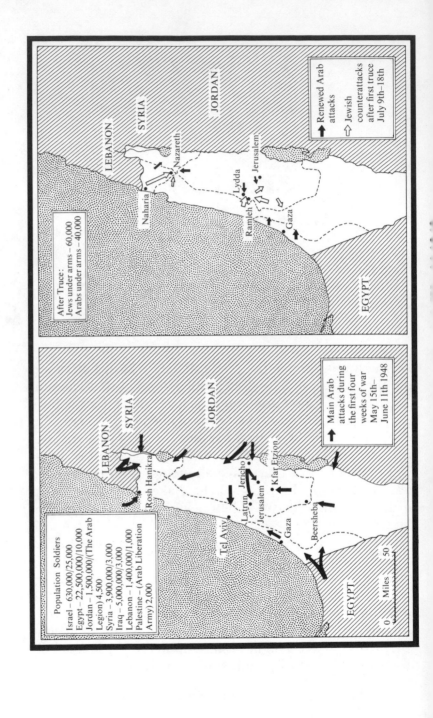

Population Soldiers

Israel – 630,000/25,000
Egypt – 22,500,000/10,000
Jordan – 1,500,000/(The Arab
Legion) 4,500
Syria – 3,900,000/3,000
Iraq – 5,000,000/3,000
Lebanon – 1,400,000/1,000
Palestine – (Arab Liberation
Army) 2,000

LEBANON

SYRIA

JORDAN

Rosh Hanikra

Tel Aviv

Latrun
Jericho

Jerusalem

Kfar Etzion

Gaza

Beersheba

EGYPT

Main Arab
attacks during
the first four
weeks of war
May 15th–
June 11th 1948

0   Miles   50

After Truce:
Jews under arms – 60,000
Arabs under arms – 40,000

LEBANON

SYRIA

JORDAN

Naharia

Nazareth

Lydda

Ramleh

Jerusalem

Gaza

EGYPT

Renewed Arab
attacks

Jewish
counterattacks
after first truce
July 9th–18th

If the Arab states had begun that first war to help their Palestinian brothers, there would have been some justification. But the truth is, not one of them had anything of the sort in mind. They were interested in one thing—trying to grab as much of the disputed territory as possible, or at the least to prevent one of their rivals from gaining anything that could help them in the endless power-struggle that was, and is, going on between the Arab nations.

This war, of course, was fought before the Law of Conquest was called into question. It was an unwritten law, chiefly because it had always been taken for granted: when talking failed to settle disputes about territory, nations could fight—and what they gained by fighting, they kept. Certainly that law was fully operational in 1945, when the victors in the world war hung onto their conquests and divided up the spoils.

So three years later, when the Jews were attacked, they felt free not merely to defend themselves but to enlarge their state if they could. Neither they nor the Arabs accepted the partition lines as final—in fact, as we've seen, the Arabs didn't accept partition at all. So as the Egyptian, Syrian, Iraqi and Transjordanian armies marched on Israel and Israel marched to meet them, it was in the minds of all that war would draw the borders and that the world would accept the outcome. It always had.*

If you look at a map of the Middle East and North Africa and compare the vast territories and populations of the Arab states with Israel and its few hundred thousand Jews, you may jump to the conclusion that it was a case of David against Goliath and that nothing could be more unfair. However, you'd be wrong. The odds were surprisingly

---

*It wasn't till after the Six Day War in 1967 that UN Resolution 242 announced that it was no longer acceptable to world opinion to keep land conquered in war. This was to oblige the Israelis to give back what they had taken. It may have been yet another great step forward for the civilized conscience, but so far I must say it has only been applied to Israel.

even. The Israelis actually had rather *more* fighting men, while the Arabs had the advantage of far more arms. But the Jews had some "secret weapons." And these were not so much the wealthy Jews of the Diaspora, who were more than canceled out by the vast resources of the Arab world.

The grim joke among Israelis, then and later, was that their secret weapon was having "no alternative"—they had to win or go under. But that hadn't kept them from disaster before. Their real secret weapons were the three things necessary to win wars: good leaders who have the support of the majority; territory to stand firm on and defend; and the power-giving conviction of being one nation. None of the Arabs had these. In fact the Jews' other great asset was the disunity, corrupt leadership and lack of motivation of their enemies.

Mind you, the Jews were not exactly models of unity themselves. Few people, in or out of Israel, knew about the burning quarrels raging among their leaders, which endangered not just the outcome of the war but the future of the State itself.

Ben-Gurion had three driving priorities: to hang on to every one of the twenty-five Jewish settlements on the wrong side of the partition lines; to secure Jerusalem, which lay like an island in the midst of Arab territory; and to unite the various "private armies"—Haganah and the Palmach, the dissident Irgun and Lehi—under one command. His generals were pulling in all directions; but most of them argued for concentrating their limited resources on the Jewish heartland within the UN borders, even if it meant sacrificing the outlying settlements and Jerusalem, most of which had been under attack since long before the war started.

As to the different "armies," the Palmach could not stand out against appeals to their loyalty, though there was much bad feeling when their kibbutz-raised commanders were replaced by regular army officers. But the Irgun and Lehi caused endless trouble. At one point there was nearly a civil war right in the middle of the other one, when the Irgun tried to bring in its own weapons and recruits by sea, and only yielded up its separate identity after a pitched battle with the regular troops. The spectacle of Jew shooting Jew on the shores of Tel Aviv shocked the whole nation; but the fact was, Begin didn't have the support of the majority, whereas Ben-Gurion did.

But in the main, the war itself was a unifying factor.

Much of the manpower for the Israeli army was "raw." As soon as the refugees started pouring in from Cyprus and Europe, every able-bodied young man and woman had a gun clapped in their hand and was sent off to fight. Many hardly knew one end of a rifle from the other, nor could they distinguish between the Hebrew for "advance" and "retreat." Small wonder that lives and battles were lost in the resulting confusion.

But your father remembers one occasion, near the beginning, which shows how this motley crew was welded into one army and one people.

A raw recruit himself, he took part in a "training battle." It was a real battle; there was no time (or ammunition) to waste on maneuvers. But the commanders knew that the Arabs in that particular sector wouldn't put up much resistance, so they sent these learner-soldiers against them for practice.

The battle was over almost as soon as it began. The Jewish troops, still taut with nerves, found themselves clustered in a valley. They looked about them. They were very mixed—many of them were sabras, native born Palestinian Jews; some were immigrants from ordinary backgrounds like your father; and some were survivors of the Holocaust, still smarting from their cruel and humiliating ordeal. They hardly had the look of soldiers—some were not even in uniform, but wearing their civilian clothes, in a few cases white Sabbath shirts, now stained with sweat and dust from their first inexperienced charge.

As they stood there, one of them pointed suddenly upward. Over a hilltop appeared a line of heads, which grew into figures; then another rank, and another, marching in good order down the hill towards them. From a second direction came more, and more—Jews coming, marching, rank on rank. Ill equipped, oddly dressed, half trained, but a lot of them, coming together. A Jewish army.

None of them had ever seen, or felt, anything like it, and nor had their forebears for 2,000 years. They experienced a wild elation. Threatened once again with disaster, now they were together on their own soil and they were going to fight. If you can't imagine what that moment meant, I have not told this history properly.

Moments like that—of high drama, inspired by a conscious sense of heroic role-playing in history—were rare, of course. That war, like every war, was ghastly, full of its own immediate agonies, and pregnant with the seeds of future suffering.

The general pattern of the war was this: the Jews took a battering in the first four weeks of the fighting. Then a truce was called by the UN during which no one was supposed to improve their position, or obtain more arms, but everybody did. After that, the Jews, having reorganized their forces and increased their strength, counterattacked with such telling effect that historians now say the final outcome was never in doubt. Easy now to say! There were doubts in plenty at the time among those in the thick of it.

But on the whole, Ben-Gurion's stubborn determination to hold Jerusalem and the outlying settlements paid off. Though the Old City, with its ancient Jewish quarter, surrendered to the Arab Legion after a fearful ordeal by siege and shelling, the New City, which was nearly all Jewish, managed to hold out, thanks to the courage of the soldiers (your father among them) who ran the gauntlet of Arab fire along the road from Tel Aviv bringing supplies, and the ingenuity of others who built a new road through the hills right under the Arabs' noses. Jerusalem was thus split down the middle, half in Jordan, half in Israel.

As to the settlements, only a few were lost; and just as Ben-Gurion had expected, the final armistice lines were drawn round those that held out, which meant that the eventual State of Israel was much larger than the UN had intended.

The Egyptians' first devastating push up through Gaza and eastward into the Negev was eventually foiled, and the Israelis might have captured the whole of Sinai in its counterattack but for the British. *Their* machinations had not come to an end with their departure at the close of the Mandate. They had done all they could, as they left, to give advantages to the Arabs; it was they who delayed the first UN truce while the Jews were losing, and they who rushed in a second truce when the Arabs were. As the war was ending, and in a decisive Jewish victory which was the last thing the British had expected or wanted, they threatened to join in on the Arab side if the Jews didn't give the Egyptians back the part of the Sinai that they'd taken. Though completely defeated, the Egyptians refused to sign the armistice until the Israelis had released the remains of their army, bottled up in the Gaza Strip. As a result, the Strip, filled with refugees and under Egyptian control, remained pointed at Israel's heartland like a festering finger for years to come.

The Transjordanians didn't do at all badly out of the war. They took over a large part of the central sector of Palestine which had been allotted to the Arabs under partition. This is the much-disputed West Bank, which the Israelis in turn captured in 1967. The religious Jews call it Judea and Samaria, say it's part of biblical Israel, and that it would be blasphemy to give it up. The Jordanians say it belongs to them, which is cheeky, because they only got it themselves through marching in and taking it in 1948. The Palestinians who live there obviously have the best claim to it, but the burning question is, what would they do with it? Turn it into a state of their own? Use it as a base for attacking Israel? Or get into such a mess the Russians would take over?

In the first decade after that war, though, the main trouble was firstly that that "bulge" gave Israel a very narrow waist near its most thickly populated area, and, secondly, that the armistice line was drawn *through* the lands of a number of Arab villages. This led to a lot of farmers creeping across the border to tend their land, together with a lot of terrorists creeping across for acts of sabotage. Since the Israelis couldn't tell the difference and were nervous anyway, a lot of both sorts got shot, which bred more hatred.

Abdullah, incidentally, also tried to grab the Negev, which had been allotted to Israel, but the Israelis grabbed it back.

The Syrians got nothing for their pains, in fact they lost some farming land at the foot of the Golan Heights to make a buffer zone between it and Israel. This zone was also the subject of twenty years of strife. Ignoring the fact that it was officially No Man's Land, the Syrian farmers tried to go on farming. The Israelis fired on them. The Syrian guns above would shell the Israeli valley settlements. The Israelis would send planes to bomb the guns . . . and so on. By the time the Israelis stormed the Heights in 1967, the bitter hatred on both sides was as deeply entrenched as the Syrian emplacements, and much harder to root out.

The Lebanese got nothing either, but since they hadn't fought, a sort of tacit agreement came into being between them and Israel. For many years, even after the Six Day War, that border was the quietest. It wasn't till the Palestinians were thrown out of Jordan by King Abdullah's grandson, Hussein, in 1970, and moved their bases to Lebanon, that that front became "hot"—a mere prelude to the inferno of civil war that ruined that unlucky country.

In January 1949, the war was over. An armistice—not a peace treaty, just an agreement to stop fighting—was signed between all the warring countries. It was supposed that, when a few problems had been ironed out, a proper peace would follow. Thirty years later it still hasn't.

The victory cost 6,000 Jewish lives, 2,000 of them civilians, and the Arab casualty figures were higher.

But the dead don't make trouble later. It was the refugees who ran away and "lived to fight another day"—or rather, their children did—whose tragedy cost the Israelis the final security they hoped to win as a result of their military triumph.

Zionists keep saying, "If the Palestinians cared about their land, why didn't they fight? Why did they run away?" To such people, nothing ever changes; their arguments are always fixed in the past. Might they not as well ask why the Jews of other times "ran away"? The answer, in both cases, is the same: they lacked the three essentials I mentioned before. They did not *feel* their nationhood. Even those few who owned the land they occupied lacked a full realization of its value to them—until they'd lost it. Then they knew. As the Jews knew, thousands of years ago, only when they found themselves cut off from it.

As to leaders, the Palestinians had one, of a sort. Not the Grand Mufti, of course—he cared nothing for their cause, and egged his terror gangs on in the hope of ruling the whole country. The Palestinians' hero was a soldier, Abd el-Kader, and while he led them they did fight—but he was killed even before the real war started. And the men they should have been led by, the rich and influential members of their communities, abandoned them—packed up and pulled out at the first sign of trouble.

Left leaderless, and hearing horror stories, one or two of which were true, many of the ordinary people panicked. The Israelis not only did nothing effective to stop them from going—for which it's hard to blame them—but in some cases speeded them on their way. Though I truly believe few Jews in the Yishuv thought of dispossessing the Arabs to begin with, when they saw them beginning to leave they were not sorry. They needed their room, for all those thousands of homeless, wretched Jews from Europe;

and besides, their more militant Arab neighbors had been
causing them a great deal of trouble, at least in places
like Jaffa where Jews and Arabs lived close together.

Once again there was no black-and-white, only the gray-
ness of faults on all sides.

Little did the Arabs realize, as they fled, the years of
exile, poverty and frustration ahead of them. Little did the
Jews foresee how those streams of refugees, conveniently
vacating towns and villages, would pollute the Zionist river
with their misery and anger, their growing sense of their
own deprived nationhood, until that once-clear current
turned murky—so murky that few Israelis today can see
what is causing their loss of vision and sureness, nor the
periodic whirlpools of war that suck down so many to their
deaths.

To put it at its simplest, the Palestinians of 1948 craved
safety, while the Jews craved a country. In a war of survival
it's hard to look ahead to a time, thirty years later, when the
Jews would be desperately seeking safety and the Palestinians a country. By which time—had they but known it then
—there would be such mountains of distrust on each side
that it would seem to many too late to make the adjustment.

Every war makes echoes, which resound, often distorted,
for years. Victory echoes are triumphant, satisfying—
deceptively healing. Those echoes, singing sweetly in the
ears of the Jews who for so long had been helpless before
their persecutors, led them to believe that military might
was the eternal answer—not only to the "Arab problem"
but to the righting of all their own wrongs, past and future;
to the restoration not just of their country, but of their
self-respect.

So crisis after crisis, war after war since 1948 has been
met with strength. Strength was what they had lacked
throughout their exile. Not moral strength—without that
they couldn't have survived; but crude physical strength.
The sweet echoes of victory had the power to hypnotize
them—they would not look for other solutions.

For the Arabs, the echoes were discordant—the maddening, perpetual jangling of failure and defeat. To silence those echoes became their entire preoccupation. First by denying Israel's existence; then by trying to wipe her out.

Only when war after war had decimated both peoples and kept their countries poor and dependent for two generations did a movement for reconciliation and compromise begin to make any real impression on the deadlock. The victory of this movement—despite the peace-treaty that was signed between Israel and Egypt—is far from won. But a few echoes from it have started to cut across the angry vibrations of all those wars and of all that bitter hatred, interfering—no more as yet—with their deafening supremacy.

Is it too late? I met one army colonel after the Yom Kippur War who had just lost his son in battle. He seemed to accept completely that that was the price that had to be paid by the Jews for a place of their own—repeated wars, repeated sacrifices. His consolation for this terrible outlook he expressed in the words, "Here at least we die fighting."

If I shared his pessimism, I would not have bothered to write this book. I would instead offer you two words of advice about Israel: "Forget it." But I believe in the power of the Jewish survival instinct. It has triumphed, in its time, over worse even than the very bad situation Israel finds herself in today.

However. No one committed to the survival of Israel can put complete trust in anything—from God's care for his "chosen people" to the strength of Israel's right arm, from the wavering commitment of the United States to the inscrutable maze of history through which the Jews have, so far, miraculously found their way. None of these alone will preserve them—they must take steps to preserve themselves.

And no matter what that colonel may think, military strength alone will not do it. If Israel were to extend her borders for fifty miles more to the north, east and south—

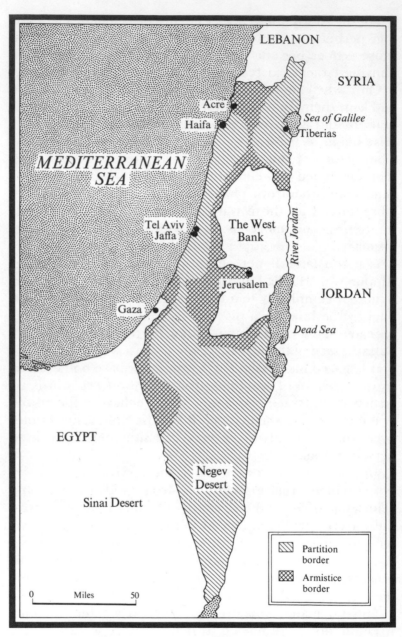

Israel's First Borders

if she were to mobilize every able-bodied Jew in the world
—if she were to smother the surface of her soil with tanks,
bombers and artillery of the latest sort—her safety would
still not be assured.

Only one thing has a hope of doing that. *Israel must integrate into her region.* It's no use her going on pretending she
occupies a rather remote bit of Europe or America. The
Jews chose that location for what seemed to them good
reasons. It will only be through reaching a reconciliation
with their fellow Semites that they will find peace at last.

Neither the Jews of Israel nor the Palestinian Arabs can
have all they would like. The Talmud says that when two
men both claim the same prayer-shawl, it must be divided.
I mention this because it is the religious faction in the
Jewish world which lays claim so immovably to the whole
of "Biblical Israel." It is the fanatics among the Palestinians
—the Rejectionists—who still call for Israel's destruction,
and demand the whole of Palestine for themselves. There
will have to be compromise.

In the past year, there has been one—a compromise of
a kind no one could have foreseen even a few years ago.
Egypt, the most powerful of Israel's enemies, has renounced war as a way of solving their differences. Israel, in
response, has agreed to hand back—has, in fact, pretty
nearly done so—the whole of the Sinai Desert, which she
has had to capture twice from a warlike Egypt at tremendous cost.

And at tremendous risk she is giving it up—greater risk
than the world has so far given her credit for. Well may the
Israelis tremble at their own boldness. For who knows who
will rule after the intrepid and peace-minded President
Sadat of Egypt? What if it were another leader like Nasser?
Then the possession of that stretch of desert might be a
vital strategic factor.

Besides, there are the Sinai oil fields. When Israel took
them in 1967 she developed them to supply a considerable
proportion of her oil needs. I need not spell out the impor-

tance of such a source of oil these days. But she has handed them back.

Then there are those settlements south of Gaza, and the town of Yamit, where we once had a pleasant seaside picnic among the keen and carefree young Israelis who, at their government's urging, came to make the desert bloom. Someone else's desert. . . . Of course they should never have gone there before peace had been made, any more than the West Bank should be "permanently" settled in the absence of a final agreement with its indigenous inhabitants. Nevertheless, there they are, and there they won't be for long. They face the prospect of abandoning their homes with bitterness and heartbreak.

All this was done, in the face of much anxiety and not a little fury from Israelis, by a right-wing government which had pledged not to return a single inch of captured Arab territory, because the prize was peace with Egypt. (And also, of course, because the penalty for not doing it was loss of American support, without which Israel could not survive.) But even this sacrifice will not be enough. The key to the whole dangerous mess really lies not westward with Egypt, but eastward with the true Arabs, and especially with the Palestinians.

The risks here are even greater. The Palestinians have not yet renounced their stated determination to destroy Israel. Until they declare their willingness to co-exist with her, it's hard to see how even the most oil-hungry outsider could seriously expect Israel to hand over control of the West Bank to the PLO. One look at a map will show why.

But a way must be opened for some form of self-determination for the *one million* Arabs over whom Israel now most uneasily rules. Mr. Begin is talking of "autonomy" for them, but he is playing with words. Autonomy means self-rule, but in Mr. Begin's mouth it means Israeli rule in a modified form. It won't do. Nothing will do, unless it gives the Palestinians a part of what they want—only a part. It cannot be all. But a part they must have, for Israel's sake as well.

I didn't open any champagne when that peace treaty with Egypt was signed. I believe it could do more harm than good in the end, if it leads anyone to imagine that the root-cause of the trouble can be bypassed. Israel is now sitting on a large powder keg watching a flame creeping along the fuse. She can't keep control of those million unwilling Arabs forever.

Not if she wants a Jewish state, because, in a few years, there will be more Arabs in it than Jews. Not if she wants a Zionist state, because the Zionist ethic, based on Judaism, opposes oppression and exploitation of one people by another. And not if she wants a democracy. A democracy gives equal rights, including voting rights, to all its citizens. Once you have a majority of Arabs inside the State, with full civil rights, then you must get an Arab-dominated government. And the only political party in Israel that Arabs in general vote for is the Communist party. If there is one thing most of her supporters, including the Americans, would like even less than the present government, it would be an Arab-dominated Communist one.

A well-known Israeli journalist to whom I talked last April was very angry about the situation. He said this:

"As long as Israel occupies the Territories, she is steadily corroding her own Jewish ethic. I want to see her give them all up—all except East Jerusalem, though there's a solution for that too: a joint council and an Arab mayor.

"But I don't see *how* we can ever give up the West Bank. Who can we give it up *to*? We can't hand it over to the PLO while they're still threatening us, and who else is there? The West Bankers haven't the guts to stand up for themselves apart from the PLO. They're afraid of us, but they're more afraid of the PLO intimidators. And they're afraid to risk their own lives or even, in the case of most of their leaders, their positions and comforts. They just sit there saying, "We've lived through the Turks, the British, the Jordanians, and we'll live through you Jews." Only they won't, because we're not leaving. That's what they won't accept—that if they want their independence they'll have to

claim it in their own name, and not let a terrorist organization do it for them."

So—what? Hand the West Bank over to Jordan? I don't
think she'd have it as a gift. A United Nations trusteeship
for a given period—say five years—to see if relations could
be normalized, and then a separate state? Better.

But one way or another, the Arabs and the Jews must
learn to live together again. Fanatics on both sides are a
menace, and to encourage them—whether it's the Gush
Emunim or the Palestinian Rejectionists—is simply to increase the likelihood that Israel will remain what she has
been for the whole of her short, modern life—a nation at
war. And that the Jews, your people by birth and mine by
adoption, will remain what they have been for 2,000 years
—a nation living with a lighted fuse, with no place of refuge
that is really safe.

Well lads, are you still with me? If so, I hope you've learned
something. There's nothing like reading a book for finding
things out. Unless it's writing one.

The irony for me is that what I originally intended to do
was write the history of modern Israel. But it very soon
became clear to me that unless you know the history of the
Diaspora, half your argument for a national home for the
Jews is lacking. So this has been the story of how the Jews
coped without a country. The rest of the story—of how they
are coping *with* one—has to be a book on its own.

But until it's written—and it's hard to see how it can ever
be called finished, because new developments are happening every day—just bear this in mind. You belong, on your
father's side, to an amazing people: champions of survival,
challengers of frontiers, torchbearers and trailblazers and
scalers of summits in every field of human effort. So they
shout "Jew!" at you in school? That is their ignorance; let
it be your pride. Zionism and Israel are under attack? Let
the attackers point to some greater, more flawless achievement, some commitment of their own which has called for

more vision, determination and courage, some ideal which has stood without impairment against a lifetime of bludgeoning by the hard, destructive sledgehammer of daily reality.

A close friend of ours said to me only yesterday, "I couldn't live there now. It's a society poisoned by unease and doubt." Unease and doubt are harder to live with, certainly, than smugness, indifference, insular concern with one's own narrow world. But they are not toxic. They're signs of health, signs of awareness of the flaws in their society, signs of caring and vitality, of the mind and the conscience hard at work.

It is part of what I love about Israel, what I miss so terribly, what draws me back again and again. It is part of what I hope will eventually take you, whose blood and birth give you the right *not* to be outsiders, back there at last, of your own free choice.

Bibliography

Avnery, Uri, *Israel Without Zionism,* New York 1968

Begin, Menachem, *The Revolt,* Steimatsky 1972

Ben-Gurion, D., *Recollections,* Macdonald 1970

Childers, E., "The Other Exodus" from the *Spectator*
  May 12, 1961

Crossman, Richard, *A Nation Reborn,* Hamish Hamilton
  1960

Crossman, Richard, *Palestine Mission,* Hamish Hamilton
  1947

Dayan, Moshe, *My Life,* Weidenfeld & Nicolson 1978

Dimont, Max, *Jews, God and History,* New American
  Library 1962

Elon, Amos, *Herzl,* Weidenfeld & Nicolson 1975

Elon, Amos, *The Israelis, Founders and Sons,* Weidenfeld &
  Nicolson 1971

Flapan, Simha, *Zionism and the Palestinians,* Croom-helm
  1979

Gilbert, M., *The Arab-Jewish Conflict, Its History in Maps*, Weidenfeld & Nicolson 1969

Gilbert, M., *Jewish History Atlas*, Weidenfeld & Nicolson 1969

Glubb, Sir John, *A Soldier with the Arabs*, Hodder & Stoughton 1957

Hellman, Peter, *The Garden of Righteous Gentiles*, Seaview Books, New York 1979

Keller, Werner, *The Diaspora*, Pitman 1971

Kimche, J. and D., *Both Sides of the Hill*, Secker & Warburg 1960

Koestler, Arthur, *Promise and Fulfillment*, Macmillan 1949

Kurzman, Dan, *Genesis 1948*, New American Library 1970

Levin, Meyer, *The Story of Israel*, Putnam 1966

Litvinoff, E., *Ben-Gurion of Israel*, Weidenfeld & Nicolson 1954

Meir, Golda, *My Life*, Weidenfeld & Nicholson 1975

Parkes, James, *Whose Land?*, Penguin, Revised Edition 1970

Ruppin, A., *Memories and Diaries*, Tel Aviv 1968

Senesh, *Hannah Senesh, Her Life and Diary*, Valentine Mitchell 1971

Sykes, Christopher, *Cross Roads to Israel*, Collins 1965

Weizman, C., *Trial and Error*, New American Library 1977

Yaari, A., *The Goodly Heritage*, Jerusalem 1958

Yanayit, Rachel, *Coming Home*, Massadah Press 1963

Index

DATE DUE